YANKEE CITY SERIES

VOLUME

III

THE
SOCIAL SYSTEMS
OF AMERICAN
ETHNIC GROUPS

BY
W. LLOYD WARNER
AND
LEO SROLE

NEW HAVEN AND LONDON
YALE UNIVERSITY PRESS

THIS VOLUME IS DEDICATED TO

Mark A. May

YANKEE CITY RESEARCH STAFF

	Writer W			Field Worker F	
		Analyst A			
W. Lloyd Warner	W	A	F	Dorothy Moulton	A
Leo Srole	W	A	F	Alice Williams	A
Paul S. Lunt	W	A	F	Sylva Beyer	A
J. O. Low	W	A	F	Margaret Mack	A
Eliot Chapple		A	F	Viola Vanderhorck	A
Buford Junker		A	F	Mildred Warner	A
Solon Kimball		A	F	Joseph Weckler	A
Marion Lee		A	F	J. O. Brew	F
Conrad Arensberg		A	F	Dorothea Mayo	F
Robert G. Snider		A	F	O. S. Lovekin	F
Allison Davis		A	F	Gwenneth Harrington	F
Elizabeth Davis		A	F	Hess Haughton	F
Burleigh Gardner		A	F		

ACKNOWLEDGMENTS

THE research staff of the Yankee City Series are indebted to many people for aid in the inception, course of research, and publication of this work. We cannot thank all of them here.

Above all we wish to express our appreciation to the citizens of Yankee City who generously gave their knowledge of the community and maintained a coöperating interest in our work. We are grateful to the Committee of Industrial Physiology of Harvard University for sponsoring and financing the field research. Professor Elton Mayo and Dean Wallace Brett Donham of the Graduate School of Business Administration of Harvard University have contributed incalculably to the study by their wise guidance, insight, and understanding.

The entire series is dedicated to our generous benefactor, friend, and colleague in social anthropology, Cornelius Crane, as an inadequate recognition of his deep and sympathetic interest in our work and of his consuming concern for the problem, the nature of man.

The authors are particularly indebted to Professors Edwin B. Wilson, Carl R. Doering, and Earnest A. Hooton, all of Harvard University, and Professor Samuel A. Stouffer, of the University of Chicago, for advice and assistance on statistical problems.

We wish to thank Professors John Dollard and George Peter Murdock, of Yale University, for their interest in the publication of these volumes and for their unerring aid in the editing of the manuscripts.

Miss Alice Marsden White and Mrs. Mildred Hall Warner have contributed their skill in the preparation of the manuscripts for publication. We wish to thank our friend and colleague, Dr. Mark A. May, and his staff of the Institute of Human Relations at Yale University, for the encouragement they gave us by their critical and sympathetic interest.

To John Dollard of the Institute of Human Relations we owe a very special debt of gratitude for his recognition of the significance of the scientific problems we attacked and for his help in the solution of many of them. The searching questions he asked us and the generous acclaim he gave our research have been deep sources of scientific and spiritual strength to all of us.

Part of the material in this volume was written as a doctor's thesis by Dr. Leo Srole. (*Ethnic Groups and American Society: A Study in the Dynamics of Social Assimilation.* Typewritten thesis, Ph.D., University of Chicago, 1940.) For the use of field reports on the several ethnic groups, the authors wish to thank Dr. Burleigh B. Gardner, Dr. Solon Kimball, Dr. Allison Davis, and Dr. Conrad Arensberg.

CONTENTS

TABLES

CHARTS

PREFACE

THE "Yankee City Series," of which the present work is the third volume, will be complete in six volumes. Each deals with a significant aspect of the life of a modern community as it has been recorded and analyzed by the combined and coöperative labors of a group of social anthropologists. The same techniques and viewpoints applied by them to the study of societies of simpler peoples are here subjected to empirical testing in a concrete case study in modern American society. The town chosen (for reasons given in Volume I) was an old New England community.

The first volume, *The Social Life of a Modern Community*, by W. Lloyd Warner and Paul S. Lunt, describes in detail the cultural life of the community, emphasizing particularly the way in which these people have been divided into superior and inferior classes. It also presents the reader with an interpretation of the techniques, methods, and conceptual framework used in the research, a summary of the findings, and a general orientation.

The second volume, *The Status System of a Modern Community*, by W. Lloyd Warner and Paul S. Lunt, gives a detailed description and careful analysis of the social institutions of this community. It shows how our New England subjects live a well-ordered existence according to a status system maintained by these several social institutions.

The present volume, *The Social Systems of American Ethnic Groups*, by W. Lloyd Warner and Leo Srole, is a detailed study of the social life of a number of ethnic groups, including the Irish, French Canadians, Jews, Armenians, and Poles; it explains how they maintain their old cultural traditions but at the same time undergo social changes which make them more and more like the larger American community.

The fourth volume, *The Social System of the Modern Factory*, by W. Lloyd Warner and J. O. Low, is specifically concerned with the study of the social organization of the modern factory. It shows not only how industrial workers coöperate in producing manufactured goods, but also how they fit into the larger community.

The fifth volume, *American Symbol Systems*, by W. Lloyd

Warner, deals with the conceptual processes which Americans use when they think about themselves and their own behavior. It analyzes the myth and ritual as well as the secular behavior of the members of Yankee City.

The concluding volume, *Data Book for the Yankee City Series*, by W. Lloyd Warner, supplies additional data for those who wish to examine the more detailed aspects of the subjects treated in the other volumes.

THE MELTING POT; SEVEN PERSONAL HISTORIES

1. Who They Are

IN most cities and large towns of the United States there are
"foreign districts" known as Little Italys, Little Bohemias,
Polack Towns, or by other appellations, which refer to con-
centrations of ethnic people in a particular section of a community. The mere presence of these cultural minorities has modified
the form of American society and indisputably changed our social, economic, and political history.

Each of these populations has developed a semi-autonomous
social system. Despite their diverse cultural backgrounds, the social structures of these ethnic communities and their social histo-
ries, from the time of their landing on American soil through
generations of development, are remarkably similar.

This volume is concerned with the study of the ethnic groups of
a representative American town we have called Yankee City. The
ethnic groups are the Irish, French Canadians, Jews, Italians,
Armenians, Greeks, Poles, and Russians. The present social organization and the social history of each group have been investigated to learn something of the nature of the ethnic group, its
place in American life, and the changes which occur through the
generations.

Yankee City is a small industrial community in New England.
It has a history that began with the early settlement of the Atlantic Coast. The heirs of the Yankees who founded it are still powerful and dominant, but the ethnic population, composing about
half the total, is increasing in power and in prestige.[1]

The research in Yankee City was done between the two World
Wars (1930–1935), as a part of a larger investigation of the social life of the New England community. In the first two volumes
that were published in this survey we described the six social
strata of the community, which are of importance in determining

1. See W. L. Warner and P. S. Lunt, *The Social Life of a Modern Community,*
"Yankee City Series," I, 76–80 and 422–450; *The Status System of a Modern
Community,* "Yankee City Series," II, 3–106.

the behavior of everyone in the community. The top level, or upper-upper class, consists of members of "old families" who are born to their position; their family genealogies show them to be products of several generations of upper-class living. This old aristocracy is the keystone in the Yankee City status system. Below this level are the "new families" or newly rich (lower-upper) who are busy transforming their money into acceptable behavior through participation with those who preceded them to the top level. On the step below them are the "pillars of society," the successful men and women, who are the powerful upper-middle class who do things and see that things are done in Yankee City. These three classes, comprising no more than 15 per cent of the total, are "the big people" who are above the common run of men.

Below them, but at the top of "the little people," are the members of the lower-middle class, the small tradesmen, the skilled workers, and the white-collar workers who cling to the virtues of the "protestant ethic," despite the fact that many are members of other religions. Beneath them are the poor and respectable workers, who hope and strive to do better than they are doing, but who worry for fear of falling into the class below them, the lowest in society, where the "shiftless Yankees" and the "ignorant immigrants" are found.

This social order is built on an industrial foundation of shoes, silverware, and textiles. In the 1840's, the expanding Yankee City industrial life welcomed the Catholic Irish as workers in the factories, the first of the principal ethnic groups of the city. Except for the Irish, many of the original immigrants are alive and members of the contemporary ethnic groups.

This book tells part of the magnificent history of the adjustment of the ethnic groups to American life. What has happened in Yankee City illustrates much of what has happened and is happening to the "minority groups" all over America. Each group enters the city at the bottom of the social heap (lower-lower class) and through the several generations makes its desperate climb upward. The early arrivals, having had more time, have climbed farther up the ladder than the ethnic groups that followed them. It seems likely that oncoming generations of new ethnics will go through the same metamorphosis and climb to the same heights that generations of earlier groups have achieved.

Many of the children's children of the early arrivals have ceased participating in the ethnic life of their ancestors and have disappeared in the larger American world. Others are on their way to assimilation. Some, partly through frustration in not gaining easy acceptance into the common life of Americans and partly through clinging to the ways of their fathers, have constructed separate social worlds of their own. Each group, without conscious imitation of others, has fashioned "an ethnic subsystem" much like that of the others, and each system seems to undergo the same changes as the systems which preceded it.

Since most of this book is devoted to analyzing the facts of these systems and no attempt is made to communicate how it feels to be a member of an ethnic group, the remainder of this first chapter will be devoted to letting one of the ethnic groups, the Irish, tell their own story. The Irish were chosen to represent all other ethnic groups because they are the oldest and have climbed the highest in the status structure.

The first episode, a critical moment in the life of Daniel Corbett, illustrates a few of the problems of some of the upper-middle class Irish. The other episodes tell the story of the Fahertys, an Irish family which has climbed to the lower-upper class, and the O'Malleys, who are in the upper bracket of the lower class.

As we said in Volume I of this series[2] about similar episodes: "The several sketches which follow are intended to do no more than illustrate how the several social levels appear to the observer and how it feels to live in the class system of Yankee City. The people described, as well as their families, cliques, associations, political and economic institutions, are presented as examples of what the researcher observes while doing his field work.

"Each person, each institution, and each incident in each essay is a composite drawing. No one actual individual or family in Yankee City is depicted, rather the lives of *several individuals* are compressed into that of one fictive person. . . . The justification for these changes lies in our attempt to protect our subjects and to tell our story economically. We have not hesitated to exclude all material which might identify specific persons in the community; and we have included generalized material wherever necessary to prevent recognition. The people and situations in some of the sketches are entirely imaginary. In all cases where changes were introduced in the reworking of our field notes, we first satisfied ourselves that they would not destroy the essential social reality of the points of the original interview. Only then were such materials included in our text."

2. *Op. cit.,* I, 127. For composite drawings illustrating class behavior of the Yankees, see pp. 127–201.

2. *"I'm Not Getting Any Place"*

IT was one o'clock Saturday afternoon. Dr. Daniel Corbett was filling the last cavity for his last patient of the week. He was anxious to get through, but he was afraid to think about what he would do after his patient had gone. It had been a very busy week. Dr. Corbett had started practicing in University City in a small, unpretentious office. Many of his patients were from Yankee City, for he had grown up there and his present social life was in that community. Through the years Corbett's clientele had improved in numbers, in quality, and in ability to pay. Now he was a successful dentist.

Corbett tried to keep his mind on his work, but found it continually wandering to the thoughts which had been keeping him preoccupied. "I've been worried for months," he thought. "Months, hell, it's years. Years it's been. This can't go on forever, my being in a jam, and am I in a jam? Oh, Jesus, am I in a jam!" He pressed the drill against the tooth. He found himself repeating, "In a jam, in a jam, in a jam, in a jam," in rhythmic time to the sound of his drill. Suddenly the patient jumped. Surprised, Dr. Corbett tried to withdraw the instrument too quickly. It cut a small wound in the patient's lower lip, which began bleeding. He stopped the machine. He was almost trembling. The patient sat up.

"I'm terribly sorry, Mr. Rogers, terribly sorry." While he attempted to stop the flow of blood he stared anxiously at the patient's face. Mr. Rogers did not appear to be angry, but you could not always tell about him. Corbett knew that the accident would not have occurred if he had had his mind on his work. This was the second time it had happened this week, and he had had a more serious accident the week before. "I hope it didn't hurt you too much, Mr. Rogers."

"Not at all, it was my fault. I jumped. I guess I can't take it any more. I'm just a baby in a dentist's chair."

By this time Corbett had regained control of himself. He took advantage of the situation and, with his usual calm, while telling Rogers how bravely and courageously he had behaved in the chair, Corbett let his patient feel that he lacked self-control and that really it was the patient's fault. The flow of blood was staunched; and Corbett finished the grinding and started filling the tooth.

"Thank God," he thought, "it was Ez Rogers instead of old lady Faherty. She'd have ruined my reputation yelling all over

Yankee City about it. Ruined my reputation, that's good. And what the hell are you doing, Corbett, outside your office but ruining your reputation? By your own actions too. God, my mind's off my work already. You're going crazy, Corbett, unless you do something about this jam you're in. But what to do? What to do?"

He forced himself to give close attention to the job at hand and soon completed it. Ez Rogers left. Corbett cleaned and sterilized his instruments. He had let his nurse leave early. He removed his white coat and changed to street attire. He went over and sat down by the telephone.

"What the hell am I going to do? Go home or go see Betty? Which is it?" He absent-mindedly fingered a coin in his pocket. "Heads or tails," he thought, "heads or tails." He laughed nervously, remembering the old joke they used to tell at dental school about the bright young dentist who was trying to decide whether to spend the night with a beautiful blonde and thereby ruin his chances for an A in his final exams or go see the old professor and get his A and forget the blonde. His friends told him to toss a coin to see whether it would be heads or tails. Corbett took the coin out of his pocket and tossed it in the air. It came down tails.

"By God, that settles it. I'll call Molly and tell her I can't come home and that I've got to go see someone in Boston on business. Then I'll get to see Betty. See her is right." His mind filled with memories of the last time he was with her. What a time they'd had. They'd spent the whole weekend at a Boston hotel. Everything was wonderful. It was lovely. It was swell. It was grand. No worry, no thoughts about the consequences, just a lot of fun. You didn't have to think about getting her pregnant. She knew how to take care of herself. He didn't have to do anything. Why couldn't Molly be like that?

"It was all right to be a good Catholic and all that, but what was he going to do with another kid now that Molly was pregnant again? How the hell was he going to support the six that she had already? And when does it stop? Six now, seven tomorrow, eight, nine, ten maybe. But this can't go on forever. Yes, but it does. I can't send six kids through school, let alone seven. You can't keep up appearances and support seven kids. Why the hell can't Molly act like other sensible women and let one of us use something to stop her from having a new baby every time I shake my pants at her?"

His thoughts were interrupted by the phone ringing. It was

Bob Cameron, a doctor from Elmwood, who was in town on his way to Boston. He was calling to find out if it were too late for a couple of drinks and a shore dinner. Corbett accepted, called his wife, and told her his plans. In a few minutes they were in the doctor's car on the way to a roadside restaurant.

After having several highballs from a bottle of bourbon which the doctor had with him, the conversation flowed easily. They talked while they ate their grilled lobsters.

"Bob, you got me at the right moment, at the right moment," said Corbett. "I was sitting there at the telephone trying to decide what to do. Jesus, am I in a jam!"

"What's the trouble, Danny?"

"Well, Molly's higher than a kite again. I can't learn to keep away from her. I don't know what to do. I can't make ends meet now with six kids, let alone seven. And when does it stop? Eight, nine, ten? I'm in a spot."

"What do you mean?" the doctor asked.

"Well, instead of the Corbetts living in a nice house in a nice neighborhood, we have to live down on a side street. I feel guilty as hell every time I buy a drink. We don't go around with our Yankee City crowd as much as we used to. It isn't that they've dropped us, but we can't afford to go to the places and spend the money they do. The kids need shoes, the kids need clothes, there are doctor bills, and God knows what else."

"But you've been a success in your profession," his friend said.

"I've done my best. I've increased my income a hell of a lot. I've got the largest practice in this town. I've worked hard. But what good does it do me? I'm not getting any place. I'm falling behind. I keep on having kids. God damn Molly! Why won't she be sensible and fix herself up or let me do something so that she won't have any more kids?

"The priest tells her it's a mortal sin for her to do anything like that. And she won't let me. I tried to fool her a few times, but she was too smart. I got to give her credit, she has more self-control than me. She won't have anything to do with me if I try to do anything about it. I try to stop having relations with her, but I can't. Not little Danny. Oh no, I've got to get hot pants and before I know it she's pregnant again. It raises hell with our feelings about each other."

"Was it always like that between you?" his friend asked.

"For a long time it wasn't. I thought it was wonderful when our first child came. And I was certainly glad when the second one came along. A boy and a girl, that's what I dreamed of. I could send them to school, dress them well, and they could bring their friends home to a nice house in a nice neighborhood. I was making more money all the time. And I had visions of moving out of this burg and of getting a house up on Hill Street and living with my friends in Yankee City.

"But about that time Molly started to have another child. I had a hell of a fight with her. I said we had to stop. She came back from confession and said it was a crime for either of us to practice birth control and not to have babies. I said it was a crime to keep on having kids and not give the ones we had a chance. I said I'd never sleep with her again. She said she'd never sleep with me if I tried any funny business. Well, you know how it is. She was with child, and I'm a passionate guy, and she couldn't have any more babies while she was like that. So we went back to staying together.

"After she had Tommy, he was our third one, I moved into a separate bedroom and tried that for a while; but hell, I couldn't sleep. Jesus, what a spot! I couldn't sleep if I didn't, and I couldn't sleep if I did. I was ready to turn atheist and tell the Pope to go to hell. I ask you, what does a priest know about paying the bills for fifteen kids? Kids for those peasants down in the clam flats are swell. But what the hell can a modern professional man like me do with a whole mess of kids? I'm right behind the eight-ball, right behind the eight-ball."

They mixed another drink. The waitress brought the coffee and left.

"Well, Tommy was a cute little devil. And I felt guilty as hell thinking about how sore I was when I heard he was coming. And that's the way it's been ever since. Except after the last one I threatened to divorce Molly. I used to love her, and maybe I do yet. But not the way I did once. You can't love a woman and be scared to death she's going to produce twins every time you hold her in your arms. It kills something in you. But I can't divorce her. Being a Catholic, my conscience won't let me. I've tried to be a decent guy. With another one coming, I can't walk out on her and the six kids. I come home some nights and look at them all. I love every one of the little guys. I wouldn't give one of them up now. But what the hell am I going to do? I'm more in debt than I ever was. Yet I'm making more money than I ever did. I'm getting less and less out of life. I'm getting no place fast."

"What's happened to the young widow—what was her name—the blonde, I mean?" his friend asked.

"Oh, she's around. She's not a bad girl. She wants to have a little fun. She got used to having it before her husband died and she says she can't quit. And would you believe it, she's an Irish Catholic, but you'd never know it. She undresses and gets into bed just like a man. I don't know what's happening to the Irish in America when the women lose their modesty like her. She stands there without a thing on looking like a million dollars and she has no shame. I can't help it, but it bothers me. I like women to be modest. I'm Molly's husband, but I never saw her undress. She's modest and I like it. I'd hate to leave Molly. I don't think I could. But what am I going to do? I can't go on like this. I'm so jittery, I'm making mistakes on the job. I almost drove a hole through one of my best customers a while ago because I had my mind on this thing. I've got to calm down or they'll have me over in an institution."

"You're a level-headed guy, Danny. You don't have to worry about that."

"You're wrong. While I'm there working on a patient you'd be surprised what goes around and around in my head. Every time I see Father Dunn I feel, by the way he looks at me, that he knows the awful things I got on my mind. God, do I feel guilty and ashamed! I feel like I'd killed an unborn child."

"Why? You haven't done anything like that, have you?"

"No, but sometimes that's what I get to thinking about. I get to thinking of that shyster doctor I know. He could operate on Molly and fix her up so she'd stop having kids. I keep thinking maybe the first time she gets a little sick I could tell her she ought to go to a doctor and see what's the matter with her. She's been sore at old Doc Kimball, so I could tell her she ought to try this man. I could see this fellow ahead of time and let him know what the score was.

"Well, my thinking goes swell up until that point, then I can see Molly looking at me and I get uncomfortable as hell. I know I'd turn red or something and give the show away. Then she'd smell a rat—and what a rat she'd smell! She'd never say a word about it, but I'd know what she was thinking and I know how I'd feel. I'd feel like a heel! Just like I'd tried to murder her! And when Father Dunn would look at me I'd know what he'd be thinking. He'd be remembering what Molly told him, and he'd be thinking, 'Danny, you Irish renegade. So you'd do that to your own wife, and you a Catholic.' "

The waitress presented the bill. They paid it, left the place, and drove back to University City. The drink was beginning to wear off and the two men were quiet and lost in their own thoughts.

"I guess I'd better go straight home, Bob."

"Aw, come on, let's go to Boston and have a little fun."

"I'd like to, but I can't afford it. And I'd go to see Betty as soon as I got there."

"Well, I wouldn't blame you for that."

"Yeah, but I would," said Danny.

Daniel Corbett got out of the car, said good-by, and went into the house. Two of the children were crying. One of them was standing on the davenport. Corbett had an impulse to turn around and leave. He saw Molly. She smiled at him and said, "Danny, I hope you had a nice time. You sure deserve it. I was telling the Father today that you were the best husband in this whole world." She moved toward him. He kissed her. He knew that things would go on as they always had.

3. *Shanty Irish*

MR. TIMOTHY O'MALLEY unloosened his belt; he stealthily unbuttoned the two top buttons of his trousers before pushing his chair back from the dinner table. He hoped his wife was sufficiently busy clearing the table not to notice this "act of an indecent man who shows no respect for his wife in her own home." Mrs. O'Malley swept a pile of empty clam shells into a pail. During Timothy's supper the shells had spilled from his plate and slipped across the oilcloth around his place at the table. Four empty beer bottles, all Timothy's, were carefully hidden behind the kitchen stove. Mrs. O'Malley got up a few minutes early every morning to collect Timothy's bottles and hide them in the cellar before she went to Mass. Timothy went to Mass once a year. He felt that Annie more than made up for his church going. He carried a string of beads in his pocket, and he had another in the bureau drawer with which he sometimes did a few "Hail Marys" when he was worried about losing his job, when he caught a cold, or when he put too much up on the horse races.

After she had cleared the dishes from the table, Annie O'Malley turned to the sink. With great effort and heavy breathing, Timothy leaned over, untied his shoes and slipped them beneath his chair. The beer had made him feel overly bold. He took further liberties. He tipped his chair back and cocked his feet on the table.

His stomach bulged pleasantly; he felt sleepy. His wife carried the dishes she had dried to the cupboard. Timothy watched her from beneath his half-closed lids. Mrs. O'Malley stopped her work to inspect her husband's appearance.

"And what kind of table manners are those? Timothy O'Malley, you set up now and button up your pants. What would Mrs. Meeghan think if she came in, with you there in your undershirt, your shoes off, your feet on the table, and your pants unbuttoned? What would she think?"

"That old hen! What she needs is a rooster. Vinny Meeghan! What kind of a man would he make for a woman's husband? I don't know what that old bag would say, but I know what she'd think. She'd wish———."

"Timothy O'Malley, you shut your dirty mouth and button up your pants. That old mother of yours may have been a good mother, but she never taught you your manners. And your old man! Him! A drunken bum and you just like him. His reputation was known and yours is known and it's low-down shanty Irish. It's people like you that spoil the good name of the Irish. My mother said when we were married that the O'Malley men———."

"Your mother, that one—that old cluck! May God strike me dead and may I go straight to hell if your mother's reputation would stand investigation. She was a dirty liar and everyone in Yankee City and all County Kerry knew it. When she spoke to you she kept her nose high in the air like she was smelling manure —and maybe she was. Maybe she was remembering that pigpen her folks lived in before they got here. My old man told me that your old lady's folks lived back of three bogs in a shanty that housed a dozen pigs and a dozen O'Callahans. They was all so filthy that nobody in the whole of Kerry could tell which dozen was O'Callahans and which dozen was pigs. My old man said the only time the O'Callahans washed was when they got their passports to come to America. There was so much mud from the pigpen on them and they smelled so bad no one would give them a passport in Galway until they washed up and proved they were humans and not hogs."

During the argument Timothy opened the icebox and uncorked another quart of beer. He was enjoying himself but he felt the need of added strength and more confidence in his own powers.

"Timothy, you have had too much to drink already. I can always tell."

He took a long draught from the bottle and set it down beside him for ready use. He now directed his remarks not to Annie but to the world:

"And what kind of an Irishman is it who wouldn't take a drink?" He turned his aim on his wife, "And now, Annie, who was your old man? He was the poor, miserable down-trodden husband of that old battle-ax. I can remember her with her nose in the air. To see her you'd think she had to shove her head through ten feet of lace curtains to look out her window. And who were her people? Why, your old grandfather was pure shanty Irish and so were his whole crew. They might act like lace curtain but they were plain shanty."

Timothy held the bottle to his lips and let the beer flow freely down his throat. Annie heard him but gave no attention to his words. She always stopped listening when Timothy reached what she recognized to be the onset of the chamber-pot stage in their genealogical discussion. She left the kitchen and walked into the parlor. She was reluctant to forego the great pleasure of reciting for Timothy's benefit her version of the O'Malley family tree. Each branch, each limb, and each tiny twig were given detailed attention, starting with the first O'Malley and working through each generation, male and female, with the story of O'Malley economic inadequacy, moral delinquency, and the increasing deterioration of its men. She always concluded the O'Malley family history with an analysis of Timothy's character. But Annie had remembered that it was time for her favorite Wednesday evening radio program, and she did not permit anything to interfere with her listening to "John Muldoon, the Great Irish Tenor."

She turned on the light in the parlor and stood back to view its gleam on the surface of a large cabinet radio that held the place of honor. She tuned in a Boston station; words poured out about the insidious influence of bad breath on the career of the socially ambitious. She waited patiently. An orchestra played "When Irish Eyes Are Smiling." She sat back in an overstuffed chair; she laid her hands on her large heavily-corseted stomach and relaxed into quiet contentment. Timothy listened in the kitchen while he finished off the last of his bottle of beer. The announcer said that the Great Irish Tenor, John Muldoon, would sing "My Wild Irish Rose." Timothy sneaked into the bedroom. In a few minutes he entered the parlor and sat down in a rocker. His shoes were laced and his pants buttoned. He had put on a clean white shirt. Timothy believed that the kitchen and the parlor were two different realms. In the first, you could act the way you

wanted to—the way you really were—and, in the second, the way
you had to act for company and for your wife. The parlor was
"Company room"; you had to dress up for it.

A quartet sang an old Irish medley telling of the beauty of all
Ireland, Killarney, the Blarney Stone, and the beauty and purity
of all Irish women. The two moved their heads in time with the
music. The Great Irish Tenor in a high, androgynous voice sang
"Ireland Must Be Heaven for My Mother Came from There."
The listeners remained silent. When the voice had reached its last
high note, the announcer said that modern science had added a
remarkable element to a mouth wash that miraculously destroyed
the menace of bad breath. The two came out of their reveries.

Timothy said, "Jesus, Annie, you can't beat the Irish, can
you?"

"No, Timothy, and wasn't it grand? It made me think of your
dear old mother and mine when they used to talk about County
Kerry in the good old days."

"Now, isn't that strange for I was thinking of the same thing
myself. And how your mother used to make the best cake in
Yankee City. She was a wonderful cook. She was all of that."

"And your mother," said Annie, "used to make beautiful
dresses for me. And your father always told me he wished he was
a young lad like you 'cause he would run off with me. He was a
one, wasn't he? Always full of fun and a laugh for everyone."

"Ah, yes," said Tim, "and your father was so kind. He worked
hard all his life and saved his money and sent his kids to school,
and he was a fine man and good to his wife."

They plunged into a long sentimental discussion in which it
developed that all the O'Callahans and O'Malleys were descendants of Irish kings and Tim's and Annie's immediate forebears,
if not kings and queens by title, were certainly such by word,
deed, and character.

"Maybe we haven't made a million dollars, but our house is paid
for and out of honest wages, too," said Tim.

"Still, Tim, we haven't done so bad. The Flanagans came here
when we did and what's happened to them? None of them is any
good. Not one of them has moved out of the clam flats."

"You're right, Annie, we are a lot better than some. Old Pat
Flanagan, what is he? He is worse than the clam diggers themselves. He has got ten or twelve kids—some of them born in wed-
lock and with the blessings of the church, but some of them are
from those women in the clam flats. He has no shame."

"His children," said Annie, "are growing up into heathens. Two of them are in the reform school, and that oldest girl of his has had two or three babies without nobody admitting he was the father."

While Annie was speaking, Tim turned on the reading lamp which stood by the chair. He glanced lazily through the *Yankee City Herald*. The radio meanwhile announced that Adolph Hitler had confiscated the property of the wealthy German Jews. Timothy and Annie agreed it served them right. He continued to thumb the pages, too sleepy to give the headlines enough attention to comprehend their meaning. He turned through the pages looking for the box scores of yesterday's ball games. The headline at the top of the women's page struck his attention: "Hildegarde Faherty Returns from Europe." He laboriously read the rather long story beneath the headline. He re-read each word again.

"Well, I'll be damned. I'll be a dirty name."

"Timothy, watch your language. Sometimes I am glad all our children are married and gone. What's wrong? What's the matter with you?"

He paid no attention to her.

"I'll be double damned and I'll be ten dirty names," as he looked over the headlines again.

"Timothy, what's the matter with you?"

"There's nothing wrong with me," said Timothy. "It's the cock-eyed world. I never read such crap."

He rose from his chair. He held the paper in his two hands before him. He bowed ostentatiously before his wife. He read the account of Miss Faherty's return from Europe to Yankee City in a la-de-da accent he had once heard a comic English lord use in a talkie.

"Miss Hildegarde Faherty returned yesterday from a three months' tour in England and the Continent ('The Continent, and what the hell is North America—England's backyard?') to the home of her parents, Mr. and Mrs. Edward R. Faherty of 81 Hill Street. Miss Faherty visited London, Paris, and the south of France, following her graduation from Vassar last June. While in Paris, she spent several happy days visiting with Katherine and John Starr, the daughter and son of Mr. and Mrs. Philip Starr of 86 Hill Street.[3] In London, Miss Faherty stopped at the home of Caroline Washburton, daughter of Sir Frederick Washburton, Undersecretary for the Colonies. She also spent some time with

3. *Op. cit.*, I, 141–152, for a description of the lower-upper Starr family.

Mr. and Mrs. Frederick Fitzpatrick, who are the younger members of well-known Yankee City families. The Fitzpatricks returned here last March.

"Hildegarde's brothers, Elliott and Harold, came up from New York to meet her. Elliott is a younger member of the old firm of Breckenridge, Low, and Faherty. Harold is a well-known novelist.

"They joined their mother and father and the family met Hildegarde at the boat."

Timothy sat down in the rocker. He dropped the paper to the floor. Annie waited appreciatively for Timothy's analysis of the whole situation and for his detailed characterization of the Faherty family tree. She had heard it many times before and had given it herself, with equal feeling and with equal insight, but she always enjoyed Tim's version.

"So it is announced by the *Herald*," said Timothy, "that Hildegarde Faherty has returned from a tour of the Continent to the home of her parents on Hill Street. Not a word spoken about going to Ireland to see the land of her own people. Ah, no, she must go to England to kiss the behind of an English duke who would be kind enough to let her do it. She was ashamed of her own people; she has got too good for them, so she goes to Paris with a lot of frogs and Johnny Starr. What happened there won't be known but I gotta damn good idea. They were doing that before they left here."

He paused for breath.

"And what the hell kind of a name is that for her to be having? Hildegarde Faherty. Why I can remember old Mike O'Flaherty, her great granddaddy, and was his name Faherty? It was like hell. It was plain Mike O'Flaherty. In the name of Jesus, what would old Mike say if he found that son of his was too damn proud to wear the great Irish name of O'Flaherty. And Hildegarde! Mother of God, what a name for the granddaughter of Old Katy and Old Mike! It couldn't be plain Margaret or Annie or Kathleen or some fine old Irish name. No, it had to be something fancy. And those brothers of hers, Elliott and Harold. What would an Irishman be doing with names like that?"

This last remark was Annie's cue. She knew it was her turn now.

"They are doing the same thing that their sister is, with that lousy wop name, Hildegarde. Her with that freckled Irish puss and that black Irish hair and them with their flat Irish pans looking like Paddy's pig. Hildegarde and Elliott and Harold! It's their mother, everybody knows that. She ain't satisfied with their just being good Irish Catholics. Ah, no, she wants to marry them into the Hill Street aristocracy. And that's what will happen, you mark my words. Why did she send Hildegarde to that fancy girls' school, Vassar, or whatever you call it, and not to a good Irish Catholic college? And why did the boys go to Harvard? Why didn't they go to our high school instead of that fancy school for the filthy rich? For one reason and one reason only! Old Flossie Faherty wants to be one of the big bugs. They already go around with the Starrs and the Wentworths and the Breckenridges.[4] People like the Donovans, the O'Malleys, and the O'Reillys ain't good enough for them now."

Timothy claimed his turn. "Well, I can remember old Mike Flaherty walking along River Street when we all used to live down in the flats. I was but a lad when he died. My granddad and him came from Casey's Bog in County Kerry. His old lady and my grandmother came from the same parish. They had a brogue you couldn't cut with a knife. They was all as poor as Job's turkey. Him and the granddad got a job working at pick and shovel. Common laborers, they were, that's all, just common laborers. Mind you, there's nothing the matter with that. My father said by the time that he was old enough to remember old Mike was the head of a section gang on the Boston and Maine and his wife was running a little corner store for the Irish people here in town. They was poor but saving. She squeezed every penny and filled that big sock of hers. Jews is tight, but any Irish countrywoman could run a kike out of town and starve him to death.

"Old Mike and his wife had nine kids. Most of them died and the others went to Boston and didn't amount to a damn."

It was Annie's turn again. "And isn't it odd that Flossie only had three children, three and no more. I wonder where she says her confessions. I know she doesn't say them to Father Dunn. No, she's got a Polack priest in Boston she goes to. It's enough to make decent people sick. Three and no more. And that son Elliott. He's got one child and him married five years. He married a Protestant too, and called his boy Elliott II. Mary Flynn says his wife brags she ain't going to have any more. Now, what kind of a woman is that?"

"And what kind of an Irishman," asked Timothy, "can a man grow up to be with the name of Elliott II? The good Irish are all passed away. God knows the clergy do their best to keep us good

4. *Idem.* See pp. 128–141, for a description of the aristocratic Breckenridge and Wentworth families.

Catholics and good Irish, but by the time a man and his family move from River Street up to a house on Hill Street, they ain't Michael Flaherty any more but they are Elliotts and Lowells and Harold Fahertys. It's enough to make you sick. They act like they are ashamed of being Irish."

"And so they are," said Annie. "Mrs. Meeghan told me that Mrs. Riley's daughter who works for the Starrs told her that Mrs. Starr told her that when Hildegarde was at that college she went to, she wasn't Irish at all. She went to the Episcopal Church. Mother of God, old Katy O'Flaherty must have turned over in her grave the first time that happened."

Tim had paid little attention to his wife's speech. He was still thinking about what he had been saying: "Old Katy soon dropped the 'O' from the name and it was only a few years until that young James had got rid of the 'L.' My old man told him he could knock the 'L' out of Flaherty, as they sing in the old song, and to some it turns into Faherty, but to the O'Malleys it still was O'Flaherty."

Timothy left the parlor. He put on his hat and coat and went out the front door, reassuring Annie as he did so that he wouldn't stop to have a few with the boys at the Antlers. He walked out into the narrow street with its sidewalks out of repair, up through the side streets toward Hill Street. As he walked, he left the region of little houses and broken fences; the streets grew wider and the houses larger. He turned into a wide avenue; giant elms, ancient and quiet, stood there on each side of Hill Street, block upon block, mile upon mile.

Back of the elms and across the wide sidewalks and beyond the iron fences, lawns gleaming mirror-like in the bright moonlight led up the hill to rows of white Georgian houses buried in trees and shrubbery. It was here that the "old families" had lived for generations, and it was here that "new families" were turning their recently acquired dollars into a way of life which they hoped would transform Side Streeters into accepted members of Hill Street. The distance from River Street and Market Square to Hill Street is very short. It is less than a mile. Timothy had walked most of the distance in a few minutes. But the social distance is so great that it had taken most if not all of the new families several generations to move socially from the clam flats through the society of the Side Streeters to the social heights of Hill Street. They were the fortunate ones. The vast majority of the descendants of the first Irish settlers remained in the river flats, or they had filled the numerous houses which crowded the side streets.

Timothy O'Malley lived at the lower edge of the side streets and the upper side of the river flats in an area of little houses. While the Fahertys moved out of the flats and up the side streets to Hill Street in a march which claimed three generations, the O'Malleys spent their three generations to get no more than a short step beyond where their first ancestor lived. Old Michael Flaherty changed from a common laborer to the head of a section gang; his son, James Faherty, from a small clerk in an office to the owner of a contracting firm; his grandson, Edward Faherty, the present occupant of 81 Hill Street, became a respected corporation lawyer and man of property; and his great-grandson, a junior partner of an old Wall Street firm and member of the board of several New York corporations.

Meanwhile the generations of O'Malleys marked time, or took one step forward and another backward. Old Pat O'Malley, great friend of Mike O'Flaherty, worked in the same construction gang with him as a common laborer and shared the same pail of beer. He tried to be a policeman, but he had too many rows with his immediate political superior and soon returned to unskilled labor. His son went into a shoe factory and became a skilled worker. His grandson, Timothy, quit high school in his first year to learn to be a mechanic. Timothy's two sons were bus drivers in Boston, four of his daughters had married firemen and policemen, and two were the wives of saloon keepers in Boston.

Old Mike and Pat could sign their names and read with great effort. Mike's son went through high school and took a course in accounting; Pat's son dropped out of public school in the seventh grade. Edward Faherty went to a Catholic college and his sons went through Harvard; Timothy's sons and daughters did not complete their high-school courses.

Timothy O'Malley and Edward Faherty, the present senior members of the two families, are sufficiently well acquainted to speak when they meet on the street. Whereas Timothy knows everything about the Fahertys, Edward is only aware of the O'Malleys when one of his Yankee City enemies obliquely refers to some new piece of gossip that Timothy remembers to tell about Edward's father. Edward never replies directly or indirectly for he himself is not too sure but what some of it might be true.

Timothy walked down Hill Street toward the Faherty residence. He passed the great three-story house with its captain's walk. The porch light revealed the beauty of a carved door with its brass knocker and the clear white of surrounding walls. All the windows gleamed in the darkness. A chauffeur was parking an oversized empty motor car in the graveled driveway. The driver got out of the car.

"Hi, Tim," he called. "What the hell are you doing up here?"

"Hello, Ted. Oh, I gotta go see somebody."

Timothy walked off.

"Well, if it's somebody about a dog," said Ted, "don't use one of our trees."

"Nuts to you, wise guy."

"And the same to you, Shanty."

4. *Lace-curtain Irish*

HILDEGARDE, Elliott, and Harold Faherty were gathered around the fireplace in the library having their after-dinner liqueurs. Hildegarde was smartly gowned in the latest creation of Mainbocher. She thought her brothers' well-tailored dinner jackets provided a fitting background for her white evening gown. This was the first time since Hildegarde's return that all three of them had faced each other without their parents' presence. She knew she could depend upon Elliott to say the proper things, but Harry was never easy to manage. Elliott was a gentleman. He hadn't gone to Andover and Harvard for nothing. He knew all the rules of good behavior and obeyed each with meticulous care. Sometimes it was annoying to see it keep on happening no matter what, and you wanted to stick a pin in him "to see if he'd give up his broad A and lose his presiding-at-the-board-of-directors manner."

She was conscious of her disbelief in Elliott's behavior as being the real Elliott. Elliott's wife acted like that too, but she was real. She was an Endicott, and that was the way Endicotts had always acted. But still Elliott was like that when Hildegarde was a little girl and he was a boy in long pants. One time when two of his Andover friends visited them she had sat on the davenport with her legs in the air and showed her pants. Elliott's friends giggled, but he told her in his best pre-Harvard manner to pull down her dresses and go wash her face. His friends said he acted exactly like the headmaster and that he even talked like him.

Elliott, she thought, was easy to handle once you knew how to do it. His personality was like a game of cards children play. The rules never changed. Once you learned them everything was easy.

You could go on with your own thoughts. Maybe Elliott was real; maybe a Faherty had got to be more like an Endicott and less like a Faherty than she believed possible.

But Harry was something else again. He had grown up very different from his brother. He was hard to figure out. Everything he did seemed to contradict everything else he did. He never seemed to add up. One day he was the perfect brother and it was "Sis, this, and Sis, that," with a rose and a sardonic little poem or an amusing song with cute little lyrics; and next day he was withdrawn from her and everyone else and when he spoke he was hard and bitter and his words hurt all the way through you.

When he was a little boy he was a devout and faithful attendant at the church. His father half jokingly, half seriously, and with some anxiety, had said that it looked as though the first Jesuit was about to appear in the Faherty family. Harry had wanted to go to a Catholic prep school, but his mother had very quickly put a stop to that. He lasted one year at Andover.

Following one or two escapades and consequent expulsion at other prep schools he finally graduated and went on to Harvard. At prep school he had turned agnostic and was bitterly and aggressively anti-Catholic. During this time his mother and he fought openly. She, because he embarrassed her before her friends with his comments on Catholicism, and he for reasons he found hard to put into words.

His academic career at Harvard produced no more than a "gentleman's C," but his extra-curricular activity included intimate acquaintanceships with a number of ladies (one of them cost his father a substantial sum), long bouts with the bottle, writing for the college publications, and a furious study of books on modern social history and current psychology. When graduated he got a job in New York with one of the literary magazines. He published two novels about the upper classes in small towns; the hero of the first committed suicide, and the hero of the second failed as a revolutionary labor leader and betrayed the group he led because he couldn't find the ultimate moral resources within himself to have faith in his, or any other, cause.

Harry had finished his second liqueur. Elliott still sipped his first.

"Well, Sis," said Harry, "now that Mother and Dad are away you can tell us what you did on your vacation. I know that the Cathedral of Notre Dame is lovely in the moonlight, and that the Paris art galleries are too, too divine, and that the changing of the guard at Buckingham Palace is something that no American, particularly if he is Irish, can afford to miss. Ah, yes, there is nothing like travel to educate one. But tell us, dear Hildy, did you have fun in Paris? And how are all the bars? And did Johnny Starr make any new assaults?"

Hildegarde looked at Elliott to see how he was taking it. Harry was going to be hard to handle. Elliott had a look of polite expectation. He seemed to have missed all the implications of Harry's remarks, "Yes, Sis," he said, "tell us everything from the time you left New York until you returned. Give us your complete itinerary."

"Yes," said Harry, "and don't leave out the part Pop asked about, on why you didn't visit Ireland. Of course I know you were busy, and you didn't have time, and that Lord Sweetpapa was panting in London to give you the key to the city or a remarkable facsimile. But Hildegarde, sweet daughter of the clan of Faherty, why didn't you touch foot to the sacred sod of the Emerald Isle?"

Hildegarde stuck her tongue out at Harry. Elliott still sat at polite attention. She didn't like the way the conversation had developed, but it was a safer subject than the previous one. Harry knew too much about her and Johnny Starr and was too indifferent to the implications of such things to curb his remarks in front of Elliott. Or maybe, she thought, he was too interested and too concerned to be able to keep his mouth shut.

Hildegarde's face became serious. "O.K.," she said, "you are going to get it. Like it or not, you asked for it, so you're going to get it. All I ask is that you don't tell Dad. I think Mother would understand; use your own judgment. But Dad is far too nice and too much of a sentimentalist. I don't want to hurt him. Of course, I never believed Dad's description of our ancestors. Somehow I knew that he knew better too; but I guess some of it had seeped into my way of thinking. Anyway I expected to see something very different from what I did.

"I lied at dinner. I did go to Ireland. I did go to County Kerry. I did see the dear little town of Casey's Bog. I did see the great farm of the O'Flahertys, pardon me, the Fahertys, all two acres of it, where Father's O'Flahertys and Mother's O'Mahoneys were kings and queens. Believe me, I saw all of it, every bit of it. I saw and passed cousinly greetings with our Irish kindred. I saw every filthy one of their ten thousand children. They spawn like—like— well, like nothing but the Irish. And I talked with their dull fathers and stupid mothers.

"I couldn't tell Dad all that, could I? Dad, with his sentimental Maxfield Parrish pictures of the beauties and virtues of Ireland?"

"No, Sis," said Harry, "you couldn't. I'm glad you didn't."

"I don't think it would have been proper or wise, particularly at the present time," said Elliott.

"It would have hurt him to hear you say it. After all," said Harry, "you are his favorite."

"And he'd find it hard to believe me."

"That's right," said Harry, "his ideas about his people's background have been screened through three generations of sentimental reminiscence about Ireland and the Fahertys. But what else can you expect with the Yankees keeping the Irish on the defensive about their origins? To hear the Yankees talk you'd think all of them came from the Court of St. James instead of the slums of Liverpool, Glasgow, and London."

"Wherever they came from," said Hildegarde, "it wasn't as bad as what we came from. I arrived in Dublin from London. The Washburtons had sent a letter to some friends who were something at our legation in Dublin. They gave a dinner party for me. There were a number of very amusing and very charming people present—most of them Irish, many of them Catholic, and all of them with connections in London. It was Friday, and they served roast beef as well as fish. I noticed several of the Catholics present took beef as I did. Lady Cadfield said it was so difficult after a number of cocktails to tell Irish fish from Irish beef. In London the better class Catholics I met were very much like us, only more so. They all have small families, many of them are married to Protestants, and none of them are stupidly fanatic about their religion."

Elliott nodded his head approvingly. "But what about County Kerry?"

"I told my Dublin hostess what my plans were, and she sent a note of introduction to a prominent Irish Catholic family in Kerry. I should have known better. They were very nice and picked me up at the train and took me to their lovely old house that looked out over the Atlantic. I told them that I wanted to look up the O'Flaherty and O'Mahoney families because they were my ancestors. They asked a lot of polite questions. I could see by the way they acted that something was up. It came out soon enough. Their cook was an O'Flaherty, and several of their retainers were O'Mahoneys. It turned out that it was a tradition in their family to have O'Flahertys and O'Mahoneys for servants.

They spoke politely of what good cooks and servants they were, honest and faithful, and always respectful."

Elliott carefully trimmed a pale, thin cigar and lighted it. Harry poured a round of highballs from a decanter that had been left for them on the library table. Hildegarde took out a cigarette; Elliott got up from his chair and lighted it for her. "Warm tonight, isn't it," he said. "We may have a thundershower before Dad and Mother get back."

Meanwhile Harry brought his drink back from the table and sat down on the davenport beside his sister. He put his arm around her, "Well, go on, Sis," he said. "It was kind of hard to take, wasn't it?"

"It certainly was. If my hosts had been trying to rub it in I'd have felt different, but they weren't. They were being nice and trying to do all they could to ease a difficult situation. They knew the spot I was in."

"You can bet they did," said Harry. "Being Irish they were being just as snobbish as you were."

"Don't be nasty."

"I'm not, I'm just telling the truth. We're all snobs. Pop and Mom, Elliott and you. And so are all the Irish. What do you think the expressions lace-curtain and shanty Irish come from?"

Elliott examined the end of his cigar. "I don't believe I can be fairly included in your list."

"Dear brother," said Harry, "when the Faherty in you died, Irish snobbery was buried with it, but Yankee snootiness sprang fullborn from the corpse to take its place."

Elliott ignored Harry. "Hildegarde, did you actually speak to any of our relatives?" he asked.

"I'll say I did. They brought the cook in and told her who I was. She was an O'Flaherty by birth. Of course we had to try to trace connections. As near as I could make it out great-grandfather's brother was her great-grandfather. When I drove down to the village with my hostess I met sloughs of them. O'Flahertys to the left of me, O'Mahoneys to the right of me, in thatched huts and on poverty-stricken farms. The clam flats of Riverbrook are a paradise compared with what I saw. They were all polite to me, but I could see they didn't like me. Some of them were almost rude. Some of them acted like I wasn't real or I was a fake. They asked leading questions. I felt like a criminal. One day of that was more than enough. My friends put me up for the night. My host tried to cheer me up. He gave me a few Irish whiskeys and told me funny stories about the other 'returned Irish' and their difficulties with the natives, and he told me about the little folk and the banshees. But next morning I went back to Dublin and got the boat the following day for London, and was I glad to get back to civilization!"

The three were silent. Elliott looked at his watch. "I think I'll be turning in. I have a long day ahead of me tomorrow. Good night, Harry. Good night, Sis." He kissed her forehead and left the room. "Thank you for telling me."

"I guess Elliott couldn't take it," said Harry.

"I hope I didn't hurt his feelings by talking too frankly."

"He ceased being vulnerable when he gave up being Irish at school. Our brother, sweet sister, is nerveless and bloodless."

The doorbell rang. Harry answered it. Nancy and Frederick Fitzpatrick, with Janet and Roger Wadsworth, son and daughter of old Frederick Wadsworth, all friends of Hildegarde's and Harry's, were calling to welcome Hildegarde home and to suggest driving to the beach for a few drinks and a dance or two at their favorite night club. Nancy and Frederick Fitzpatrick had family backgrounds very similar to that of the Fahertys. The Wadsworth family history, according to Roger, started with God and then built up as it went along. Hildegarde had confided to Harry that Roger was the only boy she could ever consider seriously. Harry had replied, "My dear sister, my dear Mrs. Roger Wadsworth, nee O'Flaherty, all I can say is that when the Irish get on the make nothing can stop them. They've got themselves a Jewish God and an Italian Pope. But everything else below that they keep for themselves, and I'm only waiting for the day they make up their minds to move up the next two rungs of the ladder."

5. *Mrs. Roger Wadsworth, nee Faherty*

HILDEGARDE and Harry, accompanied by the Wadsworths and Fitzpatricks, were being seated by the headwaiter on the veranda of a fashionable north-shore night club. Steps led down from the porch to a private beach. A few couples were dancing to the music of "Stardust" played by a small orchestra. A round of drinks was drunk to welcome Hildegarde home, and another round was ordered "to make it old-home week for everyone." They had all known and liked each other since they had gone to grammar school.

After the second round had started Hildegarde and Roger and

the Fitzpatricks joined the dancers. Harry Faherty and Janet Wadsworth sipped their highballs. With considerable amusement they watched Johnny Starr dancing with a lady whose ample figure curved under her black gown and moved noticeably beneath its glistening surface. Harry looked at her with an approving but critical eye.

Many women had attracted his attention but few had interested him. The psychiatrist who treated him when he had a nervous breakdown which put him in a sanitorium for several months said that "few" was an overstatement. "You've had ten dozen women, Harry, but none of them ever had you."

"Then, doctor, I suffered from an optical and tactile illusion."

"No," said the doctor, "you've been there in the flesh, Harry, but never in the spirit."

Hildegarde and Roger left the dance floor and walked down the steps toward the beach. They were holding hands. Everyone in Yankee City knew that "Roger was crazy about Hildegarde," and that his family had opposed his interest in an Irish Catholic. But everyone knew that some day they would have to give in to Roger. Nancy Fitzpatrick and Janet Wadsworth left the two men at the table while they went to the powder room because, they said, Harry and Freddy had begun their interminable argument about Catholicism and they had heard all of it too many times before.

"Freddy," Harry had begun, "how can you go on taking it the way you do? The Church, I mean. What is it but a place for ambitious and selfish second-generation Irish to get an easy living and an arena for them to fight among themselves for the prize of a bishopric or maybe a cardinal's ring? The Catholic hierarchy has opposed every decent reform that has been proposed in the last generation."

"Such as and for instance," said Freddy.

"They've actively lined up with every exploiter of child labor in this state as well as New York. They're busy scaring the hell out of state legislators so that knowledge about birth control won't become useful to the poor and those who need it. We can't see a serious play on any social issue because of the Church. The Church backs the censorship and lets it front for it to prevent people from reading honest books about contemporary problems. A play or a book can't treat sex seriously without being barred in our great metropolis all because of the Church. But the night clubs and the burlesque houses can pour their filthy sexual jokes all over their audiences and display their women in every dirty kind of situation, and that's O.K. by them. They seem to think that's swell."

"You don't honestly think, Harry, that the Church approves of that kind of filth, do you?"

"Maybe not, but God knows whenever I go to a sexy musical comedy I see the audience filled with Irish politicians and all of them getting a big kick out of it. The Irish Americans are the most conveniently inconsistent people in the world. They are always yelling about the bigotry of the Yankee Protestants. What do you suppose would happen to the Protestants if the Irish Catholics came into power, as they soon will in Massachusetts? Look how the Catholic Poles and the Catholic Italians, their own co-religionists, are treated in the Church. They never get their rights; they are always discriminated against. Look at the fight the French Canadians have had to put up to be given even halfway justice."

"But, Harry, you worry about the things that ultimately don't matter. I know such things exist, and I know they are wrong. I realize the Church, as a political and secular institution throughout history, has often been wrong."

"Change it to 'usually' and I'll agree with you," said Harry.

"Its position on birth control, I think," said Freddy, "is barbaric, and a lot of Catholics agree with me. But you only have to look at the birth statistics of the second generation Irish to know that most of them are devout practitioners of the arts of Mrs. Sanger and not of the tenets of the Church."

"But what about suppressing all the good plays and their attempts to censor serious literature?" asked Harry.

"Now about the plays. I saw *Within the Gates* by Sean O'Casey when they did it in New York, and I thought it beautiful and a true work of art."

"Then how can you defend the Church for banning it in Boston?"

"I don't try, Harry. The truth of the Church is not to be found in its public and outward acts but in the inner life of those who are devout members of the faith. When I go to early morning Mass and kneel before the altar I become a free soul. I come out strengthened and ready to face a world I know is cruel and sometimes evil. You see, it's what the Church stands for spiritually that counts. Think of the millions of little people who are frightened and would be lost without the guiding arm of the Mother Church."

"Freddy, did you ever try to analyze objectively the meaning of some of the Church doctrine? It doesn't make ordinary sense."

"It's not supposed to make ordinary sense. It's only supposed to make extra-ordinary sense, Harry."

"But some of it is more barbaric than a Hottentot myth," said Harry.

"Outwardly, yes, some of it is. I grant that. But the inner meaning of its symbols refers to mysteries men cannot hope to express in tangible form. The accumulated spiritual truths gathered in man through the ages can only be understood by those who approach the truth with humility and with a willingness to know it. I confess I'm not very good at it, but I keep trying."

There was a long pause. Harry took several drinks.

"You know, Freddy, I sometimes envy you. I've never forgotten the shock of losing my religion when I was a kid at prep school. I remember how bitter I was. I was all mixed up with learning what the sexual score was. Somehow I blamed Mother for fooling me on both of them. I guess I'm not over that yet. But what the hell, it's too late now. I can't be objective about it. I think the Roman Catholic Church and the Irish in it are socially dangerous. For every decent-minded one like you, there are a thousand who would return to the days of the Inquisition if they could. No child of mine will ever be permitted to do anything but hate the whole business—and hate it the way I do."

"The way you try to do, Harry," said Freddy.

"No, the way I do."

"Hell, Harry, you're still a Catholic, only you're a Catholic in reverse."

Hildegarde and Roger returned to the table. They were whispering together.

Hildegarde said, "Listen, kids, Roger and I have something we want to tell you. Keep it a deep dark secret, but the Fahertys and the Wadsworths are about to announce a merger."

Congratulations were said, hands were shaken, wise cracks were made. Someone said that this called for a bottle of champagne. Someone else said this called for several bottles of champagne. After many toasts were drunk everyone got up to dance and left Harry and Hildegarde alone.

"You'll call me a damn fool, Harry, but I made one stipulation when I agreed to marry Roger."

"What was that?"

"I insisted we be married in the Catholic Church. Roger said no Wadsworth had ever done that or ever would. I said if that was so no Wadsworth would ever marry a Faherty. He said that that would be practically a world-shaking catastrophe. I said I felt the same way and that he'd better save the world by forgetting his family traditions just a little."

"My God, Hildy, all you're asking is that ten generations of Wadsworths turn over in their graves."

"Well, they'd better start turning, because that's what's going to happen."

"I don't believe you."

"Well, we worked out a compromise," said Hildegarde. "We're going to be married in Boston in the Episcopalian church. We'll have a very small wedding; his family, ours, and a very few understanding friends. Then we're going to sneak off to New York with Pop and Mother (if they'll go) and do it all over again in a Catholic church. That way I can publicly become a part of the ancient and honorable Wadsworth family and at the same time leave off being a Faherty the way the Faherty women have always done."

"God, what a mind. King Solomon was a piker. And, dear sister, what will the children be? I suppose Episco-Catholics."

"Don't be silly. That'll be easy. We've decided there ain't goin' to be any for at least five years."

"Thank God," said Harry, "you've lost at least some of the peasant's conscience you inherited from the Fahertys."

The music stopped and the others joined them at the table. Roger told Nancy Fitzpatrick that Hildy and he planned to be married the following month.

Nancy, who was a little tight, said, "Hurray for you, Hildy. The repression will soon be over, for matrimony is practically around the corner. Freddy and I can recommend both of them."

"You bet we can," said Freddy, "and who knows, maybe prosperity's right around the corner too. I wish getting over the depression was as easy and as much fun as getting over the repression. I could do with a little more of what it takes to keep Scotch in the Fitzpatricks. And that reminds me— Waiter, another round, please."

6. *When They Arrived*

THE Fahertys, O'Malleys, and the Corbetts tell us much about the social life and personalities of the Yankee City Irish. They illustrate some of the differences and similarities which characterize the Catholic Irish group of Yankee City and, for that matter, of the United States. The stresses and strains of their daily living have been employed to bring out more sharply what it means to be Irish at the several class levels. Essentially, the problems of the Irish are the same as those of the other people with divergent cultural traditions.

The social history of the ethnic groups was studied from the time of their arrival in the town until the time of the research to discover what residential, economic, class, and institutional developments had taken place and ascertain if there were common tendencies and determinants in the life of each group. The three chapters which follow examine residential, economic, and class developments. The remaining chapters deal with the family, school, church, and associational organizations of the several cultural groups.

The term *ethnic* refers to any individual who considers himself, or is considered to be, a member of a group with a foreign culture and who participates in the activities of the group. Ethnics may be either of foreign or of native birth. For example, a Greek born in the United States who regularly attended the Greek coffee houses, participated in the Greek associations, and served on the school and church committees of the Greek community was classified as a member of the Greek group.[5] In the present volume greater emphasis is placed on descent (by use of genealogical materials) than in Volume I. Because of this there are occasional minor differences in count between the two volumes.

The ethnic groups entered Yankee City in this order:

	Decade of Arrival	Population 1933
Irish	1840–1850	3,943
French Canadians	1880–1890	1,466
Jews	1890–1900	397
Italians	1890–1900	284
Armenians	1900–1910	246
Greeks	1900–1910	412
Poles	1910–1920	677
Russians	1910–1920	141

The eight ethnic groups present differences in the number of their external relations with the Yankee City social system and in the proportion of American culture elements which have infil-

5. For a general discussion of the classification of ethnics, see I, 211–214.

trated into their internal community relations. Also within each group there are individuals, or social personality types, exhibiting variations of the same character. All the individuals of any given ethnic group can be arranged in continuous order from those whose external relations with the Yankee City social system are most restricted and whose behaviors in the group's internal relations conform with the ancestral culture to those whose external relations are widest and whose internal behaviors are predominantly of American type. These differences vary with the length of residence in Yankee City as measured in terms of the generations intervening between an individual and his immigrant forebears.

II

METHODS FOR THE STUDY OF ETHNIC GROUPS

THE ethnic generation born abroad and migrant to this country is the one attached most strongly to the ancestral social system and its derivative, the ethnic community in Yankee City, and least to the Yankee City social system. In this study this will be called the "parental" or the "P" generation.

The offspring of these immigrants, the "filial first" or the "F¹" generation, having been born, reared, and schooled in the United States, know nothing of the ancestral society of their parents except as it is partially represented in the ethnic group's community organization. The members of the F¹ generation acquire wider external relations with the Yankee City society than their parents and bring more elements of American culture into their internal group relations. The children of the F¹ generation, whom we label F², and the children of the F² generation, whom we label F³, exhibit similar progressive shifts in social personality.

A final differentiation is made by dividing the immigrants into two distinct generations, the P¹ and the P², on the basis of a marked difference in social-personality reorientation which is observed between those who migrated as mature, crystallized personalities and those who migrated as immature, "unfinished" personalities.[1] The latter, quite aside from the fact of their American schooling, are able to shift their social orientation more quickly and easily than can the older immigrants, as is suggested by the fact that in social-personality type the P² generation is intermediate in orientation between the P¹ and the F¹ generations. We have set the migrational age of eighteen as the line distinguishing the P¹ from the P² generation.

The whole classificatory scale of ethnic generations takes the following form:

P¹. The immigrant generation which entered the United States at an age over 18

1. In at least one American ethnic group, the Japanese, the generation we have distinguished as the P² is explicitly named "Hansei," i.e., "Half immigrant." Likewise, the P¹ generation is called "Isseis," i.e., "immigrants"; the F¹ generation group is labeled "Niseis," i.e., "first native-born generation"; and "Sanseis" is applied to the generation we have designated F². Cf. Magner White, "Between Two Flags," *Saturday Evening Post*, CCXII, No. 14 (September 30, 1939), 14.

P². The immigrant generation which entered the United States at an age of 18 or under

F¹. The native-born offspring of P¹ and P²

F². The native-born offspring of F¹

F³. The native-born offspring of F²

F⁴. The native-born offspring of F³

This generation scale makes possible a more refined analysis of status mobility and progress of assimilation than is permitted by the analysis of historical source materials alone. We were able to follow the rise of each group through the community as a unit and also to isolate variations in mobility among successive generations within the group. Further, we were able to compare corresponding generations among the various ethnic groups for variations and associated factors in status movements and processes. We could also follow the internal changes of the ethnic communities in the order of the successive generations.

We shall attempt to place in a measured time perspective the changes in the internal and external organization of each ethnic group and also to compare the original contexts of the ancestral societies from which these groups were derived. Characterizations of the major aspects of these societies are presented in the chapters which follow.

Of course, the complete context of Yankee City, presented in Volume I of this series, must be kept in view. General aspects of the society will be referred to whenever they are related specifically to developments in the ethnic groups. Here, however, we may indicate the conditions in Yankee City during the nineteenth century which made it possible for the ethnics to find a place and a livelihood in the city.

The earliest of the ethnic groups, the Irish, began their important incursion in the 1840's, soon after the textile and other manufacturing industries had secured their first local foothold to supplement the city's original shipping-shipbuilding-fishing economy. Openings created by the general expansion of the economic system, particularly by the establishment of large factories, were filled almost entirely by natives from within the city and without. Only unskilled occupations were available to the Irish as farm laborers, stevedores, carters, hod carriers, and domestics.

Through the 1860's employment in the factories seems to have been associated with middle-class status. Then the free competition of American industrialism adversely affected wage scales and working conditions, depressing the prestige value of factory work.

The maritime enterprises of the city ceased in the early 'eighties. This fact, together with the deflation in the industrial occupations, induced the movement of natives of the middle class, especially of the young people, either to the larger urban centers of the East, or to the West, to find the opportunities for suitable economic status and advancement which Yankee City could no longer provide. At the same time the birth rate among the natives of both the middle and upper classes began to decline. These two developments account for the fact that, in spite of only a slight expansion in local economy since the Civil War, Yankee City has been able to accept increasing numbers of ethnics into its economic system.

All but one of the ethnic groups in Yankee City stem from a rural-peasant type of social system. Are there cultural differences which have had special effects on the course of group interaction in Yankee City? What effect, if any, has a variant social background of a group on its Yankee City development?

If age of the group in the city is a critical variable, what is the influence of the particular order of appearance in the city upon the eight ethnic groups? That is, will an earlier group have more difficulties, or less, and experience slower advance, or faster, than the group which follows it? Further, what weight must be assigned to changes in the Yankee City social system itself which may present the earliest group with conditions not faced by the group last to enter the city?

In summary, this study is an attempt to accomplish the following:

1. To describe in detail, through two time scales and in terms of the relevant contexts, the steps and processes by which eight ethnic groups have

a. progressively advanced in the major status hierarchies of Yankee City and

b. progressively adapted the internal organization of their community systems.

2. To analyze the factors, constant and variable, attending these processes, including the interactive role of Yankee City itself.

3. To abstract wider generalizations concerning the nature of social assimilation and acculturation.

The underlying problem of this study is an examination of the validity of America's conception of itself as the "great melting pot."

III

THE SPATIAL DISTRIBUTION OF THE ETHNIC GROUPS

SOCIOLOGISTS at the University of Chicago have discovered that urban residential arrangements are not haphazard and formless.[1] On the contrary, a society's territorial system exhibits clear-cut and pervasive order and pattern. For example, a city is not an amorphous population congeries, but a pattern of neighborhood areas having significantly differentiated social characteristics. Groups of these neighborhoods are sufficiently similar in certain more general characteristics to be included in the same zones. Each of these areas operates selectively to attract individuals similar in status to those already living in the area.

Thus the different areas of a city acquire different status values, relative to each other. The status value of an individual's area of residence is one of the factors determining his status in the social system of the community.

1. *Ethnic Background*

THE ethnic groups of Yankee City, with the exception of the Jews, originated in a European rural-village type of social economy. They lived in scattered households, each identified for generations with its own small holding of farm and pasture land and joined by a network of dirt roads which converged on the village center. This center generally consisted of the parish church and cemetery, the village mill, smithy, tavern-clubhouse, and open market place. Near the village were the estate and grand manor of the aristocrat landowner to whom the peasant villagers were related as servant tenants. The villages generally comprised from twenty-five to one hundred families.

Typically this was an unchanging and undifferentiated folk society in which an event affecting the individual was also the affair of the entire group, and an event affecting the group was

1. An extensive and significant literature has arisen in sociological studies applying the "ecological approach," especially in the works of Professor R. E. Park and his students. For definitions of the concepts of human ecology see E. W. Burgess (ed.), *The City* (Chicago, University of Chicago Press, 1915).

at once the affair of every individual.[2] Attachments to the land, locale, and group, and family tradition had strong holds upon the sentiments. These sentiments were at times reinforced by the solidarities of a larger area such as the county in Ireland, the province in Poland and Russia, and the section in Italy. These solidarities often were so strong as to be directed antagonistically against comparable neighboring areas in the same country.

This pattern is in contrast to the urban type of residential system represented in Yankee City. The ecological base of the city is only secondarily and remotely the land as such. Identifications with place, strong in the peasant village, are shallow and weak in large American cities, although they are reorganized in a diluted form around the unit of the neighborhood. Yankee City, however, is unusual in its preservation of a strong sense of locale, attributable unquestionably to the part its geography played in the period of its maritime importance. But even in Yankee City neighbor relations are much compressed compared to those in the folk communities of Europe. As a consequence of spatial crowding and competition for place, impersonal, somewhat formal relations among neighbors in Yankee City replace the intimate give-and-take of relations in the peasant village.

The ethnic in his native village was identified with a plot of land which had been tilled for generations, often centuries, by his forebears. Moreover, his relations with the more distant members of the community were almost as close as with his immediate neighbors. In a relatively homogeneous ecological order, he could visit about freely. In Yankee City, however, in spite of relative instability of residence in the areas originally open to ethnic settlement, the ecological system provides barriers limiting the range of residential movement and the range of possible social relations as well. One is a relative stranger in most areas other than the one in which he lives.

The ethnic group, soon after settling in Yankee City and achieving adequate population numbers, is segregated in the most accessible, i.e., in the lowest-grade, areas of the city and remains identified with those areas, often for decades. However, once the group has adapted itself to the new order, it breaks from its isolation and begins moving into the larger community.

2. The folk type of society is a major category in the scheme for classifying societies that has been defined by Professor Robert Redfield. For enumeration of the attributes of the type, cf. Robert Redfield, *Tepoztlán, A Mexican Village* (Chicago, University of Chicago Press, 1930), pp. 1–14.

2. *Residential Zones of Yankee City*

TERRITORIALLY Yankee City is a long narrow rectangle which stretches along the side of a great river. Some few blocks from the river and up the side of a gentle slope is Hill Street. This is a broad, elm-lined residential street which runs from one end of the town to the other. Side streets connect Hill Street with River Street, which runs along the bank of the river. The business area in the center of the town is bisected by Commonwealth Street.

There is a continuous shading off in status value from Hill Street down to River Street on the waterfront. Residence on River Street has the lowest status value in the residential hierarchy, while residence on Hill Street has the highest value. This is approximately true at almost any point on the city's long axis.

For purposes of analysis and definition, we have constructed a schematized version of the city's residential areas based on four zones, as represented in Chart I. Zone I is at the foot of the city's slope directly fronting the river. Here are concentrated most of the factories, coal yards, storage tanks, warehouses, and smaller retail establishments. The houses are usually small, frame, somewhat flimsy, often abutting on the sidewalk. Some are of the box-tenement type. Many are from one hundred to one hundred and fifty years old, often in disrepair. The streets are narrow and some are still unpaved. In population, this is the largest of the zones and also the most dense. The zone has been divided into two sections along Commonwealth Street. Section I-E (East End) is somewhat older than Section I-W (West End), has fewer retail stores, and is more crowded. Houses in I-W are one degree better in quality and upkeep. Section I-E is associated primarily with the lower-lower class and secondarily with the upper-lower class, whereas in Section I-W the order is reversed. Wharf Square, a point of concentration for several ethnic groups, is at the intersection of Commonwealth and River Streets, where Sections I-E and I-W join.

CHART I

RESIDENTIAL CONFIGURATION OF YANKEE CITY

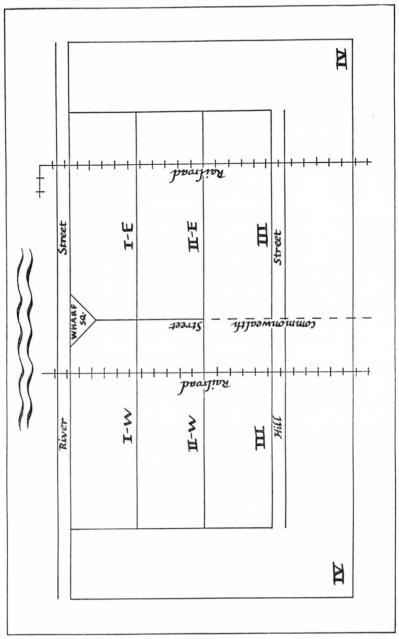

Zone III runs the full length of Hill Street and includes the residences immediately adjoining on the side streets. In contrast to Zone I, the finest and largest houses in the city are found here —those which in an earlier period were known as "princely mansions." Many are set far back from the street with well-kept gardens and shaded by old trees. Hill Street itself is forty feet wide and covered by an arch of ancient elms. There are no business establishments, with the exception of an ice-cream parlor beside the high school and a garage and small store where railroad tracks cross the street at the only low-evaluation spots in the zone. This is the smallest of the four zones, both in area and population, and the lowest, except for Zone IV, in population density. We have already indicated that this zone is primarily identified with the upper classes, although it is now also occupied by an important part of the upper-middle class.

Zone II extends between Zones I and III, has few factories, but contains all of the better retail shops, including the central business section with its stores, offices, theaters, banks, clubrooms, and public buildings. The houses are midway in quality between those of Zones I and III and in better condition than those of the former. Generally they are set back from the walks which, like the streets, are uniformly well paved. In area covered and in the size and density of population, Zone II is second only to Zone I. As in the case of Zone I, we have divided Zone II into two sections, one on each side of Commonwealth Street. The important differences between the two sections are that II-W is newer than II-E and its houses, on the whole, are one grade better and not quite so crowded. The zone is primarily associated with the middle classes. However, by far the largest part of the upper-middle class not in Zone III is collected in the western section of Zone II (Section II-W).

Zone IV is a thinly settled peripheral area. House types range from medium grade to lowest. Many houses, particularly on the southern side, are on unpaved streets, in small groups separated by considerable expanses of field. Gardening and a little light farming are still carried on here. There are no business places. It is the largest of the four zones in area and, Zone III excepted, the lowest in population density. In class composition Zone IV is the most mixed, ranging from the lower-lower class through the lower-middle.[3]

3. The regions called zones in the present volume correspond only roughly to the "areas" in Volume I. The "residential zones and sections" of the present volume were fashioned to meet the needs of the ethnic analysis. They are based on

These zones can be arranged in a graded scale according to status value:

1. Section I-E: lower-lower and upper-lower classes.

2. Section I-W: upper-lower and lower-lower classes.

3. Zone IV: lower-middle, upper-lower, and lower-lower classes.

4. Section II-E: lower-middle and upper-lower classes.

5. Section II-W: lower-middle and upper-middle classes.

6. Zone III: upper-upper, lower-upper, and upper-middle classes.

Up to this point our account has consisted of enumerations of the distribution of families in each ethnic group among defined residential areas of Yankee City, a statement of the changes in distribution, and a description from the spot maps of the detail of these changes and the changes in the group's own internal relations. It is obvious from our figures on the residential scatter of the ethnic groups that mobility has occurred to some degree in each group. We shall now summarize the facts of such mobility in the more convenient form of a statistical average or index.

3. *The Residential Status Index*

THE various residential areas of Yankee City appear in a continuously graded series according to their status value. To determine the average residential status of a group in any one year, we shall utilize a status index. Such an index is computed, first, by assigning consecutive numbers in a series from one to six to each successively higher level (residential areas) in the hierarchy. The group's population by household in any given year is multiplied by the number value allocated to the area of residence. The sum of these products is then divided by the total number of household

the more general evaluation of the territory of Yankee City made by its citizens. The Hill Street region has higher social value, the Side Street region intermediate, and the River Street area low value. They are respectively Zones I, II, and III. Zone IV is the less well-settled region which surrounds the rest (see I, 81–87).

For the benefit of the reader who is interested in the degree of correspondence between the sections and zones of this volume and the "areas" of Volume I, the following classification is given: Section I-E includes all of Riverbrook and those parts of Oldtown, Uptown, Business District (up to the railroad tracks), Downtown, and Middletown which are nearest the river; II-E includes the remainder of the six areas up to Hill Street; I-W includes all of Littletown and the river sections of the Business District beyond the railroad tracks, Homeville, and Newtown; Zone III includes all of Hill Street, the central section of Newtown and Oldtown, and the territory of Middletown, Uptown, Business District, Centerville, and Hometown contiguous to Hill Street; and Zone IV includes the extremities of all the areas which extend beyond Hill Street.

units in the group for the given year. The quotient is an index number between one and six expressing the status of the group as a whole in terms of an average.

The distribution of the Irish in 1850 is an illustration:

Area	Value	Number of Households	Product
I-E	1	48	48
I-W	2	41	82
IV	2.5	0	0
II-E	3	13	39
II-W	4	2	8
III	6	0	0
		104	177

The summation of the products (177) divided by the total number of households (104) gives a quotient of 1.70, the residential status index. Were the entire Irish group in 1850 in Area I-E, the index of course would be 1; and were the group entirely concentrated in I-W, the index would be 2. Hence, if we suppose that the Irish index in 1840 had been 1, the 1850 index of 1.7 expresses the fact that for every ten households in the group there has been an average upward mobility of seven steps (in terms of the series of graded areas) during the decade. Had there been an average advance of ten steps, then of course the index would have been 2.[4]

Table II presents the status indices of each ethnic group by decades through its occupation of Yankee City in significantly large family numbers. The figures in this table reflect the ethnic residential movements which are treated comprehensively in the appendix to this volume. However, manifestations of accelerating mobility in successive ethnic groups may now be pointed out.

4. It must be emphasized that the values attached to the several areas are arbitrary and have a serial value principally. The fact that Area I-W is given a numerical value of 2 and Area I-E is given a value of 1 does not imply that the former has twice as much status value as the latter. It means only that Area I-W is one level higher in the residential scale than is Area I-E. Our purpose is to measure the average advance of a group in terms of such levels.

We have allowed two exceptions to our assignment of values in a series of 1. Given the residential and social-class characteristics of Area IV, it is felt that movement to this area, let us say, from Area I-W cannot be considered equivalent to an advance of a full level, such as, for example, would be represented by movement from Area I-E to I-W. Hence, we have considered Area IV as being a half-step between Areas I-W and II-E. On the same grounds, movement from II-W to Area III, covering Hill Street, is by no means equivalent to movement from II-E to II-W. For that reason movement to Area III has been considered the equivalent of two steps upward from II-W, and its value has been fixed as 6.

TABLE 1

Residential Status Indices of Eight Ethnic Groups, 1850–1933

Group	1850	1864	1873	1883	1893	1903	1913	1923	1933
Irish...........	1.70	1.95	2.11	2.11	2.12	2.22	2.37	2.57	2.85
French Canadian	..	..	..	..	1.67	1.78	1.77	2.13	2.43
Jewish.........	..	..	..	..	..	..	1.93	2.14	2.77
Italian.........	..	..	..	..	..	..	..	2.21	2.38
Armenian......	..	..	..	..	..	..	..	2.39	2.57
Greek.........	..	..	..	..	..	..	..	2.40	2.54
Polish.........	..	..	..	..	..	..	..	1.25	1.40
Russian........	..	..	..	..	..	..	..	..	1.32

Four of these groups appear in their first important decade year with a higher index than did the group preceding; three—the French Canadians, Poles, and Russians—are lower. The factor responsible for retarding mobility, and consequently the residential index, of the two latter groups, namely, industrial displacement early in their Yankee City careers, will be discussed in the next chapter. The concentration of the French Canadians in the city's East End has tended to depress their index. However, these three groups excepted, the first decade-year indices increase as follows: Irish, 1.70; Jews, 1.93; Italians, 2.21; Armenians, 2.39; and Greeks, 2.40.

A second instance of accelerating mobility is seen especially in the case of the three oldest groups. On the basis of the indices above, the average mobility each decade by the Irish is .14; by the French Canadians, .19; and by the Jews, .42. The most striking advance made by the Irish is in the last three decades, by the French Canadians in the last two decades, and by the Jews in the last decade—each progressing about .66. That is, in these periods fully two families in every three, on the average, moved upward one whole level in residential status.

Chart II plots the index of each ethnic group for the year 1933. The Irish and the Jews have already reached a status slightly higher than that of the native population (2.75). The Armenians, Greeks, French Canadians, and Italians are somewhat below the status of the natives, while the Poles and Russians are still very near the bottom of the scale.

What conclusions and generalizations of significance may we

draw from this evidence of the movements through the years of the ethnic groups?

4. *Ethnic External Pattern in the Residential System*

First and most important is the fact that all ethnic groups, in relation to the Yankee City residential system, behave with a varying degree of uniformity in a definite pattern. The elements in this ethnic pattern are as follows:

1. All groups concentrate first in Zone I and within Zone I on River Street. However, Zone IV represents a secondary gate of ingress.

2. Mobility upward into Zone I from River Street begins early and progresses continuously through the zone and out of it into Zone II.

3. Within Zone I every group, except the Irish, confines itself predominantly either to the East or to the West End Section and remains fixed.

4. In corresponding periods for successive groups the trend of mobility seems to be accelerated.

We shall discuss each of these four points in turn.

The question arises as to the conditions which influenced the first settlement of all ethnic groups without exception in Zone I. Many ethnics give as their answer that industry was concentrated in the zone, and they established residence convenient to their place of work. Of the early Irish, one Irishman said: "They took a job where they could and settled near by." A Polish informant said of his own group: "The Poles are concentrated on River Street because that is where the cotton mills were and where now are the shoe factories."

But it is clear that convenience to the city's workshop area was only an apparent factor in the ethnics' first residential selection. The Jews, who have never had more than a negligible representation in the factories, were no less concentrated in Zone I.

Three factors seem pertinent, two of which are suggested in the remarks of a Greek informant: "The Greeks, coming like this to America, live in with the lowest classes of Americans. It is because of poverty that they have to go into the poor district to live. But actually it isn't so much different from the way they lived in Greece."

First, then, is the fact that the standard of housing, even on River Street, is no lower and probably considerably higher than that which the ethnics were accustomed to in their native villages, and hence sufficient, at least in the beginning, for their level of need and taste.

Second, even had their demands been higher, the ethnics, on the whole, arrived in Yankee City in a poverty-stricken condition. With rentals continuously graduated upward on the city's incline, the lowest rents were in Zone I on River Street.

The third factor, related to the second, is that upward from the waterfront the proportion of homeowners increases regularly. Zone I, with the lowest proportion of homeowners, is the most accessible to an ethnic group since there are more places to occupy by tenancy and a greater degree of residential movement.

In all these respects, except in the number of rentable houses, the sparsely settled peripheral Zone IV, at certain points, closely approximates the conditions in Zone I, accounting for the fact that as a threshold to the city for the ethnics it was second in importance to Zone I.

The second element in the pattern is that, once established on River Street, the ethnic group begins to advance, slowly but certainly, in one direction predominantly, southward and upward toward Hill Street. We shall undertake an analysis of the force which impels the undeviating ethnic drift up the city's incline and of the factors which have influenced the rate of progress.

Such movement on the part of all eight ethnic groups in Yankee City may be attributed to what we shall call "hierarchical attraction," a force which disposes those resident in any one area to aspire to a home in the area next higher in the scale. The act of translating that aspiration into movement into the higher area is what has been constantly referred to here as residential mobility. This force operates in the three status hierarchies of Yankee City studied in this volume.

It is true, of course, that conditions both in his background and in the Yankee City system compel the ethnic to settle first on River Street. Influenced early, however, by the attractions of the Yankee City hierarchy, the ethnic takes his first step upward by moving from his original River Street house to a residence somewhat higher in Zone I. But each step upward immediately defines and presents the next higher step. Hence the ethnic at intervals continues his ascent, pausing only as long as his income or other considerations preclude his paying the added cost and until a dwelling place for him in the higher area is available. The latter is no minor condition, as we shall soon see. Residential mobility, par-

CHART II

RESIDENTIAL STATUS INDICES OF ETHNIC GROUPS IN 1933

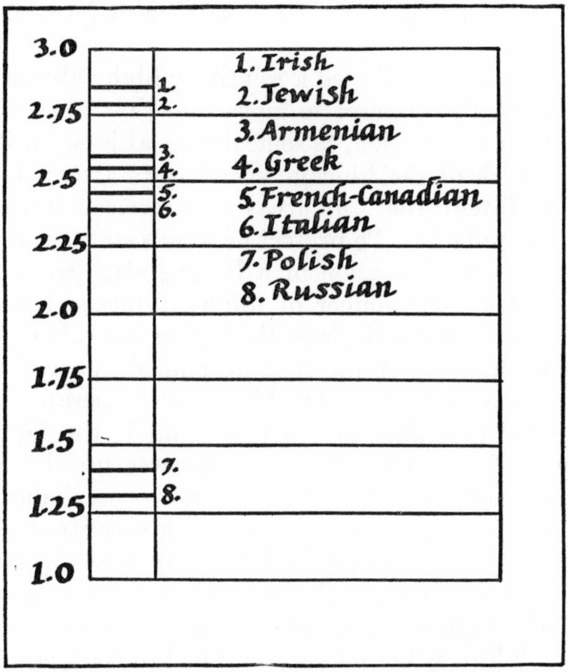

tially at least, is contingent upon economic mobility and is almost an indispensable condition for social-class mobility.

Insight into the process of residential mobility is afforded by the remarks of an elderly Irishman: "The Irish were laborers, but they were thrifty and saved their money. Just the minute they had enough, they took it to buy property in a better section. The same thing is true of the French, and the rest of the new workers. So there was considerable movement." The key to the thinking here lies in the "but" which implies the tentativeness of the status value identified with "laborers"; and the "but" hinges this tentativeness of status upon the acquisition of a home "just the minute they had enough money" in a section, which we know from evidence already reviewed, was upward from River Street.

Similarly, a Jewish informant told us: "First the Jews were all around Wharf Square and River Street. When they made money they bought up property gradually more and more outside the Square."

As in the physical realm, where attractions are partially counteracted by resistive frictions, mobility in social hierarchies does not proceed free of resistance. In fact, at each successive level the resistance tends to become more active. Such resistance is an aspect reciprocal to attraction and takes different forms in different hierarchies.

If a given area is attributed a relatively high value, and if persons of lower status attempt to move into that area, the area is threatened with a reduction, to some degree at least, of its current values. The work of the Chicago sociologists attests to the "decline" or "disintegration" of areas in American cities through shifts in the population. To protect an area's status value, its residents will resist the incursion of a lower-status group. This resistance appears in a number of different forms, both systemic and individual. In the first place, the higher the value of the area, the higher is the level of the rent demanded. There is a money sacrifice involved in residential mobility which operates as a highly selective factor to reduce mobility. Second is the fact that the proportion of family-owned homes increases up the residential scale, so that progressively fewer houses are available for rent. Hence mobile families are confronted with a contracting supply of places open to tenancy and the increasing necessity of purchasing a house. The latter, together with the rise of property values in successively higher areas, acts as an even more rigorous resistive force. Third is the pressure applied to counteract mobility by property owners who, in defense of the area's status and property values, refuse to sell or rent to "undesirables." A fourth form of resistance is the social ostracism practiced by residents of the area on those who have succeeded in "crashing." One Jewish woman, after ten years of residence in Zone III, complained bitterly of her neighbors that "they are not friendly at all."

Finally, when all else fails, more drastic steps may be taken. For example, one upper-class woman, in discussing the house occupied by her daughter, added: "The landlord has just rented the next house to some terrible Jewish family, so my daughter must move." It is significant that the imperative "must" is used here. Similarly, one Irish informant related that immediately after he had purchased a house on the edge of Zone III, the owner-occupant of the next house "came to us and offered to pay us a thousand dollars more than we had paid, because he didn't want to have us living next to him." The offer was turned down, and the discriminating gentleman who had made it soon after sold his place and moved to Hill Street.

Another incident was reported by a Jewish informant: "Mr. Cohen was the first one on Apple Street [Section II-E]. And the people around objected to his horse and wagon and the junk in the barn. So right away houses on both sides and across from him went on sale, and other Jews came in and bought these. So now there are six Jewish families on Apple Street where there used to be none. That's the way it went." Today these six families form a closely knit nucleus on Apple Street, such nuclei having been found from time to time among other ethnic groups who were beginning to penetrate Zone II. In fact, of the fifteen Irish families who were in Section II-E in 1850, ten are arranged in exactly such a nucleus along a single street.

Still another instance of resistance exerted not against an ethnic family but against the ethnic group at large was described by an old Irish gentleman: "When the Irish built their church here they had to have someone else buy the land for them because no Protestant would have sold them the land in that place (Zone III). And when the people found out about it they were very sore." Some eighty years later, when the Jewish community came to buy a vacated church building in upper Section II-W for use as a synagogue, the families in the area again "were very sore," and a petition was circulated to influence the mayor "to keep the purchase from being made."

At certain points in the city this type of resistance has operated successfully to bar entrance of ethnics, as in the case of one special area in Section I-E, almost completely devoid of Irish or other ethnics. An Irishman said of the area: "There is plenty of room in it, but the Irish never made much headway in it. They all hate the Irish."

Certainly, resistance has not stopped ethnic mobility in other areas, Zone III not excluded, but it has greatly impeded the rate of advance. How else can one explain the phenomenon that a group as socially aggressive as the Irish went through almost eighty years of slow "inching along" before its members reached representation on Hill Street?

Furthermore, but for the regular emigration of natives from Yankee City, such resistance would have been even more effective; the emigration opened houses for rent and sale, especially in Zone II, that would not otherwise have been available. Partially counteracting this condition were the facts, first, that natives from the lower areas were competing with the ethnics at an advantage for the openings on Zone II; and second, that the ethnic population grew faster than the native population declined, and hence increasing numbers of ethnics were competing among themselves for a relatively fixed number of places in the "better" areas.

A clear-cut manifestation of increasing resistance among areas consecutively higher in the residential scale is found in the higher rates of ethnic advance in Section I-E as against I-W, and in II-E as against II-W. In fact, this has been a condition which determined the original choice of each group between Sections I-E and I-W.

It will be remembered that the Irish in 1850 were living along most of the length of River Street through Sections I-E and I-W and that by 1873 they were beginning to move upward from River Street. While this progress was relatively slow in Section I-E, the pace was even more retarded in Section I-W. Hence, when the French Canadians first came to Yankee City in some numbers in the middle 'eighties, they found the Irish almost clear of the Section I-E strip of River Street and well up into the section, while in Section I-W the Irish were still at the bottom of the area and still well represented on River Street, which they were not to leave until 1903. Thus, River Street in the former section was open to the French Canadians, whereas in the adjoining section it was effectively blocked off by the Irish. As a result, the French Canadians settled en masse in Section I-E, especially on River Street, exhibiting here a far higher concentration in the section in proportion to the group's total households than did the Irish in a corresponding phase.

The French Canadians were followed by the Jews and the Italians who, small in numbers relative to either of the older groups, found space immediately around the Wharf Square sector of River Street, the city's old market place, where neither the Irish nor the French Canadians had settled to any great degree. The Jews selected the eastern side (I-E) of the Square, and the Italians the western (I-W). The Jewish advance, thereafter, was directly upward, whereas the Italian was first westward into Section I-W proper. Hence these two small groups found homes in the very center of River Street and Zone I. They were followed in a decade by the Armenians and the Greeks in quick succession, who would have been expected to select Section I-E as their place of residence. However, they settled on River Street in Section I-W because the Jews and the French Canadians were still well represented along the waterfront in Section I-E. Although the Italians were still on River Street in Section I-W, the Irish had succeeded in pushing into the interior of the section proper. With Section I-E relatively blocked off, the Armenians and the Greeks settled on River Street in Section I-W, on either side of the Italians.

The Poles and the Russians were the next to arrive. But the resistance in Section I-W was still confining Italians, Armenians, and Greeks to the foot of the section, whereas in the brief interim both the Jews and the French Canadians had been able to move forward in Section I-E. The Poles and Russians, therefore, had no choice but to settle Section I-E.

Thus the differential resistance exerted by Sections I-E and I-W has largely determined the shuttling selection made by succeeding ethnic groups as between settlement in one or other of these sections. There are, therefore, both a primary continuous stratification of ethnic groups between River and Hill Streets and a secondary alternating stratification between the East and West End. This is indicated in Chart III, which outlines the present position and range in Yankee City of the great bulk of each group.

The third element in the ethnic residential pattern is the tendency of each group to remain fixed in either the East or West End, depending upon where it first settled. In other words, movement has occurred from any given area to the one next higher on the city's incline, rather than to the one next higher in the residential scale. Zone IV is an exception. This pattern of movement is illustrated in Chart IV.

It has been established that each successively higher residential area exerts greater attraction and greater resistance, explaining both the fact of continuous ethnic advance and the fact that such advance is very slow through the extremely narrow north-south dimension of Yankee City.

The phenomenon of differential or accelerating mobility, observed among successive ethnic groups, is the fourth element in the ethnic residential pattern. Numerous factors are involved in this accelerating mobility among consecutive groups. The most important is that the pioneer ethnic group, the Irish, encountered resistance throughout its advance, especially since it was the vanguard in areas hitherto not entered by ethnics. However, while resistance stiffens in the path of the first ethnic column, in the "rear" it tends to collapse. Property values tend to decline, but the relative position of the area in the residential hierarchy does not change. Those residents of the area who can do so move to another area as yet unavailable to ethnics, thereby opening new places for

CHART III

RANGE OF SETTLEMENT OF ETHNIC GROUPS IN 1933

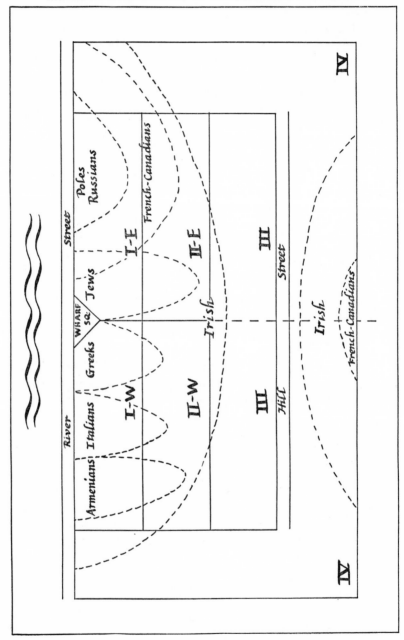

CHART IV

AREA SEQUENCE IN ETHNIC RESIDENTIAL MOBILITY

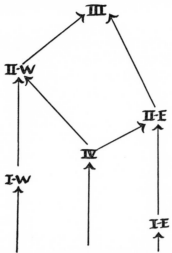

ethnics. And those who are unable to leave give up active resistance and become reconciled. An illustration of such resignation was given by a native living in Section II-E: "Some Jews have gotten in here, and they don't belong. But they have money and can't be kept out." As the ethnics push farther ahead, they leave vacancies immediately behind them. Thus the second group to arrive in the city remains on River Street only a relatively short time before it can move into these vacancies left by the vanguard group. In the wake of one ethnic group's advance, the area of exodus is left open for the following group.

The second factor in differential ethnic mobility is related to the size of the group in terms of household units. The smaller the number of such units in an ethnic group, the less resistance it encounters and the greater is its possible mobility. The reaction of a society to a social deviant such as the "foreigner" and the "alien" is generally sharp, but the intensity of the reaction is in direct proportion to the number of such deviants who invade the society. For example, in their amorphous phase,[5] the French Canadians, consisting of about a dozen families, settled as freely in Zone II as in Zone I, at a time when the Irish, numbering hundreds of households, were fighting every step of their way into Zone II. It is obvious that with a relatively fixed supply of housing facilities, a

5. See Appendix.

group of a thousand households will succeed in entering a new area in far smaller proportions than will a group of a hundred household units. The fact that the French Canadians since 1903 have never exceeded one third the size of the Irish group in family numbers has contributed without question to their greater rapidity of residential mobility as compared with the Irish. Similarly, the more rapid advance of the Jews in comparison with the French Canadians may be attributed in part at least to the fact that their household numbers have consistently been about one fourth those of the latter group. An added factor in this case is that the urban background of the Jews, as against the rural-village background of all other ethnic groups, has helped them to make a relatively quick adjustment to the urban conditions of Yankee City.

Ethnic residential mobility is conditioned by both attraction and resistance. But, whereas the force of attraction is fairly constant as a result of the unusually clear-cut configuration of Yankee City's residential system, the force of resistance varies with the order of the ethnic group's residential antecedents. Whatever the variation in resistance and consequently in the rate of mobility, the response and orientation of the ethnics to the attractions of Yankee City have been unvarying. The push of the ethnics toward Hill Street, through their entire ninety years in the city, has never ceased.

5. *Pattern of Ethnic Internal Residential Relations*

THERE are four elements in the pattern of ethnic internal residential relations[6]:

1. From an original amorphous scatter, as the group grows in numbers within Zone I, families increasingly congregate in residential formations.

2. With entrance into Zone II, large residential coagulations dissolve, but in some cases much smaller nuclei are re-formed.

3. There is a definite relation between the rate of a group's mobility and the duration of its residential formations.

4. Developments in an ethnic group's community system are related to changes in its residential formations.

Except for the Irish and the Armenians, families in an ethnic group in its earliest years and while it was small in numbers did not live near to one another in a nucleus of residences. However, with increasing numbers residences of an ethnic group congregated in progressively larger forms, expanding from small

6. For details on ecology of ethnic distribution see Appendix.

nuclei to large nuclei, minor clusters, and finally major clusters.

The increase in the group's population not only strengthens the pressures exerted against its mobility but also brings into play the internal centripetal forces which draw the group together in a community in successively larger residential formations. Mobility through Zone I is carried out largely by families gathered in these residential formations moving en masse. As the ethnic wedge approaches the Zone II line, the resistance increases to the point where the group can no longer proceed as a unit; individual families break off from the formation and push into whatever openings can be found in the higher zone. Hence there are no clusters and few nuclei formed by the ethnic groups in Zone II. Such nuclei generally appear late and only when, as in Section II-W and in the case of the Jews on Apple Street, small groups of natives protestingly move out in a body.

As crossing into Zone II proceeds, the residential formations in the Zone I area are depleted and contract successively in size and density from major clusters to minor clusters, large nuclei, small nuclei, and finally condition of dispersion.

We may conclude, therefore, that an ethnic group maintains important residential relations among its member families only as long as it remains in Zone I. Thus there is a correlation between the rate of a group's mobility and the duration of its own residential cohesion. The more rapid the advance, the shorter lived are the groups residential formations in Zone I. Up to a point, resistance tends to induce consolidation in a group's residential formations, as was observed in the greater persistence of Irish nuclei and clusters in Section I-W, as compared with those in Section I-E. But once transit is made into Zone II, the group must disperse its residences or cease its movement forward. Mobility, therefore, is the single factor in the dissolution of an ethnic group's residential base.

The three oldest of the ethnic groups have no residential base. The Irish and the Jews, their former residential coherence having disappeared, are no longer identified with a certain area but are scattered through the entire city. The French Canadians are identified with a strip in the city's East End at the center of which is their church, but with the exception of several nuclei little residential juxtaposition remains among their households. These three groups in their internal residential relations are in disintegrative stages.

The other five groups, however, in 1933 appear to be in a phase of consolidation since all are in process of expanding their large nuclei and clusters. That each of these groups has a residential base is manifest in the fact that certain parts of Zone I are identified by natives and ethnics alike as the "center" or "section" of one or other of the five groups.

The three major residential stages of an ethnic group are correlated with its own community organization. In the first and amorphous stage there is no community organization. With residential consolidation of the family structures appear ethnic stores and informal associations such as the Greek coffee shop, then formal church and school structures, and finally the first men's association. In the disintegrating phases new association structures are formed to maintain the community system in spite of the loss of the group's residential base. Therefore, there is a relation between the rate of residential mobility of an ethnic group, the degree and duration of cohesiveness of its residential relations, and the structural crystallizations of its community organization.

6. *Residential "Mixing" of Ethnic Groups*

With the spread upward of more recent ethnics, there has been an increasing degree of residential "mixing" of groups. A Greek informant's remark is typical: "I have as neighbors two Greek families, an Italian family, an Armenian family, and a French-Canadian family." A spot map for 1933 shows about one hundred cases through all four zones in which Irish and French Canadians occupy adjoining houses, thirty-five cases in which French-Canadian and Jewish families adjoin, and fifteen of Italian and Irish families. There are also scattered cases of residential juxtaposition of other ethnics in all the various combinations.

In moving out of their own residential formations, the ethnics are brought into immediate or "neighbor" relations with native and other ethnic families.

IV

THE ETHNIC GROUPS IN THE ECONOMIC LIFE OF THE COMMUNITY

I N one aspect the economic system of Yankee City appears as a
system of occupations and occupational classes which constitute highly important criteria for wider social classifications. The position of the eight ethnic groups in the occupational
system of the city was studied as well as the economic and occupational antecedents of these groups.

1. *Ethnic Economic Background*

IRELAND in 1841 had a population of 6.5 million. In 1926 it had
only 2.9 million, the loss of 55 per cent due in large part to migration. Seventy-eight per cent of the emigrants were from the villages and towns and were almost exclusively farm laborers.[1] That
most, if not all, of the Irish immigrants to Yankee City came from
a rural-agricultural type of economy is confirmed by a septua-
genarian Irish informant: "The Irish who settled here had all been
farmers, that is, those who were from Counties Cork and Kerry.
The only ones who were not adapted to tilling the soil were those
from Waterford. They were seafaring, but weren't so many."

A French historian reports of the French Canadians: "The
mass of the population was absorbed by agriculture and but few
were common labourers. . . . In the rural parts trades and professions were and still are few." [2]

An American student of Italian emigration ascribes a similar
background to the Italians:

Working upon his data of 1870, Carpi classified the emigrants according to their origin in country or town. The rural he deemed to
be about five-sixths of all. When statistics of occupation were first
officially collected, in 1878, they indicated, just as their successors

1. W. F. Adams, *Ireland and Irish Emigration to the New World* (New Haven,
Yale University Press, 1932), p. 6. Conrad M. Arensberg, *The Irish Countryman*
(New York, The Macmillan Co., 1937). C. M. Arensberg and S. T. Kimball,
Family and Community in Ireland (Cambridge, Harvard University Press, 1940).
2. J. C. Bracq, *The Evolution of French Canada* (New York, The Macmillan
Co., 1924), p. 243.

have done, that the great mass of emigrants came from the agricultural districts.[3]

Similar citations from the literature could be presented for the Greeks, but more precise figures have been made available by an occupational census of the Yankee City Greek immigrants and their fathers who remained in Greece. The occupations of these fathers were distributed as follows: agriculture, 50 per cent; handicrafts, 39; merchants, 8; and professions, 2.

The same census conducted among the Yankee City Poles shows an even more pronounced occupational specialization in the homeland: agriculture, 86 per cent; handicrafts, 10; merchants, 2; and professions, 2.

A Yankee City Pole came close to our census figures when he said: "In the old country, 85 per cent live on farms." In the United States Census Report for the fiscal year 1912–13, of 142,000 Polish immigrants with professed occupations, 72 per cent were farm or "day" laborers, 20 per cent were classed as "servants," less than 1 per cent as merchants, and about 6 per cent as craftsmen.[4]

An Armenian writer,[5] from the figures of the United States Bureau of Immigration, reports the following distribution of adult male Armenians who entered the United States from 1899 to 1917: farm laborers, 53.5 per cent; handicrafts, 31.9; domestics, 7.9; merchants, 3.7; professions, 1.8; and miscellaneous, 1.0.

The Jews are the only ethnic group to deviate from this predominantly agricultural-handicraft type of economy. They have been commonly accepted as traders par excellence, but the figures of the first Russian census of 1897 show that only about one third of the Russian Jews gainfully employed were actually tradesmen.[6] Another third fell under the official classification of "manufacturing and mechanical pursuits." These artisans were for the most part independent manual workers who carried on their handicrafts in their own homes. They included tailors, cobblers, carpenters,

3. R. Foerster, *Italian Emigration of Our Times* (Cambridge, Harvard University Press, 1932), pp. 39–40.

4. Quoted by J. Korski Grove in "The Polish Group in the United States," *Annals of the American Academy of Political and Social Science,* XCIII (1921), 154–155.

5. M. V. Malcom, *The Armenians in America* (Boston, Pilgrim Press, 1918), p. 81.

6. I. Rubinow, *The Economic Conditions of the Jews in Russia,* Bulletin, Bureau of Labor, Department of Commerce (Washington, Government Printing Office, 1908).

blacksmiths, etc. A fourth of the Jewish employed were divided among the unskilled forms of labor, such as domestics, carters, and drayers. About 5 per cent were classified under "professional service," which included teachers of Hebrew, doctors, and lawyers. The Jews, therefore, are derived from a town trade-crafts economy, rather than from a village-agrarian economy. Important consequences of this fact appear in the marked deviation of their economic behavior in Yankee City.

The Jews excepted, then, the ethnics have their source in a simple economic system which is predominantly agricultural, organized around the productive and self-sufficient family unit, and marked by only a slight specialization of occupations and relatively little circulation of labor, money, and goods. This is in sharp contrast to the highly geared economic system of Yankee City, with its narrowly specialized economic structures and occupations, lack of family self-sufficiency, complex circulation of values, and relatively impersonal, contractual types of exchange relations.

Another important aspect of the economic background of the ethnics is that in the complex of factors which contributed to the mass emigrations of the nineteenth century, the economic factor was predominant in all cases except that of the Armenians. An Irish observer visiting the United States after the Civil War writes: "The mass came because they had no option but to come, because hunger and want were at their heels, and flight was their only chance of safety." [7]

With the Irish the economic factors compelling them to leave Ireland outweighed the attraction of American economic forces. With the Jews and the Armenians the expulsive forces were even more important, the economic being aggravated by the violent antagonisms to these groups on the part of the Russian and Turkish societies. For the other ethnic groups there was a more even balance between the economic forces of expulsion in the homeland and the economic forces of attraction exerted by the United States. Had not the American economic system offered its prizes, they would not have come. On the other hand, had not serious economic dislocations occurred in their own societies they probably could not have been easily lured away from home. This has been succinctly summarized by a Greek informant: "The majority of the Greek men here came as a result of the poverty of the land in

7. J. F. Maguire, *The Irish in America* (London, Longmans, Green & Co., 1868), p. 4.

Greece, in search of the wealth they thought they would find easily in America." Poverty in Greece and the expectation of wealth in America were the related factors which induced migration.

How powerful the economic forces have been is suggested by Foerster with respect to the Italians:

> . . . there is in all agricultural folk, or at least in those that possess even a bit of land, so great an inertia, such an identification of the whole content of existence with home and habitat, that the decision to flee can only come slowly: and with the mass it has been as with the individual. That is why, as late as half a century ago, men were led . . . to regard the Italians as a people not given to emigrate— a people as attached to the soil, some one has said, as an oyster to its rock.[8]

These economic forces, apparent in the motives for migration, have had a profound effect on the relations of the ethnics to the American economic system as they have been observed in Yankee City.

2. *The Occupational System as a Hierarchy*

IN the Yankee City economy, characterized by a highly developed division of labor, each specialized type of "productive" function, carried out by a defined set of techniques, is designated as an "occupation." Each occupation is ascribed a status value relative to all other occupations, according to criteria of the importance of its function to the operations of the economic and social systems. Among such criteria are the following:

1. Range of relational controls in an economic structure, e.g., in a large corporation, foremen are "higher" than the machine operators, factory managers are "higher" than foremen, corporation executives are "higher" than factory managers, etc.

2. Degree of freedom in applying occupational techniques, e.g., the custom tailor producing made-to-order suits in a shop has higher status than has the machine-operating tailor in a factory producing ready-to-wear suits.

3. Skill, training, and special knowledge required to execute the occupational techniques, e.g., the surgeon tends to have a status higher than the general medical practitioner, the physician has a status higher than the dentist, the dentist tends to have a status higher than the chiropodist, etc.

4. Relative economic value of the occupation's product or func-

8. *Op. cit.,* p. 416.

tion, e.g., the designer of machines is above the machinist who builds them, and the latter is higher than the operator.

These criteria, among others, in combination determine the relative status values of the occupations in an economic system. The values are translated, often incompletely, in the variable money rewards attached to the different occupations.

It must be clear, therefore, that the occupational system in a complex economy appears as a graded series of positions, resembling in pattern a hierarchical organization. For purposes of tracing the occupational evolution of the eight ethnic groups, we shall arrange the occupations appearing in the Yankee City economic system into three broad, widely recognized, hierarchical categories and six classes, according to types of techniques, in the following ascending order:[9]

I. Manual techniques:
   A. Unskilled labor—involving simple, loosely organized techniques with few, if any, tools.
   B. Skilled-factory operations—involving highly specialized productive techniques in relation to complex machines and a factory organization.
   C. Skilled-craft operations—involving less specialized and wider range of techniques, with or without relations to machines, set within a relatively simple "shop" type of economic structure, e.g., tailoring and barbering.
II. Exchange-control techniques, i.e., the "white-collar" occupations:
   A. Management-aid operations—involving techniques facilitating management operations, e.g., foremen, supervisors, secretaries, bookkeepers, salesmen, clerks, etc.
   B. Management operations—involving techniques of administering and controlling market and factory structures.
III. Professional techniques—involving advanced knowledge directed toward highly important group functions, e.g., crisis stabilization—the law, medicine, social work, the priesthood; technological or symbolic creation—engineers, scientists, and artists; socialization—teachers; etc.

9. The category of professional occupations can be divided, of course, into subsidiary classes; since the number of individuals found in the professions in Yankee City is comparatively small, this division was not made. Depending upon the context, the professional occupations will be treated as comparable with either the other two occupational categories or the occupational classes.

The correlations of these occupational strata with the six levels of the Yankee City social-class system (cf. Chapter V) are broad and general rather than narrow and specific.[10] With only one exception, no occupational class in Yankee City is identified exclusively with any one social class. Rather, in describing the social-class aspects of the occupational hierarchy, it is necessary to speak in terms of the range of social classes covered by each of the six occupational levels, as in the following:

I-A. Unskilled-labor occupations—almost complete identification with the lower-lower class. (The exception cited.)

I-B. Skilled-factory occupations—range from the lower-lower through the lower-middle class, although most strongly represented in the upper-lower class.

I-C. Skilled-craft occupations—range and principal class identification are the same as for I-B, with a greater secondary representation in the lower-middle class.

II-A. Management-aid occupations—range from upper-lower through the upper-middle class, although falling predominantly in the lower-middle class.

II-B. Management-operation occupations—range from the upper-lower through the upper-upper class, but primary identification with the lower-middle and upper-middle classes.

III. Professional occupations—range from the lower-middle class through the upper-upper class, but predominant representation in the upper-middle class.

Upward from the bottom occupational stratum the social-class range tends to widen. Relative position in the occupational hierarchy is but one among a number of elements which in combination define the individual's place in the social hierarchy. The Yankee City data offer no support for the hypothesis of simple, economic determinism of social class.

3. *The Occupational Status Index*

Before an account was undertaken of the distribution or "scatter" of each ethnic group among the six designated levels of the

10. By social class we mean that the people of Yankee City participate in groups which they themselves rank. Their families, cliques, associations, and churches are socially evaluated and ranked accordingly. Terms are used to refer to the several levels which, when applied to an individual, indicate the class level he occupies. For example, "Hill Streeter" is used for the two upper classes; "old family" for the upper-upper; "new family" for the lower-upper class. "Side Streeter" refers to the middle classes. "Riverbrooker" refers to the lower-lower class.

For a full discussion of class see I, 81–126 and 422–450.

occupational hierarchy,[11] the average occupational status of each group was worked out in the form of a convenient index number comparable to the residential status index applied in Chapter IV. The occupational status index here used is computed first by assigning each occupational class a differential numerical value in terms of its distance in class levels from the value arbitrarily assigned to the class lowest in the occupational system. The weights allocated are as follows:[12]

Occupational Class	Weight
I-A (Unskilled labor)	1
I-B (Skilled factory)	2
I-C (Skilled craft)	2.5
II-A (Management-aid)	3
II-B (Management)	4
III (Professions)	6

For a given group in a given year, the absolute number in each of these classes is multiplied by the assigned value of the class, and the summation of these products is then divided by the total employed population of the group. This quotient is a number between one and six, representing the relative position of the group in terms of its average advance from the base occupational level.

Comparing the indices of each ethnic group through the decades indicates the trend of its mobility in the occupational hierarchy, and these trends among the various ethnic groups may then be compared.[13] Table 2 presents the occupational indices of all Yankee City ethnic groups in the period from 1850 through 1933.

The Irish in 1850 have an occupational index of 1.62, which means that for every hundred of employed population an aggregate of sixty-two steps above the lowest occupational level has been taken. An alternative statement is that the Irish, as a group,

11. Distribution of ethnic groups in the occupations, through time, is treated comprehensively in Leo Srole's doctoral dissertation.

12. In the above values, Class I-C (the skilled-craft occupations) is judged to be insufficiently higher than Class I-B (the skilled-factory occupations), at least in Yankee City, to warrant being weighted a full added unit. Likewise, Class III (the professionals) is felt to involve a considerably longer step from Class II-B than does II-B, for example, from II-A, and, accordingly, has been assigned a value of 6.

13. There is a large literature on ethnic occupational mobility. Representative works are: Niles Carpenter, *Immigrants and Their Children, 1920,* Census Monographs VII (Washington, Government Printing Office, 1927); A. W. Lind, "Economic Succession and Racial Invasion in Hawaii" (unpublished Ph. D. dissertation, University of Chicago, 1931); Isaac A. Hourwich, *Immigration and Labor* (New York, G. P. Putnam's Sons, 1912).

TABLE 2

Occupational Status Indices of Eight Ethnic Groups by Decades

Group	1850	1864	1873	1883	1893	1903	1913	1923	1933
Irish.............	1.62	1.76	1.74	1.76	1.84	1.94	2.14	2.31	2.52
French Canadians	..	..	..	..	1.95	2.10	2.14	2.23	2.24
Jews............	..	..	..	..	..	..	3.10	3.22	3.32
Italians.........	..	..	..	..	..	..	2.32	2.29	2.28
Armenians......	..	..	..	..	..	..	2.46	2.51	2.56
Greeks.........	..	..	..	..	..	..	..	2.53	2.34
Poles...........	..	..	..	..	..	..	..	1.88	1.97
Russians........	..	..	..	..	..	..	..	..	1.95
Total ethnics.....									2.42
Total natives.....									2.56

have a status in the hierarchy about three fifths above that equivalent to exclusive identification with Class I-A, and about two fifths below that equivalent to exclusive identification with Class I-B.

By 1864 the Irish index is 1.76, indicating that in the interim the Irish have advanced an average of fourteen occupational steps for every hundred of their employed, or that about one individual in every seven employed, on the average, has moved one level upward in the occupational hierarchy. Between 1864 and 1883, there is almost no change whatever in the indices, and between 1883 and 1903 the Irish index is increased by only .18. The period 1864–1903, therefore, is one of relative stability in Irish occupational mobility, paralleling the stability of the Irish in the residential system between 1873 and 1903.

In the two decades after 1913, the Irish index grows by about .20 each decade. These are the three phases in the occupational development of the Irish: (1) 1850–64—mobility moderate; (2) 1864–1903—mobility slight; and (3) 1903–33—mobility rapid.

The native group of Yankee City in 1933 has an occupational index of 2.55. Hence the Irish, with an index of 2.52 in that year, have reached a group occupational status almost identical with that of the city's indigenous population.

The French Canadians appear first in 1893 with an index of 1.95, an occupational status almost equivalent to having their entire employed population in the skilled-factory class (I-B). Between 1893 and 1933 the French-Canadian index increases a total of .29 steps or slightly more than the total increment to the index of the Irish in their first four decades. Although the French Canadians start their Yankee City careers at a much higher point in the occupational scale than do the Irish, their rate of mobility is no greater than that of the Irish.

The Jews, first significantly measurable in 1913, appear with an index of 3.10 in that year, indicating an occupational status equivalent to exclusive identification with the lower (II-A) of the two classes in the exchange-control occupational category. In the two decades following, the Jewish index increases .12 and .10, or a total of .22, which is exactly the increment to the index of the Irish between 1850 and 1893. Therefore, in their first decade year the Jews reach a much higher occupational status than do either the Irish or the French Canadians and are more mobile occupationally, on the average, than are the latter groups. In the period 1913–33, however, the Irish are very nearly twice as mobile as are the Jews. But it should be added that in the last decade, 1923–33, about one third of the mature members of the younger generation (F¹) Jews have left Yankee City for the greater occupational opportunities of the larger metropolitan centers. Were these to be taken into consideration, which we cannot do legitimately since we are concerned here with group status within the Yankee City occupational hierarchy, the Jewish index for 1933 would probably be above 3.75. As it is, with a 1933 index of 3.32, the Jews have a far higher occupational status index than any other ethnic group, and one considerably higher than that of the Yankee City natives themselves.

Although a handful of Italians were in Yankee City as early as the 'nineties, the number of their employed was not large enough until 1923 to be meaningful. With an index of 2.32 in the latter year, the Italians as a group are thirty-two out of a possible hundred steps beyond the status associated with the skilled-factory occupational class (I-B). After reaching this status, the Italians exhibit no further occupational mobility, although, as we shall see below, there are actually important occupational shifts among the Italians in the period. In terms of total group status, however, these tend to cancel each other.

The Armenian employed were likewise not measurable until 1913. Their occupational index for that year is 2.46, a group status equivalent to exclusive concentration in the occupational class highest (I-C) in the manual-techniques category. In the two decades following the Armenian index grows only .10, matching

the index accessions in the first twenty years of the Irish development. The Armenian occupational index in 1933 is almost exactly
that of the natives (2.55) in the same year.

The Greeks were slightly later than the Armenians in their first
Yankee City settlement, but their employed population was not
sufficiently extensive for significant analysis until 1923 when they
present an index of 2.53—the highest in that year of any group
except the Jews. Then between 1923 and 1933 the Greek index
falls sharply to 2.34, in the only instance of a marked downward
trend among the ethnics. We shall see below that this recession
was effected by a concerted movement into the Yankee City factories (I-B), while all higher classes remain very nearly constant
in number.

Up to this point each consecutive group reviewed, with the exception of the Jews, exhibits a higher occupational index in its
first decade year than that of the group immediately preceding it
in chronological appearance in Yankee City, indicating that the
occupational hierarchy had become increasingly receptive to the
entrance of new ethnics.

The Poles appear to be an exception to this trend since in their
first decade year, 1923, they have an occupational index of 1.88,
the lowest initial index for any group except the Irish. The elements involved will be considered presently. In 1933 the Polish
index rises to 1.97, approximating an occupational status equivalent to exclusive concentration in the skilled-factory class (I-B).

The Russians cannot be treated significantly until 1933 when
they present an occupational index almost exactly that of the
Poles in 1933, although somewhat higher than that of the latter
in 1923.

By 1933 the eight ethnic groups are arranged along the Yankee
City occupational scale, by index number, in the following ascend-
ing order: Russians, 1.95; Poles, 1.97; French Canadians, 2.24;
Italians, 2.28; Greeks, 2.34; Irish, 2.52; Armenians, 2.56; and
Jews, 3.32. The index for total ethnics is 2.42; for total natives,
2.56.

The occupational status index applied above is nothing more
than a device for stating in a convenient form the *average* rating
of the occupational status of a group in terms of its aggregate advance from the base of the lowest occupational class. But, as in
the case of all statements of central tendency, it is necessary to indicate the degree of scatter. This will be undertaken in the simple
form of an account of the distributions of each ethnic group,

per one hundred of its employed population, among the three major categories and the six classes of the Yankee City occupational hierarchy.

4. *Occupational Distribution of Ethnics*

THE occupational history of the ethnic groups in Yankee City follows a course which is very similar to their residential history. The workers of the newly arrived groups started at the very bottom of the occupational hierarchy and, through the generations, climbed out of it and moved up to jobs with higher pay and increased prestige. Each new ethnic group tended to repeat the occupational history of the preceding ones. By 1933 most of the ethnic groups had attained positions in the industrial life of the community which approximated that of the original native group.

Although the ethnics did not have an industrial background or the skilled-factory techniques, they made the most of the openings presented by the Yankee City economic system and adapted themselves to the special occupational demands. The extent of the ethnic adaptation to industrial conditions of work may be judged by their reaction to a situation of industrial displacement. With the exception of the Jews and the Armenians (who directly upon arrival were absorbed by the shoe factories) all ethnic groups were first drawn into the textile mills. After the local textile industry collapsed, the ethnics made a successful adjustment by widening their industrial representation, although moving predominantly into the shoe factories.

The following table shows the distribution of ethnics during their first decade in Yankee City through three of the occupational classes: unskilled labor (I-A), skilled crafts (I-C), and merchants (II-B). The first column presents each group's first-decade proportion in the unskilled labor class (I-A); the second and third columns record the deviations from I-A of Classes I-C and II-B respectively.

These conclusions are based on occupational distributions for the first decade year. Thereafter, the ethnic trend in the skilled-factory occupations (I-B) increases. However, the trend in the three classes discussed above, (I-A, I-C, and II-B) is predominantly, although not uniformly, in the direction of contraction. For example, the trend of the proportions in the unskilled-labor class (I-A) is markedly downward among all groups with one exception and that probably not statistically significant. Similarly, in the skilled-crafts class (I-C) the trend is downward, although

TABLE 3

Ethnic First Decade Proportions in Three Occupational Classes
(Percentages)

Ethnic Group	Class I-A	Class I-C	Class II-B
Irish..................	56.0	−37.0	−53.4
Poles................	32.1	−25.9	−24.1
French Canadians.....	24.7	−7.8	−19.5
Russians.............	18.7	−8.3	−14.5
Italians..............	17.1	−14.3	0.0
Greeks...............	8.9	+15.4	+14.2
Armenians...........	5.2	+5.2	+13.8
Jews.................	4.6	+16.4	+44.2

not so acutely as for I-A and with three exceptions—the Poles, Armenians, and Italians. These latter groups show increases too small to be significant. On the whole, Class I-C is one of the smallest in terms of its numbers in Yankee City and has been declining for the past fifty years.

The management-merchant occupations (II-B) present a more complex situation. This is the second highest stratum in the hierarchy and thus may be expected to provide an important avenue for mobility. However, in total numbers it is the smallest of the six classes, and with the Yankee City economy relatively static through the last three decades, it has expanded little. Until 1923 the proportions of ethnics in the class are relatively constant. That is, each group's numbers increase in pace with its employed population. Between 1923 and 1933 the proportions in Class II-B decrease. During this period the growth in absolute numbers stops. Moreover, under the economic conditions prevailing in the second half of this decade, the normal accessions from the emerging F generations decline and accrue either to the management-aid (II-A) or the skilled-factory (I-B) class, but more especially to the latter. This deflection of the normal trend of the management class (II-B), therefore, must be attributed to external economic factors and not to any fundamental change in the aspirations of the ethnics to climb in the occupational hierarchy.

In large part, although by no means completely, since the P[1] generation is itself occupationally mobile to an important degree, these decade trends are manifestations of the occupational advance each ethnic generation makes over the preceding generation. The occupations with the most pronounced upward generation trend are those included in the management-aid class (II-A). The P^1 generation of most groups has no members in these occupations, whereas the youngest F generation in five groups has from 25 to 45 per cent of its employed in the class. The generation trends in the professional class (III), in which the P^1 generation of most groups is completely unrepresented, is upward in all cases.

Ethnic mobility, apparent from both decade and generation materials, has been continuous and has effected the diffusion of the ethnics as a totality through the six levels of the occupational hierarchy. In 1933 the distribution of the ethnics closely approximates that of the natives themselves, the difference between natives and ethnics in each occupational stratum not exceeding 14.2 per cent except in the professional occupations, in which the natives outnumber the ethnics two to one. Given that the ethnics started their Yankee City course with heavy concentration in the three occupational classes lowest in the hierarchy, we may conclude that to reach a distribution among all levels approximating that of the natives, the ethnics must have exercised occupational mobility to a degree at least as great as have the natives themselves.

The point was made in an earlier chapter that the ethnic infiltration of all levels of the local economic system is directly connected with two important developments: industrialization in the 1830's, which drew middle-class natives into the factories, lower-class natives into the occupations abandoned by the middle-class natives, and Irish into the unskilled-labor occupations abandoned by the lower-class natives; and progressive emigration of natives from the factories and the city itself, after the 1880's, which opened the factories to increasing numbers of ethnics.

If we were to accept the thesis often held in the extensive literature on American immigration, we would have to hold that the natives left the city *because* the ethnics, with their lower wage demands, have forced them out. The matter is less simple than such an interpretation implies. Our evidence shows that the early Irish did not force the natives out of the unskilled occupations. Nor did the Irish or the subsequent ethnics *displace* the natives in the factories. Rather, the situation may be described as one in which the ethnics *replaced* the natives. For example, infiltration by the Irish into the textile mills was laboriously slow—rising between 1850 and 1883 from 3 to only 7 per cent of the total Irish employed. In 1893 only 60 of the 2000 employed in the local shoe factories were Irish. At the height of development of the city's textile and shoe industries in 1903, the Irish had less than 250 of their employed number in the factories, only about 5 per cent of the total factory employed in the city. The total Irish employed numbered about 850 in that year, with 38 per cent in the unskilled-labor class. After sixty years of residence in Yankee City, the Irish had less than one in three of their employed number in the factories.

The attractions presented in the Yankee City occupational hierarchy have worked to induce ethnic mobility, but native control of the hierarchy has served to resist and to retard the rate of such mobility. The ethnics are well distributed today through the Yankee City occupational strata because of the departure of natives for larger economic opportunities as well as the driving aspirations of the ethnics themselves.

The attractions of the occupational hierarchy have been exerted not only through the offer of higher occupational status in itself but also through the prize attached to such higher status—expanded money income, implying the opportunity to gather further income at an accelerating rate, bringing greater economic security with acquisition of the material status symbols to aid advancement in social class.

Some ethnics, especially among the Jewish F^1 generation, have begun to leave the city for higher economic attractions in larger places. The same forces have operated here as among the natives who emigrated: aspirations for higher occupational status; recognition that within the city's occupational system, given a contracting industrial economy, the opportunities for the acquisition of sufficient value symbols are limited. Not only is the city's economic system contracting, but the ethnic F generation's estimation of what they demand of it has expanded. The city is beginning to be too small for them. In a manner analogous to that of their immigrant parents, they have begun to seek "new worlds."

V

THE ETHNIC GROUPS IN THE CLASS SYSTEM

WITH the exception of the French Canadians, the societies in which the ethnics had their roots were all characterized by a class system similar to the feudal type. At the top was a small, tightly organized, inbred aristocratic class, founded upon extensive holdings of land, and invested, in most cases, with titles of nobility. In sharp contrast was the large class of peasants whose source of livelihood consisted of the extremely small plots of land most often rented in tithe from the landlord aristocracy. There was also a small, burgher, middle class of artisans and traders who were almost exclusively confined to the towns rather than to the villages.

Typical is Adams' report for Ireland: "All the land was owned by a superior class, and almost all of it was leased or rented to the lower orders of farmer and cotter. . . . The island was the preserve of a landed aristocracy, most of whom were members of the Irish peerage. . . . A considerable number were absentees who owned large estates in Great Britain." [1]

Similarly, in a work on the social aspects of Greece, we read: "At present the land is in a few hands . . . and the peasant is little better than a serf." [2]

One of the Yankee City Poles told us: "In Poland there were two classes, the peasants and the nobles or warriors who were called 'masters.' These had large estates and had many peasants working for them . . ."

Characteristic of this form of class system was the extreme rigidity of the strata. So small and restricted was the burgher class that the chances for a peasant's rising to it were remote indeed, and movement from the burgher into the aristocratic class was almost impossible. Thus, one nineteenth-century Irish writer observes: "In the old countries, the ordinary lot of the man born to poverty is that poverty shall be his doom—that he shall die in the condition into which he was brought into the world, and that

1. W. F. Adams, *Ireland and Irish Emigration to the New World*, p. 6.
2. W. Miller, *Greek Life in Town and Country* (London, G. Newnes, Ltd., 1905), p. 114.

he shall transmit hard toil and scanty remuneration as a legacy to his children." [3] Status in such societies, therefore, was determined almost exclusively by family antecedents and carried an absolute finality.

Among the Yankee City ethnic groups, the Irish, Italians, Armenians, Greeks, Russians, and Poles had their origins largely in the peasant stratum of this type of social-class system. A majority of the Jews were of the burgher class in Poland but were also strongly represented in the lower class of the towns, and within both were differentiated to a large extent as distinct subclasses. For the most part, the French Canadians, except in the towns, had been of one undifferentiated social level, consisting of farmers having title to their own, generally small, holdings of land. Although the rural sections of Quebec were at the same stage of economic development as the European peasant areas, and with a corresponding folk type of culture, they lacked an aristocratic landlord class.

These differences in the ethnics' social-class backgrounds will be seen later to have important bearing on their adaptation to the Yankee City class system.

1. *Ethnic Articulation to the Yankee City Class System*

UPON first establishing himself in Yankee City, the ethnic finds himself in the anomalous position of "belonging" to no local social class and having the identification only of "foreigner." He has brought with him little or no property; he has little familiarity, unless he is Jewish, with the type of economic system represented in Yankee City; he conforms hardly at all to the American behavioral modes—in short, the deviations in his social personality are so marked as to preclude relations with the natives except those of an impersonal economic type. Even in the religious aspect, all ethnic groups, with the exception of the Armenian, are variants from Yankee City's solid, native Protestantism.

At first settlement, therefore, the ethnic is an alien in terms of American law, his social personality, and social-class affiliation. An ethnic informant asserted that he felt himself looked upon as "some kind of a strange animal." The Irish relate, probably symbolically, that before their first pastor arrived the natives had pictured Catholic priests as having "cloven hoofs."

In a sense the ethnic is originally outside of the Yankee City class system, but he has a minimum of status by reason of his

3. J. F. Maguire, *The Irish in America*, p. 2.

positions in both the city's residential and occupational hierarchies. Later he appears in a partially differentiated subclass within the lower-lower class but is still not accorded complete equivalence of status with the natives of that class level.

When he has consolidated his position in the lowest class level, the P^1 generation ethnic does not always stay there. As we have observed in the two preceding chapters, he is drawn by the attractions of the Yankee City residential and occupational hierarchies and begins his upward climb in both. Positions in both these hierarchies are highly important criteria determining status in the class system. By means of these two forms of mobility; by great emphasis on the expansion of capital; by further extension of relations, formal and informal, with the natives; and by rapidly becoming more American in outlook and conduct (more slowly in matters which touch the family and the ethnic group) a substantial proportion of the P^1 generation within about twenty years after arrival compelled inclusion in the upper-lower class. On this level, the ethnics again appear as a subclass in differentiation from the natives. Within about thirty years the more successful of the ethnics (in a comparatively small proportion from the P^1 generation) managed to enter the lower-middle class, where they are too few in number at first to be differentiated from the natives. And, after about forty years of residence in Yankee City, a mere handful of ethnics in the P^1 generation succeeded in penetrating the lower border of the upper-middle class. The P^2 and successive F generations, progressively more American in the orientation of their social personalities, continue the movement of their elders in the class hierarchy, although encountering increasing resistance and using, as we shall see, somewhat different techniques of mobility.

2. *Class Distribution by Generation*

In documenting the ascent of each ethnic group in the Yankee City class system, we are not able to utilize decade data comparable to those presented in the two preceding chapters.[4] Old documents offer little material by which to judge the relative class stratifications of all individuals in a group—with the exception, perhaps, of those at the extreme levels of the system. We are necessarily confined, therefore, in rendering account of the class distributions of eight ethnic groups, to the exhaustive social

4. For an earlier systematic treatment of social mobility, cf. P. Sorokin, *Social Mobility* (New York, Harper & Bros., 1927).

personality data gathered during the course of the present investigation in the period centering on 1933. However, we are able to assess the time factor in the processes of social mobility by supplementing group distributions with the class distributions of each defined ethnic generation, as of 1933.

All of the ethnic groups have advanced themselves in the class system. Some of them have made very great headway; others show little change from the time of their entry. Despite their upward movement, none of them has advanced into the upper-upper (old-family) level. The Irish, the oldest group, are the only people who have entered the lower-upper class. The French Canadians, Jews, Italians, Armenians, and Greeks have risen to the upper-middle; and a few Poles and Russians have climbed to the lower-middle class.

The class indices[5] of the ethnic groups in 1933 are: Poles, 1.1; Russians, 1.35; Greeks, 1.55; French Canadians and Italians, 1.7; Armenians, 1.9; Irish, 2.3; and Jews, 2.4. The index for total ethnics is 1.98 and for total natives, 2.5.

Since a progressively larger proportion of individuals in each successive native-born (F) generation are not socially mature and therefore incapable as yet of rising in the social scale, any comparative measure of social mobility of different generations should be based only on those numbers eligible for class advancement. Hence the distributions presented below are in terms of that part of each generation which is above the age of eighteen in 1933. The F^1 generation, by definition, includes the offspring of both the P^1 and the P^2 generations. In the analysis of generation trends, therefore, it is necessary that the class distributions of the F^1 generation be compared with the distributions of the combined P^1 and P^2 generations. Below are presented proportions for the two P generations both separately and together.

Among almost all groups each successive generation (the F^1, of course, being considered in terms of the combined P generations) has fewer of its numbers in the lower-lower class than has the generation before it. Except for the Poles, in those groups whose modal class is still the lower-lower (i.e., Italians, Greeks, Russians) the P^2 has a larger representation in the upper-lower class than has the P^1 generation. Among all the other groups, that is, those in which the upper-lower class is modal, the P^2 generation has fewer of its numbers in this modal class than has the P^1. (Among the French Canadians the P^2 proportion in the upper-

5. See pp. 38–39 for derivation and use of the index number.

TABLE 4[6]

Class and Ethnic Group

	UU	LU	UM	LM	UL	LL	Total
Yankee	100.00 2.69	95.42 2.78	83.44 15.93	67.10 35.26	38.00 23.15	42.80 20.19	53.96
Total Ethnic		4.58 0.16	15.69 3.55	32.78 20.39	61.49 44.33	56.57 31.57	45.58
Irish		4.58 0.31	13.42 5.89	22.74 27.52	38.33 53.75	11.54 12.53	23.43
French			0.82 0.96	4.05 13.15	10.69 40.29	15.64 45.60	8.72
Jewish			0.70 3.02	3.52 41.81	3.45 47.61	0.71 7.56	2.39
Italian			0.06 0.35	0.83 13.73	2.18 41.90	2.95 44.02	1.71
Armenian			0.17 1.22	0.93 17.89	2.28 50.81	1.75 30.08	1.48
Greek			0.52 2.20	0.47 5.37	2.69 35.85	5.48 56.58	2.46
Polish				0.11 0.74	1.21 9.78	14.27 89.48	4.06
Russian				0.13 4.26	0.66 25.53	2.34 70.21	0.85
Negro			~			1.89 100.00	0.48
Unknown			0.87 19.74	0.12 7.89	0.51 36.84	0.63 35.53	0.46
Total	1.45	1.57	10.30	28.36	32.88	25.44	

6. Table 4 is taken from Volume I. For full treatment of the general class position of ethnic groups, see I, 211–226.

CLASS DISTRIBUTION OF IRISH BY GENERATIONS[7]
(Percentages)

	LL	UL	LM	UM
P[1]	27.6	62.7	8.9	0.7
P[2]	12.3	60.2	22.0	5.4
P (Total)	25.7	62.4	10.4	1.3
F[1]	13.2	55.7	26.1	4.8
F[2]	11.5	40.7	38.3	9.4
F[3]	2.3	39.2	41.9	16.6

7. Some Irish F[3] members are in the lower-upper class but too few to make a clear presentation.

lower class is very slightly larger than the P[1].) In other words, among both sets of ethnic groups the P[2] generation, in upward movement, exceeds the P[1]. In the former set of groups, however, the P[2] generation leads the way into the upper-lower class from the lower-lower; whereas in the latter set, constituting the groups older in the city, the P[2] generation is now leading the way out of the upper-lower class into the levels above. Among all groups, the F[1] generation tends to exhibit an upper-lower class proportion smaller than that of the combined P generations; and succeeding F generations among the Irish and the French Canadians continue this trend of movement out of the upper-lower class.

Every successive generation among all groups is found to have a progressively larger portion of its membership in both the lower-middle and upper-middle classes (the French-Canadian F[1] generation in the upper-middle class is an exception). This means that each consecutive ethnic generation pushes progressively farther out of the bottom level and into each of the successive levels above. That the class index of an ethnic group is related to the length of its settlement in the city is a manifestation of the continuous advance achieved in the hierarchy by each new generation.

By way of summary of the above generation distributions among the class levels, we have calculated the class index for each generation in every group and have plotted them in Chart V. As in the case of all our generation statistics, there is a wide disparity in the size of the populations, both among generations within the same group and among corresponding generations of different groups; therefore computations on such varying populations are

CLASS DISTRIBUTION OF FRENCH CANADIANS
BY GENERATION
(Percentages)

	LL	UL	LM	UM
P[1]	47.3	40.4	10.9	1.2
P[2]	40.2	42.8	15.5	1.8
P (Total)	46.0	40.9	11.8	1.2
F[1]	44.9	39.0	15.4	0.7
F[2]	40.0	37.9	21.0	1.1

CLASS DISTRIBUTION OF JEWS BY GENERATION
(Percentages)

	LL	UL	LM	UM
P[1]	12.1	59.7	25.0	3.2
P[2]	6.8	31.8	56.8	4.5
P (Total)	10.7	52.3	33.2	3.5
F[1]	0.0	39.5	55.4	5.1

CLASS DISTRIBUTION OF ITALIANS BY GENERATION
(Percentages)

	LL	UL	LM	UM
P[1]	63.1	36.9		
P[2]	48.0	48.0	4.0	
P (Total)	59.1	39.9	1.0	
F[1]	35.0	35.8	28.3	0.9

CLASS DISTRIBUTION OF ARMENIANS BY GENERATION
(Percentages)

	LL	UL	LM	UM
P[1]	29.3	63.4	7.5	
P[2]	31.9	46.8	19.1	2.1
P (Total)	30.0	57.8	11.4	0.7
F[1]	12.3	42.1	42.1	3.5

CLASS DISTRIBUTION OF GREEKS BY GENERATION
(Percentages)

	LL	UL	LM	UM
P¹	57.9	36.0	4.9	1.0
P²	52.2	38.6	6.8	2.2
P (Total)	56.8	36.5	5.2	1.3
F¹	54.8	37.1	8.1	

CLASS DISTRIBUTION OF RUSSIANS BY GENERATION
(Percentages)

	LL	UL	LM	UM
P¹	77.0	23.1		
P²	41.1	47.0	11.8	
P (Total)	67.7	29.2	3.1	
F¹	68.4	21.1	10.5	

CLASS DISTRIBUTION OF POLES BY GENERATION
(Percentages)

	LL	UL	LM	UM
P¹	90.3	9.6		
P²	86.6	6.6	6.6	
P (Total)	90.1	9.4	0.4	
F¹	90.1	7.3	2.6	

necessarily of uneven value. Nevertheless, the indices represented in Chart V demonstrate that each generation within a group consistently attains a higher average class status than does the generation preceding. No significant exception is the fact that in certain instances the P^2 index exceeds that of the F^1 generation, since the latter must be compared with the index of its parents— who, by our classification, are the combined P^1 and P^2 generations. And in all cases the F^1 index is uniformly greater than the "total P." What is an apparent anomaly, namely, that among four groups the P^2 index surpasses that of the F^1 generation, may be explained by the fact that among the Greeks, Russians, and Poles

CHART V

SCALE OF SOCIAL-CLASS INDICES OF ALL
GENERATIONS IN EACH ETHNIC GROUP

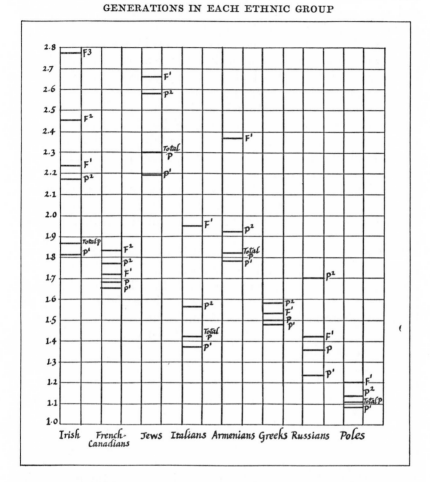

the F¹ generation has emerged to maturity in too recent years to
have exhibited the class advance normal for this generation among
the other ethnic groups. That the P² index is greater than the F¹
among the French Canadians, however, cannot be attributed to
this age condition, and the only source to which it can be traced
is, probably, the difference in the numbers within each of the two
generations (77 in the P² and 414 in the F¹).

The factor of differential age has a more general bearing upon
the ascending social status of successive generations within a

group. Progression in the class scale is a process that may begin when the individual reaches a degree of economic independence from his family through entrance into the occupational system, and may continue through his lifetime, although the greatest efforts seem to be made in the age period, roughly, of twenty-five to fifty. Since each consecutive generation in a group is twenty years younger, on the average, than the generation preceding, it is apparent that each has had that many years fewer to promote its advancement in the class scale. Hence the higher-class index of each successive generation is achieved in spite of its twenty-year handicap. By the time the age of the filial generation approximates the present age of the parental generation, the filial group would normally exhibit an even higher index than it does at present. In other words, the increasingly greater index of the generations in their order must be taken as an incomplete manifestation of status advance, for each consecutive generation in the series has progressively greater potentialities for further class mobility.

This condition is directly involved in the fact that the P^1 generation, which started on its course with an index of 1, has made a greater advance, among most groups, than has any of the following generations, each of which began its social career on the level of the parental generation. Another important factor in differential generation mobility is that the mobile individual encounters increasing resistance at each higher level in the class scale. Yet each new generation has continued its upward push, even the Irish F^3 and the Jewish P^2 and F^1 generations which now have status indices substantially higher than the status norm of the natives.

In both the total-group and the generation class indices, it is apparent that there are differences among the eight ethnic groups which are primarily related to the group's comparative age in Yankee City. The younger the group, in general, the lower is its total-population index, the smaller is its P^1 generation index, and the narrower is the margin of progressive enlargement in the indices of subsequent generations. Accompanying this general correlation, however, are certain marked secondary differences between groups which appeared in Yankee City at approximately the same time. Thus, for example, among the Jews all indices are notably higher than those of the Italians, who were their contemporaries as immigrants, and of the French Canadians, who preceded them into the city by about twenty years. The same type of differences exists between the Armenians and the Greeks, and between the Russians and the Poles, the groups in each pair being of about the same arrival date in Yankee City. Such differences where the time factor is relatively constant will be analyzed later, when an attempt is made to correlate residential, occupational, and class indices.

3. *Money and Ethnic Social Mobility*

SOCIAL mobility comprises numerous factors of varying importance, some of which have already been considered. Acquisition of material symbols, including residences, increased occupational status, extension of formal and informal relations in the society, and change in behavior modes are among these factors.

In the "old countries," with economic and social status more or less fixed, the incentive to work was essentially one of production for the needs of immediate subsistence. Adams, for example, writes of Ireland: ". . . the lower [classes], their ambitions vitiated by long continued hopelessness, lived only for the day or the season." [8] Similarly, of the French Canadians, Greenough writes:

The people are mainly industrious, but to a New Englander would not seem to be hard worked. Mechanics do not try to turn out the most and best work possible, but only enough to live on, and just a little more if the chance comes. Their habits being simple and their living cheap, they are satisfied with little, and social ambitions do not trouble them much.[9]

From this simple and static type of society, the ethnic moves into the highly fluid and dynamic American social system. There occurs a shift in his attitude in which productive labor is not merely a means to the simple ends of present subsistence but becomes a means to the end of acquiring the value and status symbols of money and property. With these are associated economic security, the only security attainable to a stranger in a new social world; status through identification with the society's property system; and social mobility.

Maguire, visiting America in 1868 and observing his former Irish countrymen established here, commented: "But in a new country, especially one of limitless fields for enterprise, the rudest

8. *Op. cit.,* p. 20.
9. W. P. Greenough, *Canadian Folk-life and Folk-lore* (New York, G. H. Richmond, 1897), p. 172.

implements of labour may be the means of advancement to wealth, honour, and distinction, if not for those who use them, at least for those who spring from their loins." [10]

Although considerably bewildered by its magnitude and complexity, the ethnic enters the American economic system determined to get ahead in it. He shows a willingness to work hard and competitively for a good week's pay and satisfaction with the increased return for labor in this country as compared with "the old country." Money becomes the immediate end of his labor and is valued in its function of providing the necessary goods to "keep alive" and in the further function in American society of acquiring status symbols. Such symbols can be classified into two types:

1. Capital, i.e., forms in which money itself is turned to productive and reproductive functions, e.g., "investments" such as real estate, stocks, bonds, savings, etc.

2. Goods, beyond the necessities, which expand and enhance the mode or "style" or standard of family life. Such goods, according to their quality and number, have varying status value with reference to different class strata in the society.

Our evidence indicates that the ethnic family upon arrival heavily emphasizes the first type of status symbol at the expense of the second, generally referred to as the "standard of living." In the societies from which the ethnics are derived, consumption consisted largely of the immediate necessities of food, shelter, and clothing. These were provided in bare minimum. A Yankee City Jew described the level of consumption in Russia: "The usual meal was dark bread, dipped into water with sugar. Milk and tea were luxuries, and meat was had only on holidays. Some Jews didn't have any even then. Clothes were all homemade out of cheap, common cloth. The wedding suit, if it wasn't borrowed, was worn only on holidays and was kept until death. The typical house was built of logs, with roof of straw, and the walls unpainted. There was no floor, only the earth. Some were without chimneys, with a hole in the roof. It was only one room, and the chickens roosted under the stove. Light was given by oil lamps. Furniture was plain, unpainted lumber. A man who had a thousand rubles [$20] at one time was a wealthy man. Yes, my friend, the very poorest in America live better than the richest in the old country."

The ethnic family on arrival in Yankee City cannot maintain any more than the minimum standard of consumption. The immediate situation is one of crisis, of adaptation to a new and strange

10. *Op. cit.,* p. 2.

social system and economy. The family must meet this crisis by acquiring the value symbols which in the new society are identified with material security, namely, money. And the whole family is organized to that end.

In the organization of the family, expansion of the family's capital is the driving force. Children, for example, are in effect turned to producing capital by being sent out to work as early as the state laws allow. In a series in the local newspaper called "Do You Know Your Newsboy?" one article, devoted to a young Pole, included the following:

There's going to be no High School career for John Bersky, 15, who faithfully appears every afternoon at the doors of 78 houses all the way from Elizabeth Street in the downtown district to Walnut Street, to the extreme East End. He's the oldest of six children of Mr. and Mrs. Alec Bersky of 19 Jones Street, East End, and although he would just love to go to High School, saying that "an education is the only chance a fellow's got of *being anybody today,*" he must forget all about school after the next term and go out and plug to help keep the brothers and sisters in shoes and see if he can't aid in giving them a "break" which is denied him.

The only P^2 Pole who has been through high school and college had this to say: "Most Polish people are after the money and send their children to work as soon as possible, but my father was the first to have any brains, and when he saw that I wanted to go to college he let me." An F^1 Italian, who is now a truck driver, was somewhat bitter when he said: "I had only a grammar-school education. My parents made me get out and work. They wanted me to be a Wop with all the other Wops, I guess."

As the ethnic family weathers the crisis, and feels an increasing degree of security, it allows the children to finish their education in the high school, and eventually they even consider college. The pastor of the French-Canadian church, speaking of the early years of his community, says: "The French Canadians couldn't send their children to school because they were very poor and had large families. But they're sending all their children to school now and have done so ever since they've become established."

Most striking in the attitude of the P^1 generation ethnic is his conception of the function of money as seen, first, in his emphasis upon saving. A prominent Irish attorney of the F^3 generation comments particularly on the Irish P generation: "I have been a lawyer in this town for sixteen years and I never settled an Irishman's estate that didn't have a savings account. There was one old man here in town who was drunk all his life, and yet, when he died he had a savings account of over $10,000. Why they save it I don't know; probably to take care of themselves in their old age. Why, even the living-out girls who work in the Hill Street homes, when they die they will have $10,000 to $15,000 saved up. The other day an old Irishman came in here, he could hardly speak the English language, but he had $30,000 saved up."

A successful P² generation Jew, in describing the early days of the Jewish community, said: "In the beginning our interest was centered on making money." And a P¹ Pole, who was little fazed by long unemployment, says of himself: "I've been in this country eighteen years. I've worked all the time and saved my money."

A second manifestation of the attitude toward money is seen in the ethnic disposition to invest savings in property. The following list records the proportion of families among the natives and in each ethnic group who own their own homes and, in many cases, other forms of real property as well: (1) Jews, 63.4 per cent; (2) Russians, 55.5 per cent; (3) Armenians, 52.7 per cent; (4) Italians, 51.5 per cent; (5) Natives, 46.9 per cent; (6) Irish, 42.1 per cent; (7) Greeks, 32.4 per cent; (8) Poles, 32.0 per cent; (9) French Canadians, 25.9 per cent.

Ethnic informants document the elements involved in the acquisition of property. We were told by an Irishman: "The Irish were laborers but thrifty and saved money. Just the minute they had enough they took to buying property in a better section. So there was considerable movement about. The same thing is true of the French. Also of the Poles, but they bought property right on River Street, while they were working in the mills."

A P¹ generation Jew, who is a cobbler, in commenting on the days before World War I when he had recently arrived in the city, said: "I was making good money in those days and had all the work I could do. Sometimes I'd work until ten o'clock at night in my repair shop. We saved money, we bought that house, I raised six children and we lived pretty well." The chronological sequence in this development, as suggested especially in the grammatical structure of his final sentence, may be outlined as follows: (1) I worked; (2) I saved; (3) I bought a house; (4) I raised children; and (5) we lived well. The buying of the house is functionally the link between the first two processes and the last two. On the one hand, it is an investment, for few ethnics have bought houses that have not at least two apartments, one of which was to bring a rental return. On the other hand, the house is both a family symbol and a status symbol ("we lived pretty well"). Possession of its own house means roots, security, and status in the society to the ethnic family.

The investment aspect is accented in the behavior of many ethnics, especially the Jews, Armenians, and Greeks, who purchase property in addition to their homes. The motive is clear in the following remarks by a P^1 Jew: "Sure, the Jews have all their money invested in property, and I'll tell you why. When they began making some money, what could they do with it? Deposit it in the bank? All you could get was 4 per cent. Or buy bonds? You'd get 6 per cent. But if you put it in property, you would get 20 per cent. So all the Jews bought property. Of course, they took out mortgages, but they haven't got too much, and they always pay." A Greek, when asked whether he wasn't afraid of bank failures, answered: "No, I have no money in banks. Everything is invested in property."

Saving, then, to the P^1 ethnic is a mode of accumulating money that might be converted to "productive" capital, principally in the form of real property.

The reciprocal aspect of this saving pattern is to be found in the spending habits of P^1 generation ethnics. One Pole stated: "I pay for the food, the coal, the rent, but other things, unless we need them, we don't buy them. I save money. I am not like some people who spend everything they make." This is a standard of living that is still confined largely to the basic necessities.

An F^2 Irish attorney, who, like all the local Irish, does not class the Irish among the "foreigners," made this observation: "These foreigners are funny people. They will work in the factory and make good money, but they will never spend any of it. They are used to eating lots of cheap foods and living in poor quarters and having little of the conveniences of life. They save their money and when hard times come they will go to the welfare board to get aid and at the same time are liable to have money in the bank. Many times these Polacks down here will not spend any money at all except for the necessities of life."

This solicitude for money, almost approximating penuriousness, is sometimes carried to the point where the Poles, for example, have asked for aid when they still had money in the bank untouched. A Welfare officer reported of the Italians: "The Italians have raised a great stink because they haven't received any Red

Cross flour. So the cases of all the Italians were investigated, and it was found that almost all of them had $300 or more stored away and yet they were hollering for free flour."

A more tragic incident occurred in a case of which a native nurse tells: "The Poles don't like to spend money. There is one family here that own their home. The woman has cancer and the doctors have told her for a long time that she ought to have X-ray treatments. But they wouldn't spend the money and now it is too late."

Behind the intense preoccupation with money on the part of the P^1 generation, there seems to be apprehension about economic status, a feeling of general social insecurity. A P^1 Pole, after railing about Bolshevism in Russia, nevertheless said this about it: "There are some good things, though, in Soviet Russia. Poor people at least have some rights. They may not get much, but they are sure of getting that. And they don't have to worry about it." It is the element of supposed economic security in the Russian system of which this Pole approves, although he disapproves of the system itself.

Hence in the P^1 generation the possession of money has meaning in terms of maintaining status, of guarding against insecurity. It is considered a form of insurance against the possible exigencies of the future. Therefore, money acquired by this generation is turned to productive, rather than to consumptive, purposes; to consolidating the family's economic status; and to establishing a minimum status in the property system, rather than to raising its social status by spending the money for a higher standard of living. The element tends to persist throughout the life of the P^1 generation and is one aspect of the general insecurity which these immigrant parents experience in the difficult processes of adapting themselves and their families to the impact of a new and vigorous social system. This insecurity diminishes somewhat as the family strikes roots and becomes "established," as the French Canadian priest expressed it, although it is never completely extirpated, since the P^1 generation never seems to lose the feeling that it is not "at home."

Beginning with the P^2 generation, however, and throughout the F generations of ethnics, this apprehension is replaced by the confidence born of having roots in the American social and economic system. Their primary emphasis is not one of saving money to assure economic status while maintaining a minimum standard of living, but of maintaining a standard of living which conforms with that of the class with which they would identify themselves. This change of emphasis from economic status to the larger social status is expressed in a shift in evaluation of money from functions of production, i.e., of increasing the family's savings, to functions of consumption, i.e., buying with money those goods characteristic of the American middle-class standard of living. Contrast the statements of the P^1 generation ethnics about their saving with the following by an F^1 Irishman of the lower-middle class. "We have always lived very extravagantly and money has just slipped through our fingers."

Another Irishman of the same generation and class related that he had saved $300 during the year and bought a car for $440 that year, meeting the difference by means of time payments. The acquisition of automobiles and the use of the credit plan rarely appear among the P^1 generation but are characteristic of all subsequent generations.

Occasionally members of these generations exhibit certain gross incongruities in their acquisition of status symbols. For example, an Irishman living in the River Street area at a low rental nevertheless has "modern" furniture, bought on the credit plan, and wears hundred-dollar suits. A Greek cobbler of the P^2 generation, living in the same type of area, first bought a Ford, but later traded it for a used Lincoln.

These differences in attitudes toward money appear most strikingly in the attitudes of the two generation groups toward each other. It will be remembered that the F^2 Irish attorney quoted above remarked that the "foreigners are funny people—they make good money but never spend any of it." The members of these younger generations, however, generally are sharper in baiting their elders. Most frequently they call them "stingy." Typical is the following estimation by a P^2 Pole of two of the most respected P^1 members of the Polish community: "Felix is a good man but stingy. He used to have a grocery store of his own. I think that is the reason why he couldn't hold his own store. He is pretty well off but he has no automobile yet. Mike ——— is the same way. He is looking for a wife nowadays, but the girls don't like him because he's so stingy. He could have a car too."

The P^1 generation, in turn, has certain strong opinions of the younger generations. An Armenian informant commented with considerable heat: "The trouble with this country is the people live too fast; they have to have cars and radios and all. I know people that are running around with cars and spending their money, forgetting all about hard times in the old country. In the old country a girl will have a coat and it will last her for six or eight years, and here they have to have a new coat nearly every year."

The P^1 generation priest of the Yankee City Greek church was no less condemnatory: "Today the [Greek] generation born in this country [F^1] no longer has the fine old grip. The attitude has changed. This is a tendency everywhere discoverable, an indictment of our civilization. These people buy new radios, cars, better houses, and so on, relying on the future to pay for them when they can't. I need a radio badly myself and would like to have one, but I am not sure I could pay for it, and to have to send it back would be a disgrace in a way."

4. *Ethnic Relationships and Social Mobility*

WE have indicated that a criterion of social status in Yankee City is the individual's relational configuration, by which is meant (1) the relative extension of one's relationships in the city's social system through such structures as the associations; and (2) the relative status superiority or inferiority of those to whom one stands in "friend," clique, and family relationships.

As illustrations of the process by which ethnics have quantitatively and qualitatively extended and enhanced their relational configurations and thereby raised the status of their social personalities, we have selected two ethnic individuals who have been among the most rapid climbers in the class hierarchy of all Yankee City ethnic groups. One of these is a Greek, and the other is a Jew. Both are of the P^2 generation; both originally settled in Area I-E, and until recently had their residence in Section II-W; both have reputations locally as gifted, "self-made" men, having risen from occupations of the I-A classification (unskilled labor) to considerable success in occupations of the management classification (II-B); and both have climbed step by step from the lower-lower class into the upper-middle class, although both are still comparatively young men—a remarkable advance of three levels.

The Greek "raised his stock" early by marrying an F^1 generation Irish woman who was of the lower-middle class. By thus relating himself through marriage with members of that class level, he helped lift himself out of the upper-lower class with which, through occupational and residential mobility, he had come to be identified at the time. Immediately thereafter, he added new clique relationships with natives and Irish of the lower-middle class to his predominantly upper-lower-class clique relations. Next, he joined two native associations which were predominantly of lower-middle-class composition. After an interval of a few years he transferred from the Greek community church to the native Episcopalian church, which has an upper-middle to upper-upper-class reputation. Then he acquired clique relations with two natives who were of the upper-middle class. There quickly followed admission to a native fraternal association which was predominantly upper-middle class in composition where, winning a reputation as a "hard worker," he was entrusted with progressively higher offices until he was elected Grand Master, an office of considerable prestige in the city. His status today is solidly upper-middle class, especially as his wife has kept step with his progress by entering native women's associations which are conspicuously upper-middle class in character.

The Jew selected as a second case of relational expansion is forty years old—about ten years younger than the Greek just discussed. In a shorter period of time his status rise has been even more spectacular than that of the Greek. He is one of the wealthier men in the city, and even natives speak of his career as one of "coming up on a shoestring," and "like an Alger story." During his climb he did not utilize the device of marrying into a higher class level, but chose a P^2 generation Jewish woman of the same status as his own, upper-lower. Nor did he abandon the synagogue congregation of his group on the way up. He was not strongly active, however, in the Jewish community system until a crisis, brought on by the death of the P^1 generation elders, carried him into leadership of the Jewish group.

We can document the range and quality of his present relational configuration by quoting directly from an interview with him. The context of his opening remarks is the campaign, which he headed, to acquire the building of a defunct native church for the use of the Jewish congregation and community.

"Some of the members of the church said, 'Why shouldn't we give it away rather than sell it to the Jews?' But this was only street-corner gossip. Of course, a lot of people made talk about it, and I went down to the editor of the Yankee City *Herald*, a friend of mine, and asked that no publicity be given to such talk. In fact, he himself lives across the way from the church building, and he said that he hadn't heard of any objections at all. I am very friendly in that section [upper part of Section II-W].

"Did you know that the Congregational Church [dominantly lower-middle and upper-middle class] gave me the pulpit once [at a Sunday evening meeting]? We had a very nice meeting and the church was crowded. Very often we have meetings of this kind. In fact, Mr. Royce [UM], the minister of the Congregational Church, is a great friend of mine. I went on trips with him many times.

"My business is 50 per cent with Christians, involving a lot of money, and I don't find much feeling against the Jews. I belong to the Yankee City Golf Club [membership from the three highest class strata] and there is not the ill feeling there that [Jewish] people imagine. They certainly all know that I am a Jew. For instance, in the Rotary Club [also of the three highest classes] I have been the only Jew for many years. Also I am the only Jew in the Golf Club. I got in because I knew the officers. A small minority of the members felt that if a Jew was brought in he would bring around *gefillte fisch*. These are the ones that feel that things must be just so—in fact, were against Catholics years ago. These they gradually let in, and have found that they are not so bad. I have a lot of fine friends, such as Mr. James and Mr. Burt [both LU], who are the governors of the club.

"I am also chairman of one of the committees of the local Republican party [leaders entirely from the three highest strata] and I have found it very pleasant. I sent letters in the last campaign to thirty-five of the most prominent [*sic*] citizens and got fine responses. I have found that in the small community you have to do work for everybody, and I find that no one has ever objected to giving money for any cause. Of course, some people afterward took back from me much more for different causes. I have always given, and it has never harmed me.

"Then, I am a director of two local banks [owned and managed by members of the two upper classes] and of the Lowell Manufacturing Company [oldest and most reputable industrial structure in the city]. I have had relations with all the mayors of the city and am now a director of the Public Library. I am in charge of book purchases and employees. The other four directors are all older men of the highest class [UU] and I am the young fellow among them, the worker. We didn't have a children's reading room so I went out to the Rotary and other organizations and raised $1,200, and now we have a beautiful reading room.

"Also I am a guardian of the Girl Scouts, that is, I am a financial director. Last year they wanted a hearth in the Winthrop woods. I sent out letters and got some of the clubs together, raised $400, and built it for them.

"Yes, this is all necessary work, and they [his highly placed social associates] appreciate it. It is a noble and fine work helping others out."

In addition to those he has mentioned, this Jew is also a member of the Yankee City Building Association (LM to LU), of the Chamber of Commerce (UM to LU), and of the local Society for the Prevention of Cruelty to Children (UM to UU).

As a result of his business reputation, his liberality with contributions to "worthy causes," his attitude of doing "good works" (which is notably associated with the behavioral configuration of the two upper classes)—in short, as a result of his conspicuous "public spirit"—he has come in contact with members of the three top-class strata. These strata define their community function as one of exercising certain central controls through such structures as the city government, the Republican party, the banks, the businessmen's associations, and the various charitable organizations. This Jew is not only a member in all such structures but within them he is an active leader. As a consequence of his formal relations in these structures he has acquired informal clique relations with natives of both the upper-middle and lower-upper classes and is on "friendly terms" with members of the upper-upper class. His wealth, his occupation, his relations, and the standard of his behavior place him very high within the upper-middle class. He has achieved such status in about twenty years of maturity; and, quite obviously, he is still "on the make," as is evident especially from the fact that in 1931 he acquired one of the city's "fine old houses" in Zone III as a family residence.

These two cases, in extreme form perhaps, are examples of the fact that broadening relations with the Yankee City social system, especially with the "right people," that is, extending and enhancing the individual's relational configuration, have been a process utilized by the ethnics to facilitate their ascension in the social hierarchy.

5. *The Behavioral Configuration and Ethnic Social Mobility*

In the discussion of the ethnics' changing conceptions of the function of money and of the extension of ethnic relations, there were scattered references to the change in ethnic standards of behavior, i.e., culture. This change in behavior constitutes the fourth process by which class mobility is engineered. Further case material illustrates two selected aspects of this process, one relating to behaviors of recreation, the other to behaviors centered in the ritual of the family meal.

Insight into the type of recreation enjoyed by ethnics of the lower-lower class is provided by the answer of a P¹ generation Pole when he was asked where he went in his spare time: "I never go anywhere. I just put on this shirt and overalls and stay this way all day. I'm not going to dress up. Well, afternoons I lay down and sleep a while. Then at night we sit about until ten or eleven and then go to bed."

Strongly in contrast are the recreational standards implied by the P² generation, upper-middle-class Jew discussed above, who, with reference to his golf playing at the Yankee City Golf Club, said:

"I belong to the Boston Jewish Golf Club, too, but I don't play there much. I belong only to help out, and because I do business with them. The Yankee City Golf Club is of higher caliber. The Christians have played golf for two hundred years, and it takes years to learn the etiquette of the game. Things at the Yankee City Club are handled a little differently, are a little quieter. At the Jewish club the men are more friendly and a little noisier, but I feel just as much at ease at the Yankee City Club as at the Boston. Between the two places, the Yankee City Club is more refined, but that is not the reason I belong there. I belong there because Yankee City is my home and I want to play among my neighbors. The Christian makes his golf club his whole life."

In his emphasis upon learning "the etiquette of the game," and in remarking on the "refinement" of the Yankee City Club, this Jew expresses his awareness of new and "higher caliber" modes of behavior.

In behaviors at the family board, there is the contrast between the "manners" of a P¹ generation Polish family of the lower-lower class and those of a P¹ generation Jewish family of the lower-middle class. The former were described by a native lower-middle-class visiting nurse, as follows:

"They are clean and neat, though they don't have our idea about things. For instance, they always eat in the kitchen, and never learn to set a table with cups, plates, saucers, knives. They just throw things down. They lay the bread on the bare table and things like that. Each one just gnaws off a hunk, never cuts it. Of course, those [Poles] that are becoming Americanized plan differently and act differently."

How differently the Jewish family referred to above conducts itself was related by the daughter of the family:

"You know, we have a new maid. She certainly is wonderful. She is a very good worker, and she has a whole-hearted interest in the house. She certainly is marvelous, and you would never recognize the house the way she keeps it up. She used to work for the Rands [LU native family]. She told us she much preferred to serve [*sic*] meals in the dining room. We used to serve all the meals in the kitchen, as you know. But because she wanted it, we are now serving all meals in the dining room. She bawls us out sometimes for the things that we do, but she is really right about it, so we respect her for her pains."

It is obvious from the above, in the change of the scene of meals from the kitchen to the dining room, in the fact that meals are served by a maid (an element of the upper-middle and upper classes) trained in the manners of the upper classes, and in the maid's general domination of the household regimen by reason of her acknowledged authority, that the influence and example of Hill Street have notably altered even the private, familial behaviors of this P[1] generation Jewish family.

The interest of the younger ethnics in measuring up to the Hill Street standards of behavior is strikingly brought out in the following remarks of a highly mobile P[2] generation, lower-middle-class Pole:

"You know, the Polish Hall [association clubhouse] was a booze joint. They had a cellar where liquor was served and cards were played. And boys and men were arrested for drunkenness and disorderly behavior on account of this, and it always has been in my mind to get rid of this. So I suggested to the girls that they shouldn't dance with men who had liquor on their breath. Now, I don't mind people drinking liquor provided they could act decently after they had done so. But, they can't. And I figure that the best way to get rid of the evil is not to have the censure of the police on the Polish community but the censure of the Polish people themselves—that of their own kind. Because that is much stronger. If a man shames himself, then the Poles could have nothing to do with him—he would be ostracized; and that is the worst sort of punishment. Now the thing to do is to educate the Polish people to see how bad drinking can be, and to disapprove of it. But this can't be done by telling them that it is bad. What I plan to do is to lead them to better things—higher things. For example a little later I plan to have a tea for the boys and the girls. Then maybe later I will jokingly suggest that they have a formal affair like the elite of Hill Street. They will take it as a joke, but they will do it. And so, little by little, they can be led by suggestion to more respectable and decent ways, and drinking and rowdyism will by comparison appear to them very low and shameful. And if the younger people will feel so, soon the older people will too. So you see my plans for the Polish community. Already we have had a couple of dances, and they were pleasant affairs. You know, for the last dance, I decided that a good way to improve the affair would be to send out invitations and make it appear as a private affair. They liked the idea of invitations, and besides, the bums were kept out."

This energetic Pole, who, at thirty, has already advanced two class levels and may be expected to rise even further in the future, explicitly attempts to orient his standards of behavior to those of "the elite of Hill Street." What is even more significant is that he is attempting to reform the behaviors of the entire Polish group by reorienting them around those same "more respectable" standards. That he has actually accomplished his own reorientation has been an important factor in his unusual rise in social status.

6. *Resistance and Social Mobility*

THE four processes just reviewed have been the means by which social mobility has been achieved by the Yankee City ethnics. As in the residential and occupational hierarchies, such mobility meets resistant forces, certain aspects of which will be reviewed here.

First, social status depends upon the combination of the four interdependent status-value attributes exhibited by the individual. If he fails to advance in any one of the four value scales, it is likely that his advance will be retarded in the other three as well. For example, if the individual is kept from moving up in the occupational hierarchy, he will be kept from enhancing his money wealth and, in turn, his stock of material status symbols. Unable to provide himself with the "better" kind of residence, clothes, car, recreations, etc., he will continue to bear the external marks of his original class association. He is thereby cut off from acceptance as an equal by those on the class level just above, and he will have little chance of extending his relations in that direction. On the other hand, even if he does rise occupationally and expands his store of material status symbols, qualitatively and quantitatively, he may still be unable to improve his relations if he does not present the behavior demanded by the members of the superior class. In other words, the resistance to occupational mobility, and in a lesser degree to residential mobility, as well as the increasing difficulty in measuring up to the progressively more precise and rigorous behavioral expectations of each higher class, have an indirect, but highly important, effect in retarding and suppressing social mobility.

The superior class group cannot directly prevent an individual from lifting himself in the occupational scale, nor from expanding his wealth, but it does make the effort to bar "pretenders" to its status by keeping them from extending their relations in the group. The attempt is made by means of the group's reassertion of the "social distance" which separates them from those of the class below—this through unwillingness to admit the parvenus to equality of status or to accept them in clique or "friend" relations.

An excellent example of the enforcement of class distance is found in the following remarks of an upper-middle-class native who is principal of one of the Yankee City public schools:

"We have the children of the upper class coming from Hill Street, middle class from the East End, and all the lower classes. There are quite a few children from Hill Street here. They mix with the others during school hours and at the playground but not very much after school. Occasionally a boy who came from a very good family would start going around with a Polish boy after school hours. His mother came to me and asked whether I could break it up. All I did was to keep the boys after school separately and keep them in from the playground, one or the other or both all the time, so they did not mix. Another boy was mixing with someone the family didn't want him to, so I went right up to him and said, 'Well, now do you want to mix with a good sort of a fellow?' and I tried to steer him off."

Children, of course, are not so rigid in keeping class distances as are adults. If there is a lapse, the parents are quick to separate them.

Class distance is likewise expressed by people of immediately contiguous strata, as in the case of an upper-upper-class girl who, when asked about the girls of a neighboring lower-upper-class Irish family, said: "I don't know anything about them, although they are of my own generation and went to school with me." Similarly, one native woman of the lower-upper class had as immediate neighbors an Irish family of the upper-middle class and admitted never having met them. She added: "Neither I nor my mother have ever called on them. I don't know quite why we haven't, but we never have." Explicit is the remark of one of the upper-middle-class Jews with reference to those of the upper classes: "Socially, we are as far apart from them as the North and South Poles."

Class distance is generally expressed with passive concurrence on the part of both those of the superior and those of the inferior classes except in cases where certain of the latter become mobile. Then the activity of the mobile individual often stimulates those of the superior class to active resistance. Certain native associations, especially those composed of members of the two upper classes, function formally to exclude such intruders. An upper-class men's association with a long history is of such a type. An F^2 generation, mobile, upper-middle-class Irishman commented on this organization: "It is too bad they don't allow any Catholics in the Washington Club so that I could get in. . . . But it is impossible to get in." Similarly, a Jewish woman only recently of the upper-middle class complained of the Yankee City Women's Club, which is predominantly upper-middle class in its membership: "I once went to a meeting, but the women were not at all cordial, so I've never gone again."

Pressures to restrain or at least to brake the pace of social advance take an early and specialized form when the mobile individual begins to assume material status symbols which are associated with a level higher than his own. For example, an upper-middle-class native was wrought up about a prominent lower-middle-class Jewish merchant: "When I purchased my red Hudson car the only other car like it was owned by Mr. Sacks. I can't stand him because in the days when cars were more rare he owned a great shiny Marmon and there was a great feeling against the Jew owning such a fine car because it was really a great car, especially as he had started as a junk dealer on Wharf Square." Here is evident a very active resentment against the Jew for acquiring a class symbol, in the form of a fine car, out of context with his class status. A strong point, also, is made of his class origins and mobility by reference to his original residence in Zone I and to his earlier occupation as a junk dealer.

A similar situation was related by the Greek priest in speaking of one of the upper-lower-class Greeks: "Varkas recently bought a second-hand Lincoln and it nearly drove him into the poorhouse. He found it cutting into his business. It was too much for him, so he consulted me about it, and on my advice he gave it up. The trouble was that it was entirely too conspicuous for Yankee City." What is meant here, apparently, is that the car was conspicuous by reason of its owner's class context, and it is significant that pressures were exerted in the direct form of a boycott of Varkas' business.

Of course, resistance notwithstanding, the ethnics have conspicuously succeeded in "getting ahead" in the Yankee City social hierarchy. Where they have advanced without appearing to "push," have slowly consolidated their new positions, and have conformed in their behaviors, they have been able to overcome resistance, and have been accepted on the progressively higher-class levels. Thus, an elderly upper-middle-class native, after relating that as a boy "we looked down on the Irish," concluded with the assertion: "Then, somehow, something happened, change came along, and I guess they got *strong*, because all this seemed to disappear, and now we are sort of taking the Irish in as one of our kind."

7. Social Mobility and the Solidarity of the Ethnic Group

ONE significant effect of ethnic mobility, apparent in complete form in the Irish group, is that the scatter of the Irish through all but the topmost level of the class hierarchy has produced a split in the group along class lines. Internally, the Irish group is now differentiated according to position in the city's class system. The growing identification with class level and the usual manifestations of extreme class distance have served to break up the Irish group's inner cohesion. The result is seen in the sharp antagonisms which exist between the Irish of the two lowest classes (lower-lower and upper-lower) and of the two higher classes (upper-middle and lower-upper). The former refer to the latter as "lace-curtain Irish," a term with reproachful connotations, and associate them with the Hill Street "codfish aristocracy." The higher-class Irish, when aroused, will apply to the Irish of the lower classes the familiar epithet, "shanty Irish." The lower-middle-class Irish seem to keep to the fence in this conflict between the two class factions in the group.

The issue between these two "warring" Irish subgroups was

clearly dramatized at a Yankee City mayoralty election when the only candidates were two Irishmen—Kelly (UL) and McCormack (UM). The former conducted his campaign largely by castigation of Hill Street for its iniquities to the poor of River Street and to the small taxpayers. He won the election easily, apparently carrying the entire vote of the two lowest classes, both native and Irish, and at least half the votes of the lower-middle class. Even the lower-lower-class native descendants of the old fishermen group, who traditionally "hate" the Irish, "lined up the two (candidates) and decided that Kelly looked less Irish than did McCormack and so they voted for him [Kelly]." Actually, Kelly conforms far more to the conventional conception of the Irish physical type than does McCormack, but these lower-lower-class natives were asserting that they were more closely identified with Kelly than with McCormack and hence felt that the former must be the "less Irish" of the two.

McCormack, on the other hand, was strongly supported by members of the three highest classes, native as well as Irish, and had this to say to the interviewer: "When I ran for mayor the last time I don't think that more than two out of every ten Catholics voted for me. I think the other eight voted for Kelly, and most of the votes I got were from the Protestants."

In other words, between the Irish and the natives of the two lowest classes today, and between the Irish and natives of the three highest classes, there is a class solidarity greater than the group solidarity between the Irish of the lowest and highest classes or between the natives of the lowest and highest classes.

In none of the other ethnic groups have sufficient numbers progressed into the upper-middle class to create the sharp class dichotomy which appears in the Irish group. But among those who have crossed into that stratum from the lower-middle class there is evident in most cases a weakening of the individual's relations with his group's community system. This was seen in the case of the upper-middle-class P^2 generation Greek who was discussed above. He has never participated in the association structures of the Greek community, and although he was once a member of the Greek church, he has now left it for a native Protestant church. The P^2 generation Pole, also referred to, now of the lower-middle class and moving toward the upper-middle, said of his relations with the Polish group: "Of course, I want to help them as much as I can. But if I don't want to be too far from them, I also don't want to be too close to them."

8. *Comparison of Mobility among Hierarchies and Groups*

CHART VI gives a graphic representation of the three corrected status indices[11] of the native and the eight ethnic groups. All groups except native appear to describe a status line approximating the shape of an "L," either in the normal or inverted position. Specifically, two facts appear: (1) All groups, with two exceptions, show an occupational index[12] higher than the residential—the deviation being relatively small for the Armenians, Greeks, and Italians, and very large for the Jews, Poles, and Russians. The two exceptions are the French Canadians, with whom the two indices are identical, and the Irish, whose residential index is somewhat the higher of the two. (2) All groups, except the Russian, have a class index lower than either of the other two indices—the total deviation being very large for all groups except the Irish. However, among the Russians the class index is slightly higher and among the Jews and Poles slightly lower than the residential index; but for all three of these groups the former is still far below the occupational index.

Do these facts mean that in general ethnic mobility is more rapid (1) in the residential than in the class hierarchy, and (2) in the occupational than in the residential hierarchy? There is a sequential pattern among the ethnic movements in the three hierarchies which precludes quite so simple a conclusion. Two further facts may be recalled from Chapters III and IV: (1) All ethnic groups (except the Irish), in their first important decade year, achieve higher positions in the occupational than in the residential hierarchy. (2) While mobility through the subsequent decades proceeds in the occupational hierarchy at a more-or-less uniform rate for most groups, in the residential hierarchy it develops at an accelerating rate.

11. The three status indices used in preceding chapters were made comparable by equating them in terms of the norm of the native group. The occupational, residential, and class indices in 1933 of the native group are assumed to be equivalent and therefore of a 1:1:1 correspondence. The status index of each ethnic group is then expressed as a percentage value of the corresponding index of the native group. For example, the occupational index in 1933 of the Irish, 2.52, divided by that of the natives, 2.55, gives a "corrected" index of 98 per cent for the Irish. The "corrected" index allows the determination of the degree to which the three indices of a group approximate each other as well as those of other groups. The writers are grateful to Dr. S. A. Stouffer and Mr. Felix Moore, of the University of Chicago Department of Sociology, for their encouraging approval of such statistical measures as have been applied in previous chapters and for their indispensable help in working out the problem presented above.

12. Unless otherwise qualified by the term "original," indices referred to in this chapter designate "corrected" indices.

CHART VI

CORRECTED STATUS INDICES OF NATIVE AND ETHNIC GROUPS

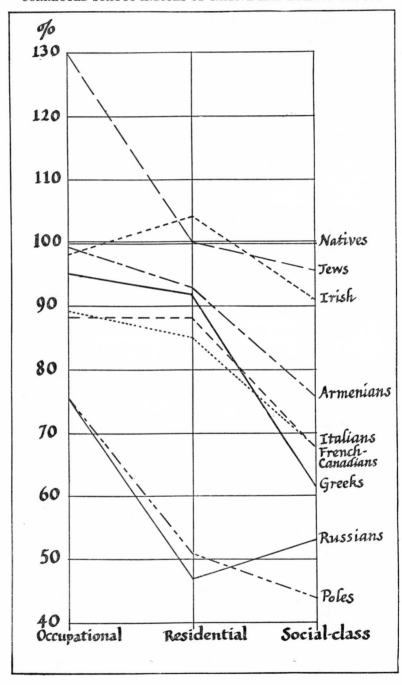

Chart VI gives evidence that while an ethnic group generally begins with the residential status lower than the occupational, acceleration of mobility in the former in time brings the two indices close together. Among the two newest groups in Yankee City, i.e., the Russian and the Polish, residential mobility has not had time to acquire sufficient momentum to cut down the considerable gap between the residential and the occupational indices. With the next older groups—the Italian, Armenian, and Greek— residential status has advanced until the index is little below the occupational index. With the French Canadians the two indices have reached a point of coincidence. And with the oldest group of all, the Irish, the residential index actually exceeds the occupational.[13] The Jews are exceptional in that they are one of the oldest ethnic groups and yet show a deviation between their occupational and residential indices as wide as those of the two youngest groups. The special factor present in this case is that the Jewish group entered at such a high occupational position and moved so rapidly in the hierarchy that its residential mobility, rapid as it has been, could only narrow the gap by 1933. With the exception of the Jews, therefore, if the ethnic groups are seen in the order of their age in Yankee City, the trend is one in which the occupational and residential indices progressively approach each other.

It is to be expected, of course, that the far more severe and complex standards and demands which govern status in the class hierarchy would retard mobility as compared with the other two hierarchies. The class index also lags far behind the others because all groups enter the hierarchy at the very lowest possible point.[14] However, it tends to approach the two other indices. For example, the smallest deviation (7 per cent) between class and occupational indices is with the oldest group, the Irish; the next (20 per cent) with the French Canadians; and the largest deviation (the Jews excepted) is among two of the youngest groups, the Greeks (34 per cent) and the Poles (33 per cent).

13. The Irish, however, present a somewhat typical case. They began, on arrival, in more or less corresponding positions in the two hierarchies, and through 1903 occupational mobility typically lagged behind residential advance. In the last three decades, however, the former has exceeded the latter.

14. It should be noted that area of residence and occupation are two important elements contributing to the determination of class position. Hence, the varyingly marked deviation of the class index from the other two indices reflects an even greater lag than the index number itself suggests in the other important elements involved in the definition of class status. These elements reflect the individual's relations and behavior.

The definite trend toward correspondence of an ethnic group's statuses among the three hierarchies, after the model of the native group, appears to be in three stages. At arrival, a group's occupational status is higher than its residential status; and the latter, in turn, is far higher than its class status. Advances are made in all hierarchies, but most rapidly in the residential and most slowly in class. The P generation, after thirty years in Yankee City, reaches equivalence in the occupational and residential hierarchies, with class status still lagging. The F^1 generation advances (over the P generation) farthest in the class hierarchy, but not sufficiently far to close the gap between the class index and the other two indices. In the case of the Irish, the gap is not closed until the F^1 generation, but it appears that the newer groups, to judge from the Armenians and the Italians, may achieve equivalence in all three statuses by the F^2 generation.

Among successive generations there are different rates of mobility in the three hierarchies—differences which carry the ethnic group in a single direction, from a condition of great disparity among the three statuses toward an ultimate condition of identity among the statuses. The latter is one more native norm which the ethnic group is progressively approaching; and it may therefore be considered as another aspect of the acculturation and assimilation of the ethnic groups within the Yankee City society.

The generalization that the degree of ethnic approximation to the status of the natives is correlated with the length of a group's settlement in Yankee City has been documented in this and preceding chapters. Examination of Chart VI, however, shows that the arrangement of the group lines on the vertical scale is by no means in the exact order of group age in the city. It is seen, first, that there are certain pairs of groups which arrived in Yankee City during the same decade, yet whose status lines are at varying distances from each other. The Jews and Italians compose such a pair, the combined status indices of the former being an aggregate 83 per cent greater than those of the latter. The Armenians and the Greeks form another contemporaneous pair; the total indices of the Armenians are an aggregate 21 per cent greater than the total for the Greeks. Three fourths of this deviation is accounted for by the difference in the indices of the two groups. The difference between the last pair of contemporary groups, the Russian and the Polish, is almost wholly in their class indices. In other words, for each of these pairs of groups the time factor is more or less constant, yet there are significant status differences between the members of each pair.

Second, the status lines of the two oldest ethnic groups, the Irish and the French Canadians, are not as high as might be expected from their age in the city and the status positions of certain younger groups. All three status indices of the French Canadians are almost identical with those of the Italians and much below those of the Armenians. In one index the Irish are below the Armenians and in two below the Jews. It is apparent, then, that although there is a broad correlation between the position of a group's status line and the length of its settlement in Yankee City, this correlation is by no means perfect.

One of the important conditions affecting the mobility rates of the three pairs of contemporary groups, especially that of the P generations in the class hierarchy, is the type of motivation which induced migration to the United States. The Jews, Armenians, and Russians, in the act of migration, "burned their bridges behind them." Arriving with the design of establishing themselves in this country permanently, they were anxious from the first to strike roots to adapt themselves to the basic demands of the American society.

On the other hand, substantial portions of the Italian (those from South Italy and Sicily), Greek, and Polish groups migrated with the original plan to settle only temporarily. Generally, their aspiration was not to rise in status in this country but to secure sufficient funds with which to increase their landholdings and therefore their economic status in the homeland. The number of those among these three groups who have actually repatriated themselves according to this original plan is comparatively small, but the decision to remain was reached only after about a decade or more of residence here; until the decision was made, there was little impetus to meet any but the minimum terms of the society. Therefore, although many P generation members of these groups were as quick as any in accepting better jobs, they were somewhat late in selecting better places of residence, and they were especially slow in adapting to the opportunities and demands of class ascent. The Poles and Russians, for example, in 1933 have almost identical occupational as well as residential indices, but the class index of the latter is 9 per cent larger.

The purchase of a house implies the acquisition of a share in the property system and a special status, through the function of paying taxes, in the political system of a society. It involves driving permanent stakes and in the case of ethnic groups may be interpreted as an indication of the degree to which roots have been struck in the society. The classification of six Yankee City ethnic groups into originally permanent migrants (1) and temporary migrants (2) is substantiated in the difference between the two groups of each pair, as late as 1933, in the proportions of families owning their homes and other real property:

	Percentage
1. Jews	63.4
2. South Italians	29.0
1. Armenians	52.7
2. Greeks	32.4
1. Russians	55.5
2. Poles	32.0

In the case of the Armenians and the Jews, additional elements appear to increase mobility. Similarities between the Jewish background and the Yankee City society have been cited. The similarity in background of the Armenians lies only in a religious affinity between the Armenian Apostolic Church and the Episcopal Church, which led to affiliation between the two and more rapid acculturation of the Armenian group.

The French Canadians present a peculiar case in that all three indices of this group are relatively low as compared even with such groups as the Italians and the Greeks. The factors in this situation are multiple and interrelated in a complex manner.[15] Many French Canadians settled in Yankee City with the intention of returning ultimately to Quebec. The fact that they are only a few hundred miles from Quebec, which they can revisit easily, has unquestionably acted to slow the pace of the group's adaptation to the Yankee City social system, especially by perpetuating the traditional lines of the French-Canadian family structure, which is strongly patriarchal. The father decides which son is to inherit the farm (for the family landhold must remain intact and un-

15. The writers have had the benefit of conversations with Dr. Everett C. Hughes, of the University of Chicago, and with Dr. Horace E. Miner, of Wayne University, both of whom have made extensive studies in the rural and town areas of Quebec. They have either confirmed or themselves suggested, in both conversation and print, the factors incorporated in the interpretation. Cf. E. C. Hughes, "Position and Status in a Quebec Industrial Town," *American Sociological Review*, III, No. 5 (1938), 709–717; and Horace M. Miner, *St. Denis: A French Canadian Parish* (Chicago, University of Chicago Press, 1939).

divided), which is to enter the priesthood, and which are to go to the industrial towns of Quebec and New England. A boy's future occupational status is the choice of the father, and the nature of the schooling he receives determines that status by restricting more or less the range of occupational mobility. Where a boy does rise, as into the priesthood, he does so not through his own efforts alone but through the combined efforts of his family. Therefore, such mobility raises not his prestige alone, which would place him above the family, but that of the entire family unit. Individuals do not advance in prestige; families do—and this only in certain narrow and prescribed channels. Initiative for mobility is not the individual's but that of the family as personified by the father. In short, the basic motif in the pattern of the rural social organization of French Canada is the family unit, and the basic "drive" is to retain unimpaired the family's identification with its land and its customary way of life, which means its customary economic status.

It was stated above that relative to its age in Yankee City and compared with other younger groups, the Irish group's status line (Chart VI) is not as high as might have been expected. Two special factors appear to be involved: First, the general rate of Irish status mobility has been retarded as penalty for the fact that the group was the first, among ethnic groups, in order of appearance, arriving in a period of a fixed native population and relatively limited opportunities for advance within the Yankee City social system; and second, as we have shown elsewhere, the larger the ethnic group, the smaller will be the proportion of those able to climb into progressively higher status levels. It is not possible to assert anything more than the fact that the size of the Irish population, which is almost three times as large as the French Canadian and many times as large as that of any other ethnic group, has directly reduced the mobility rates and status positions of the group in all three hierarchies. This likewise would seem to hold, although to a lesser extent of course, for the French-Canadian group in relation to the other and smaller ethnic groups.

9. *Summary*

To summarize, the degree of ethnic approximation to the statuses of the natives is correlated primarily with the length of the group's establishment in Yankee City. That is, all groups have progressively climbed toward higher positions in the three hierarchies. However, certain secondary factors have produced differences in the rates of mobility among the various groups:

A. Factors for retardation of status mobility

    1. Original migrational intention of temporary settlement (South Italians, Greeks, Poles).

    2. Family structure with patterns of maintaining customary status and of parental determination of status (French Canadians).

    3. Order of a group's appearance in the city, both because the earliest group encounters local conditions which no longer operate when later groups arrive and because, to a certain extent, the earliest group reduced resistance to and cleared the way for the advance of later groups (Irish).

    4. Large group population, a condition increasing the resistance to mobility (Irish and French Canadians).

    5. Proximity to the homeland, a factor for the slowing of the acculturative processes and therefore for the curbing of status advance (French Canadians).

B. Factors for acceleration of status mobility

    1. Similarities between the ethnic ancestral society and Yankee City in general social-organization type (Jews).

    2. Similarities between the ethnic ancestral society and Yankee City in the religious aspect of culture (Armenians).

VI

THE FAMILY

1. *Original Form of the Ethnic Family*

AMONG all the ethnic groups represented in Yankee City, the family in the homeland had been of the general patriarchal type, with almost complete subordination of wife and children. Maguire[1] has written of Ireland that "deference to parental authority is the characteristic of the country." Similarly in French Canada the destinies of the family group were guided by the father.[2] An Armenian informant told us: "In Armenia the father has absolute power over the family."

In an unpublished study of Italians, Adams[3] has this to say of the family in South Italy:

Family ties among these peasant folk are strong. Husbands and fathers rule their households with rods of iron and frequently when red wine has flowed too freely, reinforce their commands to wives and children with generous blows. Women are looked upon as economic assets to be used by oneself and protected while under one's control, and used for one's own ends when they are not. Young girls are taught to respect and obey the father and, in case of his death, the eldest son, who then becomes the head of the family.

Similar evidence is abundant in the literature on the Jews, Greeks, Poles, and Russians.

The patriarchal type of family structure was not merely enforced by tradition and convention but took its form in every case except that of the Jews from its functions in a relatively simple agrarian economy. The general economic background of the ethnic is predominantly agricultural, organized around a rural land system and the productive unit of the family.

With economic self-sufficiency an objective of the family, labor was divided between the sexes, and even the children had their

1. J. F. Maguire, *The Irish in America*, p. 493.
2. E. C. Hughes, *French Canada in Transition* (Chicago, University of Chicago Press, 1943); Horace M. Miner, *St. Denis; A French Canadian Parish.*
3. Helen Thayer Adams, "Italian Culture and Delinquency in the United States."

apportioned share of work. Organization and direction of the family in such a productive unit fell to the father. Hourwich[4] says of the Russian father in this capacity: "The authority of the major of the household was respected on the ground of his greater experience, which comes with age, as well as of his administrative ability."

Hence the father's traditional status as head of the family was reinforced by the fact that he managed it as a producing unit. Conversely, the subordination of wife and children was accentuated by the fact that they were subalterns in an economic enterprise.

Since the family as a productive corporation rested upon perpetuity of both land and man power, certain of the sons even after marriage remained under the parental roof. The family was thereby extended to include three generations, to compose the type known as the *grosse famille*.

Xenides[5] reports of Greece: "Greeks are strongly attached to their families and relatives. Family life in many parts, especially in Turkish sections, is of the patriarchal type. It comprises father, mother and the children, and as the sons grow up they bring their brides to the paternal home. . . ."

Typical is the information offered by a Yankee City Armenian male: "In Armenia when you get married you go and live on your father's property and in the same house. It is a disgrace to go and live in some other house, and you have about four generations living together in the same house. The oldest one in the place is the leader of the house. If the grandfather is living, he is the head of the house, and when he dies the eldest son is the head of the house, and so on down."

The result of such a succession is that the family household is never depleted and that the patriarch retains his status and hold upon his sons, even though they are parents themselves, until his death. Not even death can alter the perpetuation of such an extended family system. This is in contrast to the modern small American family which is broken up when children marry and the parents are left to an "empty" old age.

The ethnic family in Yankee City is conditioned not only by its ancestral form but also by its identification with the linguistic,

---

4. Isaac A. Hourwich, *Economics of the Russian Village* (New York, Columbia College, 1892), p. 90.

5. J. P. Xenides, *The Greeks in America* (New York, George H. Doran Co., 1922), p. 49.

nationalistic, and religious traditions and structures of its former society. The threat to the new ethnic family is not merely one of a comparative decline in parental status in conformance with the American family type, but of elimination of the family's traditional behavioral modes. Destroy these in the child and, from the parent's point of view, the result will be family chaos.

2. *Migration and the Ethnic Family*

THE ethnic family structure of Yankee City, however, has been determined not only by the ancestral social system but also, although in lesser degree, by the conditions which accompanied its transference to America. The chapter on the relations of the ethnics to the Yankee City economic system has shown that mass migrations to the United States resulted from forces of attraction exerted by the expanding American economy and forces of expulsion exerted in the lands of emigration. The predominance of one or the other of these forces varied from period to period and from country to country. Where the forces of expulsion were violent, emigration was permanent and in family groups. Armenian emigration to a high degree and Jewish emigration to a somewhat lesser degree, impelled by the Turkish massacres and the Russian pogroms respectively, are examples.

Where the American gravitational forces were dominant and there were no overpowering expulsive forces to endanger the security of the family, as in the case of the Italians, Greeks, and Poles, emigration did not usually involve whole families but generally only the younger, unmarried, more adventurous sons. Foerster[6] refers to the "strangely temporary character" of Italian migration; figures published by the Bureau of Statistics since 1876 show that in the early years nine tenths of the emigrants were males and in later years four fifths, as compared with two thirds among other groups.

Xenides[7] says of the Greeks:

It is not far from the truth to say that 20 per cent of the Greeks in America have their families with them; the rest are either unmarried or have left their families in the homeland. The number of families has been growing lately, both by marriages in the United States and married men bringing over their families from Greece or Turkey. Men came alone for economic reasons, as sums of money

6. R. Foerster, *Italian Emigration of Our Times,* p. 39.
7. *Op. cit.,* p. 76.

insignificant in the United States were of great value and service on the other side. They worked in the United States and sent money home.

A Yankee City Greek in his early forties volunteered this information: "I came over first with an older brother, then after a time a younger brother came over. That was in 1912. Then in 1921, after the War, my oldest brother went back." The return of the older brother and the remark of another Greek that "we all thought we would go back in a few years, but it seems we never did," both indicate the temporary intent in the Greek migration.

The same situation is confirmed by a Polish informant: "Very few of the Poles brought their families over. Most of them were all young men and boys who came to make money." Here is provided the motivation for temporary settlement which is a manifestation of the American forces of attraction.

Whereas the Armenians and Jews burned their bridges behind them, the Italians, Greeks, and Poles migrated to America to accumulate wealth and then return to lift their families to a higher status and a more comfortable mode of existence. That most of these immigrants have not returned may be ascribed to the powers of assimilation of the American social system.

The French Canadians provided a slight variation of this migrational mode in that at the beginning movement was for temporary purposes and yet took place in family groups. The factor here, of course, was Canada's proximity to New England, allowing relatively easy transportation. But, as in the instances just reviewed, temporary intent gradually gave way to permanent residence. Thus Greenough[8] records:

Emigration of the *habitant* class within the last twenty-five years has been enormous, and still goes on, although fluctuating from year to year according to the condition of business. There is scarcely a family in our vicinity from which some immediate member has not *"monté dans les États"* (gone up into the States). Whole families have been accustomed to go and return almost annually. A good many of them find their way back and remain at home; for even if they obtain constant and remunerative employment the civilization of "the States" does not always suit them, and they long for their own rivers and forests, their familiar speech, their churches, and their inherited customs. Then, although they earn much more in the

8. W. P. Greenough, *Canadian Folk-Life and Folk-Lore,* pp. 121, 122.

States, they are obliged to work much harder and more steadily than at home; and it is not every one that likes hard work, even if well paid. A man who lately returned, when asked why he came back when he was doing so well, replied, "*Je m'ennuyais du pays*" (I was tired of the country). He had nothing to complain of, but he was home-sick. The busy, earnest life of the States does not please the majority of French Canadians.

Within a few years, however, so many have decided to remain and make the States their home that there are now about two-thirds as many Canadians in the States as in Canada, and the regularly migrating contingent has proportionately diminished.

Between the two extreme migrational modes described there is one which results from a more even balance of the forces of expulsion and attraction. It generally takes the form of migration to the United States by young unmarried men and women who use their first savings to bring over their families. Here the expulsive forces are not sufficiently serious to dislodge the family but are so chronic in character as to make ultimate migration of the entire family an ardently held objective. Hence, such migrations are permanent. The best case in point is the Irish.

An old Yankee City Irishman said: "Usually the children came first, then sent for their brothers, sisters, and parents." And Maguire[9] writes of these young Irish people: "To assist their relatives, whether parents, or brothers and sisters, is with them a matter of imperative duty, which they do not and cannot think of disobeying, and which, on the contrary, they delight in performing. And the money destined to that purpose is regarded as sacred, and must not be diverted to any object less worthy."

What, in general, are the effects of migrational mode[10] on family structure? When whole families settle in Yankee City they succeed at first in maintaining their traditional family structure while making adjustments to the new environment. But when the young ethnics who arrived singly, expecting to stay only temporarily, settle and marry, the family structure is quite different. The individual has been independent of family controls in the intervening years and detached from his former society. A Greek-American newspaper writes of this type of young immigrant: "People were not as he imagined them to be, angels on earth.

9. *Op. cit.*, pp. 315, 316.
10. The migrational mode assigned to each group is typical though not exclusively characteristic.

There were no golden streets, neither were their any glad hands to receive the newly arrived. Unprotected and unguided he was left alone to open his way through."

The children of these young ethnics have not experienced the social background of the parent nor the period of emigration. The family, starting within the American context, is not as strongly organized as the family that emigrated as a unit.

3. *The Husband-Wife Relationship*

THE very day that the husband takes his place in the industrial economy of Yankee City, the patriarchal pattern of the family is radically altered. The new economic behaviors are observed, not within the spatial range of the family plot of land, but in specialized factory and market structures. The family ceases to be a self-sufficient coöperative producing unit, and the highly complex and differentiated division of labor characterizing the Yankee City economy is at once reflected in the sharp division of labor between husband and wife. Where before both had worked in the fields and around the home, with different emphasis as between these two areas, now the husband alone is the producer, the "breadwinner," with the result that the wife becomes even more dependent and subordinate to the husband in her role of "homemaker." What accentuates this dependence is that the husband in his economic relations soon picks up the American language, which facilitates his movement in the society. The wife, however, centering her existence about the home, has no relationships beyond it except with a few persons of her own ethnic background who may be her neighbors. She remains linguistically helpless in any relationships except those of her family and ethnic community.

Money for small household needs is portioned out by the husband only in small amounts for immediate requirements. Larger necessities, such as coal, clothing, furniture, etc., are always purchased by the husband. But even for small groceries the wife rarely ventures out to the stores, most of which are conducted by fellow ethnics who speak her language. Instead, a child is generally sent. The P^1 generation wife is tied to the home and completely dependent upon her husband.

With time, the wife's relationships begin to expand beyond the home, and with this expansion the wife starts to climb in status relative to the husband. We shall trace this process through the generations and the various communities.

Although the Greeks antedate the Poles and Russians in Yankee City by a decade, the husband-wife relation has not changed perceptibly from those in the Polish and Russian families. Hence we shall use the Greeks to illustrate the first of two changing phases of this relationship in the P^1 generation.

That the Greek P^1 husbands mean to keep their women identified exclusively with the home is apparent in the following strong words of one of their number: "What do the women do to amuse themselves? Well, they just stay at home. You know, in this country one trouble is that they give the women too much power. They have organizations, they vote and run things, and run for governor just like the men do. In Greece about five years ago they wanted to give women the vote. But they said, 'If the women want to vote and hold office like the men, they will have to serve in the army for a year, as do the men.' The Greek women here don't vote. Just the men vote. I know the American women do, but the Greek don't. They stay at home."

Greek women are not expected to be interested in anything outside of the home and children. The husband, in his new productive capacity, must be away a considerable part of the day. In his community activities in the Greek-American Progressive Association, the Greek church, and the Greek school, he is often away evenings. Other evenings he generally spends at the Greek coffee shops. To the wife falls the lot, formerly the husband's, of supervision of the children. Not that he abandons to her any of his traditional authority over the children but rather delegates it to her as his agent when he is otherwise engaged.

That the Greek women accept this position as defined by their husbands is evidenced in the following comment of a Greek wife: "No, the Greek women don't have organizations, they aren't smart enough, they just stay at home, that's what they are for, to keep house and take care of the children." This is as strong a statement as any offered by the Greek men.

As in the case of the Poles and Russians, this complete domination by the husband is extended to the control of family funds. But the Greek wife gets around, more than do the Poles and Russians, going shopping, which is generally her first step toward direct participation in the city's economic system.

However, among all ethnic groups except the Irish and the Jews, there are P^1 generation wives who are gainfully employed. (Those wives who divide their time between the home and their husbands' stores are not included.) Data show that these women are childless, have only children over thirteen, or are working while the husband is unemployed. In the first two instances, the wife is not much needed at home and her time can be used more productively in working; in the last, she is helping to meet a crisis situation, and the husband takes charge of the household. In all three instances the husband remains dominant.

While employment of P^1 generation women does not perceptibly alter the form of the husband-wife relation, it does serve to shift the wife's complete identification with the home. That employment gives the initial impulse to the expansion of the wife's relationships beyond the home became clear toward the end of the three-year research when these wives were found to be largely instrumental in creating the first association in the Polish community open to women.

The Greek wife is an ardent and regular worshiper in the Greek church—much more so than is her husband; but even within the church structure she has no status except through her husband, since only the men are recognized as members and they direct the affairs of the church through a church corporation. Further, the women are subordinated in the church ritual. In the seating arrangements there is a rigid separation of the sexes which is extended to the youngest children, babes in arms excepted. During the service the women's part is passive while the men chant the responses and act as altar assistants. On the other hand, it is the Greek wife who performs such family rituals as burning incense on Saturday night and carrying it ceremonially through the house.

Finally, although it affects status little, there is considerable informal visiting among Greek wives throughout the day and especially during the afternoon at a time when children are generally away at school.

The Armenians have been in Yankee City somewhat longer than the Greeks. Although the Armenian family structure is the stronger of the two, the Armenian P^1 women exhibit a more developed phase in change of status than do the Greek women because they have been in Yankee City approximately a decade longer[11] and, since many of the Armenians are of the Protestant faith, they have been given a special place in certain of the Yankee City Protestant churches. This relation, as we had occasion to

11. It will be remembered that the women of the Greek P^1 generation did not come over until about a decade after the men and married here.

observe in an earlier chapter, has served to facilitate the general social mobility of the Armenians in the Yankee City class system. Of all the personality types in the Armenian community, however, the wife has been least touched by this mobility.

The P^1 Armenian wife is as subordinate to her husband as are the Greek and Polish. The evidence from Armenian male informants is of the same character as that already reported from Greeks and Poles. "My wife doesn't spend much. She wants to have a home. She's not like some women. She stays at home and works and saves money. She doesn't run around. A girl should never forget she's a woman and that her place is in the home and bringing up children." As among the Greeks, the women have no formal status as members of the churches and are separated from the males in the services.

But the Armenian P^1 wives deviate from those of the later ethnic groups in that they have assumed definite functions beyond the home in the Armenian community. They have an association of their own, the Armenian Welfare Corps, which is the sole charity-dispensing structure of the community; and the committee having complete authority over the Armenian school is composed entirely of women.

Under the patriarchal family system of Armenia, the women had no formal functions in the village community. The husband-father represented the family in all the structures composing the rural commune. He was the formal link and sole means of establishing accord between the family and the larger society. And, conversely, he exercised his authority within the family in part by reason of his extensive relations in the social system. Yet here in Yankee City, among the P^1 generation Armenians who migrated as adults and fully developed personalities, we find wives carrying out definite and important community roles. This emergence of new functions beyond the home is correlated with the wife's increased leisure time, the complexity of the ethnic community organization which requires a division of labor, and the increasing impact of the American social system.

It is apparent that among the Armenians as well as among other earlier ethnic groups, the women are attracted in two directions. The forces of a strong patriarchal family keep the woman subordinated to the husband and her personality identified with the home; while the forces of a variety of types of relationships and associations tend to expand her personality. The P^1 women compromise with these separate forces by maintaining a large measure of traditional uxorial subordination and by accepting limited extra-familial relationships which have definite functions in the ethnic community. With the P^2 generation there is a more nearly equal balance typical of the American form of relationship.

The Jews as a group preceded the Armenians into Yankee City by about a decade and may be expected to exhibit a further developmental phase. The Jewish family structure was traditionally of the patriarchal type but, unlike the other Yankee City ethnic groups, it did not derive from an agrarian economy. Also, the Jews were of the petty bourgeois class in Russia, and transfer to corresponding positions in the Yankee City economy did not involve shock to the family structure's principal internal relationships. There were no productive-work functions for the Jewish wife to lose; consequently, there was not the further accentuation of the dependent status of the Jewish wife which was observed among the wives of later ethnic groups. Hence the Jewish wife emerged into a participating role in her community earlier than did the wives from the other ethnic communities.

Almost half the Jewish families in Yankee City are of the middle classes. On the other hand, only one fifth of the Armenian families, one twelfth of the Greek families, one twenty-fifth of the Russian, and one hundredth of the Polish families are middle class.

Among the Jewish P^1 generation there is still a marked subordination of the wife to the husband, but it is not as strong as among the Yankee City Armenians or in the traditional Jewish family structure. Her husband does not dole out money to her. Instead, she is generally given a weekly allowance for the immediate and small necessities of the household. Either the husband alone or husband and wife together shop for home furnishings and clothing involving larger outlays.

We have already noted that among the ethnic groups only the Irish P^1 wives (who are almost all in advanced years) and Jewish wives are not employed in the economic system. This may indicate that the wives have passed the status in which they can be turned to such economic purposes and that such behaviors, being typical of the lower class, are antithetical to middle-class standards.

The Jewish P^1 women have been organized since 1908 into an association called the Jewish Ladies' Aid Society. When it is remembered that the Jews first appeared in the Yankee City directories in 1893 with fifteen families, keeping this number in 1903, and expanding from 1905 until by 1913 they had forty-one families, it is seen that they were still a relatively small and recent group when the J.L.A.S. was established. It is certain that this organization of P[1] women appeared earlier in the development of the community than did corresponding organizations found among the Irish, French Canadians, and Armenians.

In view of the scope of its functions, the J.L.A.S. is probably the most important associational structure of the Jewish community. Like the Welfare Corps among the Armenians, it performs the charity function for the entire community. This function, it must be emphasized, was traditionally discharged in Russia by formal organizations of husband-fathers. The range of J.L.A.S. charities is almost world wide, extending to needy families in Boston, New York, Denver, Poland, and Palestine. The influence of the J.L.A.S. has reached even to the male-directed synagogue and Hebrew School, where it acts as a fund-raising unit.

It is among the P[2] generation Jewish wives, however, that the full consummation of this personality development is found. Here the husband-wife reciprocal appears in a form indistinguishable from that of the modern American family with its more equitable sharing of authority and control. In these Jewish families, the "allowance" system prevails in the apportioning of money to the wife, but it is generally extended to include the prerogative of making all purchases, even to home furnishing. The husband usually reserves the right to purchase only his own clothes, the family car, and real property. In the buying of the car the wife is usually consulted. Hence, for all practical purposes, the P[2] wife becomes the purchasing agent and business manager of the family corporation in which the husband fills a position akin to banker. This is an enormous advance over the minimum economic behaviors of the Polish P[1] wife, for example.

The P[2] Jewish women are organized into an Hadassah chapter which is linked with the American Zionist organization of the same name. Through Hadassah these women organize the community around the nationalist aspirations of dispersed Jewish society, a more important community function than any performed by the Jewish male associations.

Most striking of all is the fact that the P[2] generation wives not only represent their families in important association structures of the Jewish community but also represent the Jewish community in certain special structures of the total Yankee City social system. This has occurred specifically in the Yankee City Health

Center and on the Yankee City Community Welfare Board, both privately endowed charitable institutions serving the entire city, where Jewish P^2 wives are members of the Boards of Directors.

This highly important position of the P^1 and P^2 Jewish wives in the community system, together with the P^2 wives' conspicuous advance in the family structure, emphasizes the fact that with the Jewish P^2 generation there has occurred a revolutionary change in the traditional personality type of the Jewish wife. Certain factors contributing to the rapidity of this change have already been reviewed; the immediate single factor is leisure. In the Pale of Russia, the regimen of homemaking absorbed the full energies of the Jewish wife, whereas in Yankee City household tasks have been greatly reduced through mechanical appliances. No ethnic home is without electricity. A Greek informant said of his sisters, "The poor girls have nothing to do at home. In America the housework is so much simplified. They can get water by turning a faucet and gas light from a burner, and there is no housework such as they had to do in the old country."

However, in the adoption of the American labor-saving devices there are very real differences between the generations. The P^1 wives accept them one by one, hesitantly, and even a bit dubiously. Among them, for example, electric washing machines, carpet cleaners, and refrigerators are relatively rare, whereas in the P^2 generation's homes they are general. Further, the former never give up altogether such of their handicrafts as bread baking and garment sewing, whereas among the P^2 these techniques are extremely rare. A number of P^2 Jewish wives admitted that until the Hadassah undertook a sewing project to prepare garments for Palestinian orphans, they were unable to sew. The P^2 wives, especially those of the middle class, have taken to hiring "maids," usually for only part of the day, to help them with their more tedious tasks, but few of the P^1 wives follow this practice. Hence there is a sharp difference in degree of leisure between the Jewish wives of the P^1 and P^2 generations, correlated with the degree of their identification with the home.

Another manifestation of this difference is found in their respective associations. The J.L.A.S., composed of P^1 women, gathers once a month for what is strictly a business meeting, whereas the Hadassah of the P^2 wives meets regularly every week, business taking up only a small part of the program and a wide range of recreational activities the rest.

The most time-consuming use of leisure by P^2 Jewish wives is auction bridge. One P[1] Jewish woman, in answer to a question about bridge, expressed her indignation: "Say, don't ask. People are going crazy about it, the women especially. They can play day and night. There is a group of younger Jewish married women and they are having bridge this afternoon. Then tonight [Monday] and Tuesday night. Then again Thursday night and Sunday again they are having bridges. It's a regular epidemic and a sickness, and some of the women should be taken out and shot. They don't take care of their own children. They leave the house go, their husbands come home and find no supper. They run down to the delicatessen store, throw something together and then go out in the evening for more bridge; and believe me, in some towns, although not here so bad, there have been some serious family troubles because of it. Say, you can't blame a man if his home and family are neglected for bridge. I really don't object to cards though; when people get together you've got to do what the rest do to be sociable, but say, there is a limit to it."

Even with children in the family, the focus of the P[2] Jewish family has shifted from the home; the family's behaviors are no longer directed inward but outward to the effective community system. In this respect it has reached a form approximating that of the modern, urban, middle-class American family.

This radical change in the emphasis of the P[2] Jewish family structure is correlated with the change in the status of the wife. The P[2] Jewish wife is no longer subordinated to and identified with the personality of the husband but has acquired a distinct personality in her own right. A P[1] male informant made this typical comment: "The difference between the woman here and in Russia is like day and night. There her first interest was the family. Here it is herself." And another, speaking of some of the younger Jewish women who wear shorts and slacks and smoke, concluded: "Yeh, in America the women try to be men."

This deplored equivalence of the sexes, symbolized in such externals as informal dress and cigarette smoking, became an issue, interestingly, in a sacred context when a new synagogue was acquired for the community in 1933. By the most ancient of traditions, seating in the synagogue is arranged with males in a front section and females either in a rear section or in the balcony. A screened partition must by prescription mark off the female section from that of the males. Both these edicts signify the inferiority of the women in the synagogue.

In the old Yankee City synagogue, which was dominated by the

P[1] men, these sacred laws were observed to the letter. However, when a new, larger, and far handsomer building was purchased to be converted into a synagogue, effective control passed into the hands of the P[2] males. Immediately the P[2] women, with no voice in the affairs of the congregation, began a campaign through their husbands for abandonment of the age-old separation of the sexes. One of these women, to point her position, referred to the Reformed Jewish congregation in an adjoining city: "There the whole family sits together, but here I have to sit back in the women's section. But I never lift a sider [prayer book]. My husband sits with the men and kids around and my little boy wanders back and forth between us. Now that is no way! I have said that I will not go [to the new synagogue] unless I can sit with my husband and children. And a lot of other people are going to hold out until the changes are made. You watch and see!"

The synagogue was the only structure in the Jewish community system in which the P[2] wife had made no advance. Here is a clear instance in which physical space has symbolic value in representing social space. If the P[2] wife could have broken through the partition to invade the sacred area of the congregation which, by Hebraic Law, is a community only of males, she would have reached, symbolically at least, a status in the sacred community equivalent to that of her husband, although it could not have been recognized on the rolls of the congregation or in the ritual of the synagogue. This was the last and most difficult barrier keeping her from equality with her husband.

The P[2] generation favored seating the congregation in the new synagogue by family groups rather than in sections by sexes. But the P[1] generation, husbands and wives both, was unalterably opposed, and in turn threatened secession. The new executive committee of the congregation, composed almost entirely of P[2] men, was faced by what seemed a hopeless dilemma. If they took one position they would alienate the P[1] generation, now in the position of "elders" to both synagogue and community, and of great ritual importance to both; if they accepted the other, they would lose the P[2] generation families, who were the "up-and-coming" young blood of the community and who, at some sacrifice, had largely financed the new synagogue. In either case, this conflict of the generations would rend the community, no less than the synagogue, in two.

At this critical juncture the executive committee came forward with a proposal in the Solomon tradition for composing the issue.

Instead of having sections one behind the other, three sections were arranged running the full width of the synagogue. The section on the left hand would be reserved exclusively for the conformist males and that on the right for the conformist females. This part of the plan placated the P^1 generation. A central section between these outer sections was to be reserved for the reformist family groups. The P^2 wives and their husbands felt they had won their point.

Since the whole controversy had its beginnings among the P^2 generation wives, its settlement was for them a notable victory. They were determined to have a place in the synagogue beside, and not behind, their husbands. To them, how the "backward" wives were seated was a matter of the latter's choice and pleasure.

What of the husbands of these P^2 Jewish wives? How have they taken to the new roles and new positions of their wives? The answer is found in the behavior of the husbands during the crisis situation just described. They were in a position to enforce the traditional seating modes in the synagogue, had they been of that mind. They were in control of the executive committee and they had the power of the sacred law, from both of which there was no possible appeal. Yet they battled with their own elders on behalf of the reform. They have offered no resistance to the ascent of their wives even into the final sanctum of the "holy of holies."

At the time of the investigation, the F^1 French Canadians and the F^1 and the F^2 Irish were adult. In these two generations we can presumably continue the observation and analysis of the progressive change in the husband-wife relation to its final development. However, in extension of their social personalities and in status relative to their husbands, their wives have advanced very little, if at all, beyond the phase exhibited by the Jewish P^1 wives and even lag in responsibility for family purchases.

Not only do these Irish and French-Canadian wives persist in subsidiary roles, as in financial dependence, but they show only a slight extension of their personalities into larger community relations.[12] Of course, neither men nor women have voice in Roman Catholic Church affairs. The wives generally join the Married Ladies' Sodalities, which are direct extensions of the separate churches and are purely devices to continue the indoctrination begun by the church in the parochial schools. Educative in design

12. This generalization holds for the F generation wives of all classes except those few who have reached a status in the lower-upper class.

and strictly religious in content, they have not the larger community functions performed by the Armenian Welfare Corps and the Jewish Ladies' Aid Society. Such functions are served, though in far less degree, by two female organizations among the Irish and one among the French Canadians. However, since the combined membership of the two Irish associations is about two hundred and fifty (a figure which includes a small proportion of P generation wives and a larger proportion of unmarried women) and since there are several hundred Irish F generation wives in the community, it is evident that only a small percentage of the F generation wives is represented in these associations. The proportions are even smaller among the French-Canadian F generation wives. The Jewish female associations, by contrast, include more than 90 per cent of the wives of the Jewish community.

Since an Irish F^2 female is native born, two full generations (F^1 plus P^1) removed from the ancestral society of Ireland, and is therefore more closely identified with the American social system, how are we to account for her retarded rate of advance in status, especially since this is in such marked contrast to the P^2 Jewish wives, who were subadult immigrants?

The answer is to be found in the relation of the Catholic Church to the family structure. The Catholic Church in one aspect is exclusively a cult of the family, just as Judaism may be said to be a cult of the Jewish society. The church is a superfamily of families, with each family "a cell in the organism of the Whole Christ." Its symbolism is filled with familial elements, and its ritual has as its core the seven Sacraments, four of which are rites of passage whose foci are the family. Two others, Communion and penance, unite the individual with the symbol of Christ. The seventh is the rite of passage into the priesthood. By ritualization of family crises and by directly "embracing" the individual, the church provides the family with a matrix which shapes the family structure and keeps it inviolate. To quote at random from the enormous church literature to substantiate this thesis:

The Mother of Jesus should be our Mother. Did He not say He would not leave us orphans? But would we not be orphans without a mother? If He emptied His generous Heart by giving us His Father, His Life, His Spirit, then why should His arm be shortened in holding back His Mother? He called us to be His brothers and adopted sons of the Heavenly Father. But if He has a Mother, should not we who are His brothers also have the same Mother? Grace is the perfection of nature, and if in the natural order we receive natural life through a woman, why should we not also receive supernatural life? Once granted He has given us His Mother as Our Mother, then how true ring His words: "And all my things are thine, and thine are mine." [13]

But not only is Mary the Mother of Christ and the Mother of the family but Christ Himself is present in the home: "The Christian home became a tabernacle of religion, where the passions of man were to be controlled by the purity of Christ, where obedience was to be clothed in the tenderness of Christ, and where the power of the husband over wife, and the power of both over children, was to be exercised in the charity of Christ." [14]

In the case of the Greek and Armenian churches, which are branches of the Eastern Orthodox Church, as also in the case of the Jewish synagogue, the church is the inclusive religious structure of the community system and is only symbolically related to the churches of other such communities in this country and in the homeland. That is, the church of each of these communities is autonomous in the management of its own affairs. Each may have its priest or rabbi, but these are hired by, and are dependent for their position upon, the community.

The Irish Catholic and French-Canadian churches of Yankee City, however, are not merely autonomous *corpori* of families, but are themselves "cells" in the extended Western or Roman Catholic Church, articulated and controlled by a pyramided hierarchy, which is in effect a closely knit, highly sensitive, extremely efficient bureaucratic government. It is this "government" which directly administers and controls the church of the Irish and French-Canadian communities and, in a very real sense, transcends these communities. These churches have shown none of the internal weaknesses that are apparent in the non-Catholic churches and have maintained their controls on the family in the face of the reductive powers of the American social system. Nowhere is this more clearly demonstrated than in the contrast between the husband-wife relation in the Irish and French-Canadian families and in the Jewish family.

13. "The Spiritual Bethlehem." Address on the National Radio Catholic Hour, March 24, 1935.
14. "The Christian Life." Address on National Radio Catholic Hour, February 24, 1935.

The position of the Catholic Church on this matter is illustrated in the following excerpts from a work on the Sacraments by an authoritative Catholic writer:[15]

The husband is the head of the family. He ought to exercise his authority with charity and gentleness. "Husbands, love your wives, as Christ also loved the Church, and delivered Himself up for it. So also ought men to love their wives as their own bodies. He that loveth his wife, loveth himself. For no man ever hated his own flesh, but nourisheth and cherisheth it as also Christ doeth the Church. Let every one of you in particular love his wife as himself." (Eph. 5. 25, 28, 29, 33.)

The wife ought to love her husband and obey him. This God commanded from the beginning when he said to the woman: "Thou shalt be under thy husband's power, and he shall have dominion over thee." (Gen. 2. 16.) The Apostle also exhorts those to whom he writes: "Let women be subject to their husbands as to the Lord." (Eph. 5. 22.)

Wives are particularly admonished not to dispute or wrangle: "Let the woman learn in silence, with all subjection." (I Tim. 11. 11.)

Matrimony is typical of the union of Christ with the Church. . . . The Apostle portrays this mutual relationship in the following passage: "The husband is the head of the wife, as Christ is the head of the Church. He is the saviour of his body. Therefore as the Church is subject to Christ, so also let the wives be subject to their husbands in all things. Husbands, love your wives, as Christ also loved the Church, and delivered Himself up for it, that He might sanctify it. . . ."

The [marriage] ring is a symbol of the fetters which she [the bride] takes upon herself. She no longer belongs to herself, but to her spouse. . . .

In these quotations from a work bearing the imprimatur of the church is enunciated the unequivocal "dominion" of the husband over the wife.

And yet in more recent equally authoritative writings by representatives of the church, it is evident that the Catholic Church in America, with its capacity for yielding to changes in the social system once they are established, now concedes equality, with

15. H. Rolfus, D.D., *Explanation of the Holy Sacraments* (New York, Benziger Bros., 1898), pp. 272, 288, 292.

important qualifications, of male and female, husband and wife. Thus, a member of the American branch of the hierarchy says:[16]

Man and woman constituted the initial partnership of the human race. Each had to act in the interests of the partnership. Disassociated from the partnership of a life in common, each stood equal before the eyes of God. Whatever subordination was imposed upon woman by reason of her physical structures, was purely for the benefit of the partnership as such and not for the benefit of man as an isolated individual. . . . Where woman is subordinate to man simply for the sake of the individual man, the threshold of free love has been reached, or the tyranny of the past has been duplicated.

The fact that the rights of women are denied recognition so long in the history of the world has been due to the tyranny of man and not to the plan of Almighty God. Until modern times all civilizations represented more or less a denial of the proper status of woman as revealed in the creative verses of the Book of Genesis. Many times the Church was obliged to tolerate such tyranny. Never did she adopt it or encourage it. . . .

Today the married woman is no longer a legal slave. Today she has become what God Himself wished her to be when He created her in the morning of the world, what the Church proclaimed her to be in the noonday of Christianity, and what she herself must continue to be until the night-time of existence has come: the helpmate of man, the equal of man as an individual, the partner of man in the great partnership of the human family.

This interpretation of "equality" of husband and wife is based, in brief, upon two propositions: (1) The family is a "partnership," with both partners subordinated to the family enterprise; and (2) the differences in degree of subordination as between husband and wife imply subordination of the latter to the former not *qua* man but *qua* the status of husbandhood.

This seems to indicate that the church has made a verbal concession of equality with respect to what might be called "dignity" of wifehood status without yielding in any essential its traditional position on subordination of wife to husband. These facts come out even more clearly in the following excerpt from the article on the family in the *Catholic Encyclopaedia*:[17]

16. Rev. E. L. Curran, "The Christian Family." Address on the National Radio Catholic Hour, June 19, 1932.

17. "Family," *The Catholic Encyclopaedia* (New York, Robert Appleton & Co., 1909), V, 783.

The Christian family implies a real and definite equality of husband and wife. They have equal rights in the matter of the primary conjugal relations, equal claims upon mutual fidelity, and equal obligations to make this fidelity real. The wife is neither the slave nor property of her husband, but his consort and companion.

Being the provider of the family and the superior of the wife both in physical strength and in those mental and moral qualities which are appropriate to the exercise of authority, the husband is naturally the family's head, even "the head of the wife." To claim for her completely equal authority with the husband is to treat woman as man's equal in a matter in which nature has made them unequal.

The article continues with a discussion of the division of labor between husband and wife, the latter's share receiving heavier emphasis:

On the other hand, management of the details of the household belongs naturally to the wife. Their [children's] moral and religious formation is for the most part the work of the mother, while the task of providing for their physical and intellectual wants falls chiefly upon the father.

This evidence illuminates the function of the Catholic Church as protector and "shock-absorber" of the family against changes working into it from the social system. The roots of the movement stretch back into the nineteenth century, but it is particularly since the war of 1914–18 that the status of women in American society has risen with great rapidity. One need only examine the statute books to find the number of legal prerogatives formerly denied but now accorded the wife independently of the husband. The movement has gone so far that recently a national convention of professional women not only insisted upon complete "equality with men" but refused to endorse special Congressional legislation to protect women against industrial exploitation, on the grounds of "discrimination between the sexes."

This change in the status of women in both the family and society at large is only a symptom of complex movements in the social system, which are beyond the province of our analysis here. However, no family structure, native or ethnic, has been immune to the forces making for this change. The impact of these forces on the family structures of all the Yankee City ethnic groups was direct, the structures yielding gradually at first and at an accelerated rate later. Those families, however, which were within the supra-family structure of the Catholic Church, namely, the Irish and the French-Canadian,[18] yielded far more slowly than others because the church has a tight hold on the family, especially on the women, and the change was in a direction the church could not approve. That the Irish and French-Canadian families yielded at all is attributable to the fact that the F generation family, with the exception of its church affiliation, is dominantly American in its behavior.

To the church, the change was not merely one involving a point of dogma. Rather, it involved threats on two fronts:

1. *The Family*. The movement of the wife toward higher status might mean a closing of the gap in the unequal distribution of authority between husband and wife and weaken, by implicit challenge, the authority of both in the parent-child relation.

2. *The Church*. The extension of the personality of the wife by means of extra-familial relations would not only take her out of the home but, by carrying her out into the larger society, weaken her hitherto exclusive extra-familial relation to the church.

Faced with these threats, the church countered by according minimal equality to the wife on both fronts. As we have already observed, it explicitly conceded the wife full equality with her husband with respect to their "primary conjugal [i.e., sexual] relations." The dictum of the church, "Let women be subject to their husbands," had hitherto denied the wife such equality. By this important concession and by assigning the wife wider scope in the training of the children, the church acknowledged greater importance to the status of wifehood without retreating in its traditional position on the distribution of authority between husband and wife.

On the other hand, it has sanctioned the extension of the wife's personality but has provided the structures into which such extension may take place in the form of the church associations. These associations serve both to extend the wife's personal relationships and to keep her within the church and under its control. By the fact that its associational system provides places for both men and women the church again admits corresponding importance for both sexes; but in maintaining strict sexual

18. The Yankee City Italians and Poles, although Catholic, have no churches of their own. While nominally affiliated with the Catholic Church of the Irish community, these two groups show only minimal articulation to the church.

dichotomy between the associations it reaffirms its stand on the "distance" which must exist between the sexes.

Thus the change which threatens the family structure passes into the church system. The church, in turn, reacts by making concessions which mitigate the forces making for change, yet which neither alter the family structure in any fundamental aspect nor compromise its own position.

4. *The Parent-Child Relationship*

The primary function of the husband-wife relation is procreation of children. A corollary function, determining the division of labor between husband and wife, is the social orientation of children. The second basic relational component of the family structure, therefore, is the parent-child reciprocal with its function of orientating the child to the social system of which the family structure is part.

The relative status of husband and wife and the details of their division of family responsibilities vary considerably from society to society. Not so the parent-child relation. There can be little variation in relative statuses of parent and child; the parent-child relation is the "ideal type" of the class of relations called by Georg Simmel "superiority-subordination."

Yet within a narrow range, and depending upon the form of the family structure itself, there are variations in the aspects of the parent-child reciprocal in different societies. There is evidence of such variation between the traditional form of the relation in the original ethnic family and in the urban American family.

The ethnic family structure before migration was also an economic or productive structure. The child was subordinated not only as a child to father but as farm worker to supervisor. Arensberg[19] describes the relation as he observed it in Ireland:

The growing child ordinarily sees his father as owner and principal worker of the farm. When the whole family group of father, mother, children, works in concert, as at the potato planting, it is the father who directs the group's activities, himself doing the heavy tasks. . . . The direction of economic enterprise coincides with the dominant and controlling role of the parent in the family structure. The son is subordinated in both spheres to his parents, particularly the

19. Conrad M. Arensberg, "A Study of Rural Life in Ireland as Determined by the Functions and Morphology of the Family." Unpublished manuscript.

father. . . . The child grows up with the full complex of life within the family. The petty errands which constitute his first steps in farm work are a mere incident in the conditioning he receives. . . . The father comes, as it were, to stand for the group which he heads; the farm is known by his name.

This is supplemented by a Polish informant who, in discussing the role of the child in Poland, said: "Well, there they work all the time. It's like this—if I have a farm, there's always work to do and the girls and boys have to help on the farm."

Even recreation in the leisure hours was largely organized familially. As a Yankee City Greek tells us: "I had a fine father in Greece. When he was alive all the children had to be in evenings —not staying out late. We'd all stay home in the evening, talk, and play cards and games. Everybody was happy."

Further, the father was actually the lawgiver to the children and the law enforcer or disciplinarian. An Italian writer[20] says of his father: "He was primarily law and secondarily love . . . and made use of two methods: that of being a teacher and that of applying the rod." Similarly, the Jewish father was conceived in these terms: ". . . the father's authority over the child was supreme . . . children must respect parents as God's representatives on earth."[21] Of course, the child's attitude was prescribed in the Fifth Commandment of the Mosaic Code. Under such a thoroughgoing subordination the child's behavior was dominated and regimented by the father. An immigrant Jewess[22] writes to this effect: "In Polotzk [Russia] we had been trained and watched, our days had been regulated, our conduct prescribed."

How formalized was the child's behavior toward the parents is suggested in the account of a P[1] Armenian father: "An Armenian child has to obey the parents and be respectful to them. If they don't do it, they get hit, or beaten, and sent off by themselves. For example, if an Armenian man tells his daughter to bring him a glass of water she must come forward to within one step of where her father is, and hold the glass of water until he takes it. When he takes the glass of water, she has to step back one step and hold her hands like this [folded across her breast] and be very respect-

20. Constantine M. Panunzio, *The Soul of an Immigrant* (New York, The Macmillan Co., 1929), p. 14.

21. "The Family," *Jewish Encyclopedia* (New York, Funk and Wagnalls Co., 1906), V, 336–338.

22. Mary Antin, *The Promised Land* (New York, Houghton Mifflin Co., 1912), p. 270.

ful. When he is through drinking and hands her the glass, she has to step forward one step and no closer, take the glass, then step back one step and make a deep bow. Then she can turn around and leave the room. There are lots of customs like that."

The Armenian social system in a formal sense was a society of fathers. The status of the family in the community was derived from the status of the father. The personalities of the children were submerged in that of the father until his death. The father was the patriarch, the *pater familias,* whose authority controlled every aspect of the child's behavior.

Consider now the changes in the parent-child reciprocal induced after the family's settlement in Yankee City. The father is now productively employed beyond the confines of the family structure. Therefore the child's progressive initiation into the productive functions of the family and his progressive subordination to the father as the "head man" in the agricultural work are lost. The child, of course, remains dependent upon the livelihood provided by the father, but the immediate subordination to the father in an extensive area of behavior no longer exists.

This is implied in the remarks of a P^2 Polish mother: "In the Old Country everybody works too hard. When I was a girl of fourteen I worked on the farm all the time. I could do anything that had to be done on the farm, but my girl now never has to work. She worked for a while last year in a restaurant, but she has never worked very hard."

A French-Canadian father deplores the situation, particularly as it appears among the female children who are no longer trained in the household functions: "Everybody thinks the French are good for waiters and servants and all because they are trained even as little children to do things about the house, to wait on people and take care of things. A French girl [in Canada], even if she is only sixteen or eighteen years old, can cook, sew, and keep house. And look at the American girls [i.e., American-born French Canadians]. Not many that age can do that, and yet when they get married they have to learn how."

However, as we shall see, once the children reach the legal age at which they are allowed to work, the ethnic father within certain groups does reassert his superordination by claiming the child's pay check. But this comes rather late in the child's development and is not tolerated without some protest.

More serious, however, is the fact that the separation of the father from the family during his working hours and the separation of the child from the family by the American schools take from the father and, in a lesser degree, from the mother one of their most important sources of authority: orienting and educating their children. Not that there were no schools in the "old countries," but rural primary schools were in a relatively low stage of development in the nineteenth century, absorbed only a part of the population, taught the children for only a few years, and even then only in those seasons when their work was not required at home. Formal schooling merely supplemented the primary training given the children by their parents. In the American school system, however, the schools assume a far greater educative function. In terms of the F^1 generation child, they have almost exclusively the function of orienting the child to the American society, since the immigrant parents are themselves inadequately oriented. Not only do parent and child during an important part of the day move in separate social structures, but, as a consequence of the fact that one is in a Yankee City factory and the other in a Yankee City school, the father is no longer the supreme and sole lawgiver to the child.

The recreational organization of leisure hours was centered in the ancestral society around the family and the family hearth, but recreational forms in American society are generally found outside the home. The ethnic child in Yankee City has extensive play relations around the schools, on the playground, and among cliques and gangs which further separate him from the controls of the family.

Up to this point, we have merely outlined the general Yankee City factors which have worked to change the ethnic parent's side of the parent-child reciprocal from its traditional form. As in the case of the husband-wife reciprocal, the changes have not been immediate.

The fundamental fact facing the ethnic P^1 parent is that, through changes forced upon the family structure by reason of its inclusion in the Yankee City social system, he has lost many of the indirect controls (economic, educative, recreational) by which he had formerly maintained his all-inclusive authority over his children's behaviors. Does he capitulate to the incontestable logic of the situation and assume the father role after the American mode, converting himself from the patriarch to something more like "first among equals?"

The evidence from the newer ethnic groups—Poles and Russians, Greeks, and Armenians—is that the father reasserts his authority through direct controls with even greater vigor than before. We may take as an example of one type of parental reaction a Polish P[1] father who arrived from Poland twenty-eight years ago and is now a factory worker, unemployed for several years. He was married a year after his arrival and has been prominent in the Polish community as an officer of one of its associations. During an interview he said of his children, all girls: "You see I have nice girls. They are all very good, but I know how to treat them. Every week they bring their pay check home to me, give me all the money, and then I give them what they need. I buy everything, and then I give them a little money to spend. And then on Saturday nights they will come to me and say, 'Papa, can't we go out to the dance?' So I just drive them out to the dance, and my sister and me wait for them. They dance and they know I am there all the time. Even though they don't see me, they know I can see what they are doing. I don't dance any more. I'm too old, but young people are different. They have to have their good times, too. You have to treat them that way. Give them what they need, and let them have a good time and take care of them. If you don't, they will go and do it anyway. When we are at the dance and I decide to come home, the girls do it perfectly willingly. They don't argue.

"Other people don't care for their children. They don't look after them. They think they shouldn't have a good time, and then they have trouble with their children. Every week I give my daughter twenty-five cents to spend or fifty cents. She always says, 'Thank you, Papa.' If I don't give her anything, she doesn't say anything about it. I pay for the food, clothes, and the rent, but other things, unless we need them, I don't buy them. I save money. I always have money. I'm not like some people, spend everything they make, or like some people whose daughters pay them two or three dollars a week board or something like that, and spend all the rest themselves. They shouldn't do that. They all ought to be together. Whatever my girls spend I know about it. Whatever I spend they know about it. It's all one. The family sticks together. In that way we always get along, never quarrel like these others."

It appears that this Polish father has kept an iron hold on his children, all of whom are now over the age of eighteen. He appropriates their pay checks, which, since he is unemployed, are the sole support of the family. Obviously he feels that he has been successful in maintaining his patriarchal role of superordination over his children and thereby preserving the family's original pattern. If anything, he seems to have used the fact of his unemployment to further his claim on his daughters' earnings and to maintain himself in the home, much as did the parents in Poland who, when the children grew up, "sort of sat down and took life easy and directed the farm work."

He seems to have made no effort to secure reëmployment either with the factories or through the government agencies, in spite of the fact that he has otherwise greatly emphasized the necessity of saving money. By the device of unemployment, if the interpretation holds, he has reëstablished the family structure in almost the same pattern as that which prevailed in Poland, except that here the girls, instead of working within the family-economic structure, are now employed in the factories. He has strengthened his patriarchal position over his children, although this has meant the sacrifice of the income which his earnings would have added to the family funds.

The practice of appropriating the children's earnings is general, not only among the Poles and Russians but also among the Greek and Armenian P^1 parents. Among the latter a variation appears in that the earnings are not always taken in toto but in the form of a fixed rate for "board." Resentment of the F^1 children to this situation is expressed by one Greek high-school boy: "Many of the Greek boys and girls turn in their pay, like the R—— girls. Their father wants them to turn in every cent of their pay to him. Of course, that isn't right because it makes them hold out money on him—about twenty-five or fifty cents at a time. They save it up until they get money to buy a dress. Then they tell the parents they got it cheap. That isn't right. My sisters pay board. They used to make seventeen dollars a week and gave ten dollars to my father for board. Sometimes they would give something to my mother. Of course, if they need it, maybe they wouldn't give him that much. Of course, sometimes you have to help out; that is different. But times are pretty hard now, and they have to help them out all they can. But when they ask them to turn in every cent of their pay, it isn't good. They don't like that; they hold out money on them."

The Greek and Armenian fathers, under resistance from the children, are in some cases easing their demands for the earnings of their children, but with respect to the traditional control of courtship they have yielded very little. Here again, the children

resort to the practice of "holding out" as the only means of cir-
cumventing unyielding parents. The attitude of the Greek boy
quoted is quite emphatic that although such "holding out" of
money "isn't right," the blame for such behavior is upon the
parents. It is of interest that the girls reported to hold out
"twenty-five or fifty cents at a time" did so in order to buy their
own clothes. Apparently the father does not provide them with
enough for clothes according to their standards, pointing to the
difference in emphasis of the P^1 and F^1 generation upon such a
status symbol.

That the patriarchal attitudes of the P^1 generation are unchanged among the Greeks is suggested in the following words of
a P^1 Greek bachelor: "The Greek families always look up to the
parents. The father is head of the family, is always on his dignity,
and is close to his children. He always eats with them at meals.
You never see any joking; they are always serious, which instructs
the children. When he tells them to do something they must do it.
They don't argue about it or talk back. I visit my brother's family
in Boston, and I notice the difference between him and others
[Americans]. He lets his children have as much as others; he gives
them good clothes, money to spend, takes care of them well. His
children are always quiet and nice, and when they have something
to say it is in a quiet way. But when they want to do something
that is not good for them, they can't do it. They just do as their
father says.

"Then the Greeks have these coffee houses; they sit around,
having good fun. It is all understood. But when one goes to
another's home, he must be dignified; he won't joke with the husband or anything like that. Keep the jokes for the joking places.
The children see that their father is respected and they respect
him. You don't see any joking or arguing in the Greek families
as you do in others."

Here are emphasized the dignity and authority of the father.
The formal aspect of this dignity and authority is indicated in
the informant's attitude as to "joking" in the home. Joking relations involve informality, give and take, and "making light" of
certain aspects of personality. No joking behaviors, therefore,
may be exhibited before the child, since these would lead him
to question or doubt the father's dignity and authority.

Although the Poles and the Greeks have in large measure been
successful in their disciplinary roles, they have not been so in all
cases. Consideration of all the complex factors involved in delin-

quent behavior among the ethnics cannot be attempted here. The
ethnic groups having by far the largest crime rates among the
children are the Poles, Greeks, and Italians. In ten of the nineteen
Polish families with one or more delinquent subadult children,
one or both parents have police records. Of the eight Greek families with delinquent children, seven have parents with police
records. And of the eleven Italian families with delinquent children, the parents of six have police records.

In part, then, juvenile delinquency among ethnics is correlated
with parental delinquency. In most cases the behavior of the
parent and delinquency of the child are both manifestations of
a single fact—the disruption of the parent's personality, leading
to such behaviors on the part of the parent as assault and battery
and drunkenness, which are the predominant offenses among the
Poles, Greeks, and Italians, and to collapse of the parents' disciplinary function.

We may take as one instance a P[1] Pole who lives on River
Street, four of whose seven children have criminal records. He
arrived alone in this country at the age of nineteen and worked
in a mill town in southern Massachusetts. Five years later he
married and settled in a city some ten miles from Yankee City.
Of his eight years there we know nothing except that he was a
strike leader and that his fellow Poles considered him "no good."
Shortly before the first World War he moved to Yankee City,
and almost immediately his name began to appear on the police
and welfare records. He and his family have been receiving aid
intermittently since. On the police files he is credited with the
following offenses: nonsupport of family, violation of school law,
liquor nuisance, drunkenness, assault and battery, violation of
prohibition law, and neglect of children. Two of his daughters
and one son, the three eldest children, have no police records. Two
daughters were arrested for truancy and larceny, and both of
these have run off to New York where one has again fallen into
police hands. The three youngest sons, ranging in age from twelve
to seventeen, have been charged with truancy, larceny, and drunkenness.

A local judge who has tried most of the cases says of the family:
"The father is to blame; you can't work with him at all. Evidently
he doesn't coöperate in trying to bring the children up well. He
drinks rum and just won't work with you at all."

One of the older daughters of this Pole has said of her father:
"He used to get drunk lots, especially when I wasn't in town.

He's afraid of me because I used to put him in jail when he got drunk." The child is here disciplinarian to the father.

A school official reports of one of the younger daughters: "She was a wild one. She hated to go to school. She was all painted up, and she hated school because the kids in the sixth grade, where she was, made all kinds of fun of her, although she was sophisticated enough to be a high-school senior. The old man thinks highly of his girl in New York, who is the moll of some racketeer or gunman. You ought to hear what the old man said about his youngest son. I asked him what the boy was going to do, and he said, 'Well, we talked that over a great deal, and Danny said, "Don't worry, father; when I graduate from high school, we'll see how much money you have saved up to see whether I can go to college." ' The old man said that all his boys were fine boys and they help around the house. Huh, wait until you get the court record."—In the light of the fact that the father was unemployed and on relief, the remark of the son, "We'll see how much money you have saved," is almost insolent. That the father could voluntarily repeat the remark to a school officer apparently betrays his blindness to the son's meaning and to his own position.

This Polish father exhibits a personality with elements that seem to have no inner consistency, no mutual integration. He has repeatedly neglected his family and children and seems to feel no moral responsibility when his children run afoul of the law. In spite of their frequent troubles with the law he seems to be proud of them; while his children have very little respect for him, he apparently is not aware of it. Finally, for all of these lacks, he still is an important leader of one of the two Polish associations, and through it, of the Polish community.

Of the latter aspect of his personality his married daughter says: "Yes, he is an officer of the club [Polish-American Club]. He is there quite often. He likes the job very much, but we kid him about it. We make fun of the fact that Ladski [she calls him by his surname] should be spending all his time and money for the club and not for himself. He has a very good time doing it, but it seems a waste of time to me. He runs around all the time talking to people about club business."

The investigator reports that at open affairs of the club Mr. Ladski carries out such diverse functions as waxing the dance floor, carrying cases of light drinks, and presiding. This Pole has managed to orient himself to the Polish community, although to an excessive degree and without conception of the character of his role, just as he shows no adequate conception of his status as father. However, his preoccupation with the Polish organization, which was organized only in 1929, has given his personality a focus which it did not have before. That this development has changed certain of his behaviors is indicated by a Polish neighbor of his: "He used to drink a lot, like a fish. Now he has quit it. He hasn't had any at all since New Year's [seven months ago]. He seems to have gotten over it."

The general type of change in ethnic personality exhibited by Mr. Ladski we shall call, for lack of a better term, "personality disjunction."[23] Extreme personality disjunction appears in the Yankee City ethnic groups only among the Poles, Greeks, and Italians, and in these groups, as against the ethnic groups which were their contemporaries, the special factor was their migrational mode, i.e., they came singly and for the most part as young adults. Few of them came directly to Yankee City; they drifted in from other and larger cities. They had been conditioned, prior to emigration, to tightly held family controls and had then undergone for varying periods a foot-loose social existence beyond the controls of their families. Some of them, though by no means all, could not weather the sudden release from the family constraints, and personality disjunction followed. When they came to marry and establish families, they could not discipline themselves either in their extra-familial relations (witness their drunkenness and violence) or in their family functions as disciplinarians. In fact, there are instances in all three ethnic groups in which parent and child were apprehended together in the performance of what the society considered a crime.

To select an example for analysis: A man in his early twenties arrived in Boston from Greece, married four years later, and came to Yankee City. His occupational category is that of a skilled craftsman, and he has his shop and home on River Street. His name is found on police records with only one offense, "Neglect of children." He has five children, ranging in age from four to eighteen. Two of his three oldest boys have extensive police rec-

23. This term is preferred to the more common phrase "personality disintegration," which by usage has come to have more sweeping denotations than we intend. By personality disjunction is meant that condition in which the elements of social personality no longer show concatenation or system but appear disjointed, with the result that the individual exhibits a lack of "oneness," of consistent distribution of emphasis between these elements, and a failure to perform or appraise his defined functions within the various structures of which he is part. From the point of view of the community, he lacks attitudes of right and wrong, of a sense of responsibility, and of dignity.

ords, one with twelve arrests for the following types of offenses: larceny, habitual school offender, drunkenness, and ringing false alarm.

M. Vanzelas, the father, was interviewed. "Yes, the kid thought he'd be smart, turned in an alarm. They were watching and caught him. He just thought he'd have a good time and turned in an alarm, but they caught him anyway. Probably he'd seen some older boys doing that, because there have been lots of false alarms and he thought he could get away with it too and have some fun."

Several Greek informants deplored the conduct of the father in staying out gambling instead of going home to see that his children were off the streets and in bed.

One of the Vanzelas boys, who was still in grammar school when he should have been well advanced in high school, swore at his teacher. An officer of the school who called in the father reports the proceedings in his office: "The father said, 'You God damn little stinker. You son of a bitch. You're no son of mine; you don't show your bringing up. In the old country when my father spoke to me, we shook in our pants. When I came here I got work; I got a roof over my head. I sent my money to my father a thousand miles away. You, you have no respect for your father. What do you use language like that to a lady for? You're no son of mine.' Sammy grinned at his father. I then said, 'What will we do about this? We can't let him get away with it.' The father was as perturbed as the rest (but had no recommendations). Sammy finally said, 'I will apologize. Miss Rose has always been white to me. But I just seem always to get into trouble.' "

The outburst of Vanzelas shows a disjunctive personality. Swearing at his son is hardly compatible with the definition of a Greek father's dignity in the presence of his children, especially in view of the fact that swearing was the son's offense. His remark, "You don't show your bringing up," in the light of his neglect of his children indicates the same failure as that of the Polish father already analyzed to measure his own behavior by standards, although he does refer to his own behavior to his father as a standard for his son.

There is a parallelism between Mr. Vanzelas and Mr. Ladski, the disjunctive condition of the one being centered on liquor and of the other on gambling. Vanzelas has been a member of the Greek association since its formation in 1929 but has not been active in its affairs. However, in 1932 he was drafted to one of the lesser committees of the Greek community's church. A few months later a Greek gave this account of him: "He used to gamble a lot, cards and dice, but I don't think he does that much any more. I think he's straightened out now." In both cases, therefore, direct participation in the ethnic community has served to organize their personalities, at least to the degree that they no longer seek release in extreme forms of recreation.

There are several added observations to be made on the condition that we call disjunction among the P[1] ethnic fathers. A Pole who had no criminal record but who had a young son with an extensive police record said: "Most of the neighbors like my kids. The kids do get into mischief now and then. However, it isn't that the kids are bad, but when they get out among others, they do lots of things. They tease the lady next door a lot. She is an old lady without any kids of her own, and she complains about mine lots. I've always tried to be on the good side with her because she is old, but she doesn't understand kids, and perhaps, like so many others, she doesn't remember what she was like once. But most of the other people are all right about it. A person always thinks his own kids are the best and is apt to think that his own kids are not the kind to get into mischief, but he knows they're all alike, really. I feel that mine are best, although they are just like any others." He is here, obviously, setting mischief as a standard type of child behavior although his son's "mischief" was larceny.

Later, after he had been reading a newspaper account of a particularly brutal murder committed by a "respectable" boy in a near-by city, this Polish father discussed the case in detail and said: "How easy it is for a presumably very good person to be suddenly bad. Who knows we won't go bad, likewise?" A disjunctive personality rarely has so conscious an insight into the unpredictable, impulsive, and socially illogical character of his behaviors.

In connection with the instances reviewed of the correlation of an ethnic father's disjunctive personality with criminal behaviors of his children, native informants have frequently commented upon the mother and illuminated her function as disciplinarian among the newer ethnic groups. A welfare officer who is thoroughly familiar with the Ladski family said: "He has a good-looking wife, but I think that's the trouble. She doesn't know how to manage the children. They are always in trouble." Of the mother in the Vanzelas family, a school officer said: "Sammy's mother is living, but she has no stamina. Greek women rarely have much influence in their homes. Sammy's mother has no influence whatsoever."

And, finally, the judge who has sat on all the appearances of this Greek youth in court comments: "The father is supposed to be the disciplinarian entirely in the Greek family, but Sammy's father didn't have time to watch over the kids. They could chase around and do pretty much what they wanted because he is not around to talk to them."

Among these recent groups, then, the mother is as yet too subordinate in the family to have authority in enforcing discipline where the father fails to exercise control over the children. Among the earlier ethnic groups, beginning with the Jews presently to be examined, the mother has assumed secondary controls over the children that in functional importance exceed the father's final controls.

Heretofore we have attempted to establish that at least half the cases of children in the Polish, Greek, and Italian groups who have police records are manifestations of relaxed parental controls and the personality disjunction of the father. Among the Armenians and Jews there are no instances of a correlation of criminal behavior of parents with delinquency of children and among the Irish and French Canadians only one case in ten of juvenile delinquency is correlated with a parental police record. Each of these four groups has a juvenile delinquency rate of from one half to one third that of the Poles, Greeks, or Italians.

A disintegrated condition in the parent-child relation has been taken as one of the factors in juvenile delinquency. One form of this condition, where the father relaxes control and is himself undisciplined in his behavior, has been illustrated. Another form is one in which the parent has been overly rigid and severe in his application of controls upon his children.

This is so general a condition between P^1 parents and F^1 children that it calls for detailed analysis in terms of personality development. It will be remembered that a P^1 generation individual migrates as a matured, adult social personality, facing the problem of adjusting to a new environment. The sole structural segment within Yankee City society which offers this individual a framework that fits his own personality system and with which he can articulate is his own family. A later exception is the ethnic community. Within the family, at least, he can maintain his personality and find security and stability in a society that "tastes and smells different," as one Jewish informant phrased it. The two basic relational components within the family structure have to be preserved against radical change and transformation. We have already established that in the husband-wife relation the P^1 generation has been in large degree successful in maintaining its traditional form. Its effort to keep the parent-child relation intact has had different consequences, principally because of the personality aspects of its American-born children.

The F^1 child [24] in its first few years of life is wholly absorbed by the family, and its personality is slowly organized to correspond with the typical ethnic personality pattern. For example, the ethnic language, which is the mode of communication between the parents, also becomes the language of the child. The regulation of the child's behaviors and attitudes according to ethnic modes is typified by the accounts, presented earlier in this chapter, of the deportment of Greek and Armenian children in the presence of the father.

At about the age of three, the child is allowed to break through the confines of the family and establish play relations with children its own age, generally neighbor children of the same ethnic group. As the child grows older, his play relations expand to include children of native and other ethnic groups. Through these relations the child acquires English, which continues as his extra-familial language. At the age of six he enters grammar school. Whether this is the public, the Irish parochial, or the French-Canadian parochial school, English is the language used and is an important part of the curriculum. From that point on, therefore, English is emphasized and the ethnic language becomes increasingly less important. The ethnic school, which appears in every Yankee City ethnic community without exception, represents the community's unsuccessful effort to maintain the native language.

Between the parent and the child, therefore, there is this fundamental breach. The parent uses English only in those relations that demand it, and then hesitantly. The child, in turn, uses the ethnic language only in those relations that demand it, namely, with his parents. As he grows older and his extra-familial relations

24. In this chapter only, "F^1" will be used with special reference to the children of P^1 parents. The children of P^2 parents, who in our classification also appear as F^1, will here be referred to specifically as "children of P^2 parents."

increase, and with them the use of English, he comes to resent the ethnic language even in the home and develops a sharp antagonism to it. A French-Canadian parent commented: "The children now won't speak French. It's hard to get my own children to do it. They don't like to because they hear it only at home, and all their playmates and people they speak to all day long speak English." One Jewish boy exclaimed sharply: "It gets me mad when I hear some of the Jewish women speaking Jewish out loud on the street. This is America!"

And from his side a Russian P[1] father complained of his son: "He doesn't understand half of what I say to him in Russian. Sometimes I will be talking for a long time and he will break in [speaking Russian] with 'I can't understand half you're saying. Why can't we talk English?' It makes me sore."

Frequently when the parents speak the ethnic language the child replies in English. Each understands the other but persists in using the language to which he is predominantly oriented. This language difference is an undisguised source of conflict and antagonism between parent and child and symbolizes the fundamental difference in the orientation and pattern of their personality systems.

The effective influences in the reorientation of the child's personality are three, each of which will be taken up in turn: (1) the Yankee City schools; (2) American modes of play; and (3) clique relations.

The relation of the ethnic child to the Yankee City schools cannot be considered in detail; only those aspects will be selected that are concerned with the orienting functions of the school system.

In a series of articles "by persons connected with the school system of Yankee City" which appeared in the local newspaper, one article was entitled "The Aims of Education." Seven "objectives" of the schools were defined as follows:

1. Command of fundamental processes (i.e., the "three R's").
2. Health. Life today demands physical fitness.
3. Worthy home membership. The home is the center of our life and exerts a tremendous influence over our activities outside the family circle. The school must prepare its graduates with the abilities necessary to found and maintain happy, well-ordered homes.
4. Vocational and economic effectiveness. This includes such vo-

cational preparation as can be effectively brought about in the public schools. . . .

5. Preparation for citizenship. No one can deny that there is a necessity for the school to provide the knowledge and encourage the development of the ideals necessary to prepare each future citizen to take up his part in our national life in the way that will be best for him and for our democracy.

6. Wise use of leisure. . . . The proper use of leisure time will lead to happier lives for all of us. Too many, however, today cannot find sufficient activities of the right sort which interest them. . . .

7. Ethical character. The good of all of us is dependent upon the character of the individual members of the group. . . .

A later article expanded on the seventh objective and defined the "desirable character traits generally accepted by schools throughout the United States" as follows:

1. Steadfastness, obedience, honesty, justice.
2. Fair play or good sportsmanship, courage.
3. Mental cleanliness, thoroughness.
4. Gratitude, appreciation of service.
5. Self-control, temperance, initiative, and vision.
6. Coöperation, friendliness.
7. Thrift, ambition.
8. Loyalty, willingness to serve, patriotism.
9. Kindness, sympathy, generosity.
10. Industry and perseverance, self-reliance.

It is apparent that this list represents a catalogue of the American conceptions of virtue.

On the school's capacity for inculcating these virtues, the article continues:

It takes little imagination to see that these qualities can be developed in class room discussions, by observation and daily experiences, through general literature, the study of the social sciences, mathematics, general science, and every other school activity.

On into the secondary school this character building goes. More than ever do these traits weave themselves into the daily lives of the student. The athletic field offers a great opportunity for developing fine character, not only by the contestants but by the student spectators.

This system of logics permeates the Yankee City schools explicitly in the curriculum and implicitly in methods of grading, call of hands during recitation, study periods, student government, etc. A foreign observer[25] writes: "In Europe the main emphasis is laid upon form, authority, obedience, discipline, while in the American public schools freedom of action, imagination, initiative and self-reliance are pursued as the main goal in the training of youth."

Not only does the child acquire in the school these American attitudes of "self-reliance" and "freedom of action" with respect to his own individuality, but he becomes oriented both in the curriculum and in school rituals to specifically American symbols. Four of the courses in the Yankee City grammar schools are: Duties of Citizenship, History and Constitution of the United States, Civics, and English. The following numbers are included in the annual Memorial Day exercises held in all the city's schools in which ethnic children are conspicuous participants: "Salute to the Flag," and recitations—"What Our Flag Stands For," "Red, White and Blue," "The Meaning of the Colors," "Memorial Day," "Little Patriots," "For Our Country," and "America the Beautiful." All but one of these are presented on the programs of the First Grade.

In subjects taught, attitudes suggested, and symbols ritualized, the school effectively transforms two basic classes of elements in the ethnic child's personality—his behaviors and his attitudes. A school officer in effect states this fact: "In school the foreign kids are resocialized so that their differences, at least outside of the home, tend to disappear." The ethnic child comes to conform with the personality pattern of the American child.

How far this conformity may be pushed is revealed by a Jewish high-school boy. All classes in the public schools start the day with "The Opening Exercises," consisting of a reading by the teacher from the Bible, New as well as Old Testament, followed by recitation of the Lord's prayer by the entire class. The Lord's prayer, of course, is part of Christianity, and for a Jew to recite it is analogous to a Christian's reciting the Mohammedan prayer to Allah. Yet this Jewish informant, in answering the question whether Protestant and Catholic children use the different versions of their separate churches in reciting the Lord's prayer in

25. "Autobiography of an Intellectual Esthonian," (manuscript), quoted by Park and Miller in *Old World Traits Transplanted* (New York, Harper & Bros., 1925), p. 279.

school, answered: "The Protestant prayer is used. I myself read the prayer along with the other school children and do it the regular way because when in Rome do as the Romans do."

A school official was asked whether school children make ethnic discriminations in their relations with each other. He answered: "You ask whether the children are aware of foreign differences in school. I should answer no, except for parental differences. Children are really the best democrats alive. With this, and the mixing up of groups by the school, such awareness would never occur but for their families. When you get down to it, the only thing that rubs across the grain of a kid is a sissy or a sneak who won't play the game by the rules. You ask about the names like Wop, Mick, Sheenie, etc. You won't hear them except in fights. That is, it is used as a verbal brickbat, but it is not general."

The last comment is significant in indicating attitudes of evaluation. The stereotyped American names for different ethnic groups have opprobrious connotations. They are used only in the heat of battle when a boy will take whatever advantage he can seize.

The recreational forms of American society are based on its logics. Athletics stress equality of opportunity, individual responsibility for observation of the rules (fair play), and competition of individual skills. To the winner, moreover, go the plaudits of the society. Ethnics are prominent in participation around the city playgrounds and on the various organized teams. In this connection their names appear continuously in the local newspaper, and as personalities they are in the public eye. The "heroes" on the high-school teams are generally ethnic boys, and they are "heroes" of the community as well. Nor is there a single ethnic group that is unrepresented on these school teams. This has led the local newspaper to comment editorially: "When you talk about the melting pot of America, the game of football comes nearer to filling the bill as melter than any other movement."

A Yankee City athletic coach suggests another angle: "People don't know how important athletics are for promoting harmony. In athletics these boys [of different groups] learn to get along with each other."

Athletics perform several functions: inculcating American standards of behavior; bringing into play relations individuals of different groups and classes; and giving ethnics with athletic skills special status in the society.

Perhaps even more important than athletics in influencing the personality of the ethnic child are the "movies." Here the child receives an explicit and more dramatic statement of American standards and values. How strong a hold this recreational form has on ethnic children may be judged by the fact that the P^1 parents have sharp antagonisms to the "movies," expressions of which will be presented below.

The third effective factor in forming the ethnic child's person-ality is his informal clique relations, which in most cases extend beyond the ethnic group of which he is part. This is true in the grammar schools, as one member of the school system has already substantiated. A typical instance of the functioning of a complex clique is that of a Halloween party given by two native girls, aged thirteen and fifteen, with the following guests: eight natives, seven Irish, three French Canadians, two Italians, two Armenians, one Jew, and one Pole.

The function of the clique in converting the ethnic child's per-sonality has been corroborated by interviews. For example, one Italian boy, a sophomore in the high school, said: "There are three Italian girls and five Italian boys in high school, but they do not cling together. Mostly they associate with the Irish. But there are no distinctions made on the basis of race or nationality." A Jewish high-school girl said: "Most of my friends in the high school are not Jewish, but Catholic [Irish, French Canadians, Italians, and Poles]. We seem to be close to each other. I don't know why." A Jewish high-school boy stated: "I have many Ital-ian friends. But I mix with the other fellows [i.e., of other groups]. We never think a thing about the racial group to which we belong." Finally, one Irish boy, when asked about the various ethnic groups in the high school, said, "We're all Americans."

The ethnic child through such clique relations extends his con-tacts to children of native and other ethnic groups. The "com-mon denominator" in such relations is, of necessity, common American elements of personality. The fact that he does not often choose as friends boys and girls of his own ethnic group is evi-dence of his suppression of the ethnic elements in his personality and unwillingness to be identified with his group, and the obverse, his desire to have no "distinctions" of ethnic descent recognized. "We're all Americans."

Therefore, through the American schools, recreational forms, and clique relations, the following progressive and cumulative changes occur in the personality of the F^1 child from the time when he establishes relations beyond the family structure: (1)

orientation to American symbols, i.e., language, flag, country, patriotism, etc.; (2) acquisition of the American logics, especially the concepts of "individuality," "self-reliance," and "self-determination"; and (3) expansion of his personality beyond the limits of the traditional personality of the ethnic child.

The third change requires brief comment. The societies in which the ethnics had their origin were, in a formal sense, societies of fathers. Family status in the various structures of the society was derived through the father's position in those structures. The personalities of the wife and children did not extend beyond the family and were identified with the personality of the father until his death. The ethnic child in Yankee City, however, through school talents, athletic skills, clique relations, and associational affiliations, no longer is identified with the father's personality, except perhaps in terms of class status, but has a distinct social personality in his own right. In so far as in these relations he is beyond the authority of his parents, his independence of them has increased, and, conversely, the parents' superordination over him has declined. The child's status in the parent-child reciprocal has risen relative to that of the parents.

In addition, the specific concept of the parent-child relation held in the American ideological system intrudes upon the ethnic parent-child reciprocal. The P^1 ethnic father conceives his role in patriarchal and authoritarian terms. By the modern American conception, however, the child should not be dominated by his parents but should be given "freedom" to express his own full, inherent potentialities. The parent, it is held, should not be the child's remote and severe superordinate but should try to make the child his equal; he should not be the "master" but the "companion."

Social change is an acknowledged process in every society, although different societies exhibit varying attitudes of acceptance toward specific changes depending upon the effects of the change on the equilibrium of the social system. If a new element is admitted into the older generation of the family, it thereby takes its place in the pattern which the parents are imposing on the personalities of their children. Any single change or series of changes, passing slowly into the structure of the society through the medium of the parents, thus has its shock absorbed, and the system's equilibrium is easily maintained. What is change is a change for the parental generation only.

It follows, further, that any new trait which cannot be absorbed

without doing violence to the equilibrium will rarely pass the parental wall and hence will rarely get into the social system. Thus,
the function of the family in terms of the phenomena of social
dynamics is twofold: (1) to reject new elements inimical to the
social system and (2) to adapt and integrate new elements into
the system and to ease their transmission through the system.

The family is not only trustee for bringing the past down into
the present, but also the trainer which prepares and reconditions
the changing present for the future. The family is the link between the past and the future, assuring the continuity and stability of the society through the changes that beset it.

It is precisely this trusteeship for the past and responsibility
for the future that give parents authority over their children.
Their superordinate position derives from the fact that the past
and future of the culture lie in their hands; without them the children would be cultural orphans. Note that in essence sociological
maturity is not acknowledged until the child himself has fully
absorbed the society's pattern and through procreation fulfilled
his function of transmitting it into the future. Therein we see the
full implications of the distinction between the family of procreation and the family of orientation.

Since, however, in Yankee City the P^1 parent is neither able
nor willing to accept into the family the full complex of changes
impelled by its juxtaposition to a new social system, and since,
further, change does enter into the personality of the child, it is
the child who now has the important function of absorbing change
for the family. Thereby the authority and prestige accompanying
that function shift from parent to child. Instead of the child's
looking to the parent for the pattern and content of his social
personality, now the child cuts himself off from his parent's orientating efforts and takes his "design for living" from the social
system outside of the home. Altogether, the generations become
estranged and isolated from each other.

The following factors, then, have contributed to this condition
of the parent-child reciprocal:

1. The child is no longer dependent solely upon the parents for
its cultural orientation.

2. The child is the absorptive medium of culture change for the
family and therefore has an advanced function for the family.

3. In any judgments of rank, the American social system, being the more vigorous and having also the dominance of "host"

status, is affirmed the higher. Since the child identifies himself with it, his position in the present reciprocal is higher.

4. The fact alone that parent and child are each articulated to separate cultural groups would not be quite so serious were it not that each is eager to influence and convert the other. Neither is amenable, and hence on specific issues clash is inevitable.

A derivative aspect of the conflict affecting the parent-child relation is that of the child's challenge to the father's authority. Not only does the child resent the fact that his parents do not act after the American behavioral modes; not only does he resent pressure to act after the ethnic behavioral modes; infused with the American logics, he implicitly questions the right of his father to dominate and control his behaviors.

It is not to be inferred that parent-child conflict emerges immediately. It develops progressively in time and differentially between the sexes. While an ethnic group is still "young" in Yankee City and cohesive, the child's play and clique relations are still with children of the same ethnic group, and he is rarely admitted to relations with children of older and higher ethnic groups and of natives. For example, Polish and Greek children "mix" less in the schools than do the other ethnics. The difference, however, during this early period is only one of degree, since the conflict situation already exists between father and child, although the father with fair success still maintains his controls.

We may therefore consider the evidence of differential development in the parent-child relation among ethnic groups. To determine the time factor we shall arrange the ethnic groups, as we did in our examination of the husband-wife reciprocal, in an order from the most recent, the Poles, to the oldest, the Irish.

With respect to the Poles, the evidence already presented indicates that except where there is personality disorganization of the father, the child is still rigidly under his control. In part this is enforced by threats of extreme physical punishment.

A Yankee City judge, in generalizing on Polish families, said: "They come over and most of them don't have any education at all, even in Polish, and they have the old country ideals. They try to bring their kids up according to that, but the kids go to American schools and they learn to speak English. The kids begin to think they know a lot more than the parents and get things running along the way they want to. Sometimes the family tries to do something about it, and sometimes they don't give a damn."

Cases in which Polish fathers "don't give a damn" about their children's behavior have already been reviewed. In most cases, however, the father does "do something about it" and in such traditional and stringent fashion that the child seeks release from parental controls in his extra-familial relations. The contrast, moreover, between the pressures of the home and the "freedom" of these wider relations is so great that in the latter his behavior tends to become "wild" and undisciplined. Especially among the Poles and Greeks, the boys move in gangs whose collective behavior tends toward the type which is adventurous, aggressive, and spectacular. For example, a Greek boy said of one of these gangs: "Go down to the river any hot afternoon and you'll see them swimming. Some of the fellows dive off the arches of the bridge. It must be one hundred feet at low tide. The railroad bridge is about sixty feet at high tide, and they dive off of that. They told me of several instances where they had been diving from the arches of the bridge, cars would stop to watch them, so the traffic would almost be stopped there, watching the boys diving."

Of another type is the behavior of a Polish gang described by a school teacher: "Some boys had come in late and smelling of smoke, so I asked them what had happened. It developed that some of the older boys had built a house of tar paper and tin and so on, down on the dump, and they had taken these four smaller boys, started a fire around the house, and stuck these boys into the house. They said that they were going to start a new club and that this was the initiation, so they pushed the boys in to see how long they could stay in. They called it a crucifixion."

But such behavior is not restricted to gang groupings. A school truant officer reported that a Greek girl "took a baseball bat one day and broke a lot of the pickets in front of the school. She just got sore and went out and smashed them."

A court officer said of a Polish boy who had recently committed larceny: "Joe Wojcik broke into some place and stole a small amount of stuff so he could be sent away. He came and told me that he wanted to. His father and mother have a large family, and his brother and he were the oldest ones. Finally the boys got so fed up with the home that they went out and robbed this place so they could be sent away. They were sent to the truant school. The father and mother made life pretty miserable for them."

He added of the Poles and Greeks generally: "I think the reason why a lot of these kids go bad is that their families don't give them any rights or privileges at all. Let him do a few things that he wants to and don't force him and keep him down all the time. A lot of them don't let the kids do anything. They take all their money away if they are working."

Regarding the relation of the F^1 ethnic child's personality to his social context, he is the focus of the interaction of two types of social systems—that which is maintained in the home and the ethnic community and that in Yankee City. He participates in both, and both impose their sanctions upon him, forcing him in two different directions and causing conflict in his personality. Although his personality orientation is essentially American, the ethnic elements in it are distributed in something of a patchwork pattern. They are incongruous and overlap contradictory American elements. To the child they are meaningless and irritating, and he would slough them off if he could, as evidenced by his refusal to speak the ethnic language and his outbursts of anger at hearing it. The conflict in personality is generally resolved in one of three ways:

1. The child engages in "profane" behaviors, i.e., those which violate the standards of both the ethnic and American societies. On certain levels this attitude may be expressed in the aberrant behaviors described. On other levels, depending upon age, education, and intellectual background, his behavior may take an "intellectual" form and lead to escape into esoteric, religious, or political movements.

2. The child, when he can free himself from the home, may leave it, renounce its traditions, and embrace "100 per cent Americanism." For instance, an F^1 Italian, now married, insisted: "If I ever have any children, they are never going to know whether their parents were English, German, or Italian. I will never tell them. After all, we are in America, and that's all that counts." The principal of a Yankee City school perceived this drive when he said of the ethnic children, "They seem to become more American than the Americans."

3. Finally, rather than react against both sets of elements or against only the ethnic elements in his personality, the child may come to reconcile both. Under certain conditions to be discussed later, he may join others in his ethnic group of the same generation to form an association whose symbols are predominantly American, but in part ethnic. In certain circumstances, the F^1 generation, grown to adulthood, will take the place of the dying P generation in the ethnic community system, which will at such a stage assume many American elements. The system will both ex-

press and facilitate the reconciliation of the disparate elements in the personality type of the F^1 generation.

In general, it appears that an F^1 child normally proceeds in sequence through all three forms of these conflicts resolutions. The period of duration of each phase varies with a complex of factors from group to group, from individual to individual within a group, and even within a family. Certain individuals may remain fixed in the first or second phase. For example, in one Greek family with three boys ranging in age from fifteen to eighteen, the oldest and the youngest at last report were still running in gangs and committing petty larceny from time to time. The middle boy, however, after establishing a bad school record for truancy and seemingly being headed for the same type of career as his brothers, at the age of seventeen joined in forming the Greek-American Progressive Association Juniors, an association of the Greek community for boys of late adolescence. Thereafter he "straightened out and is a good boy," as one Greek adult phrased it. Ultimately the great majority of those in the F^1 generation strike a balance between the conflicting elements of their personality by orienting themselves principally to the American social system while still maintaining a limited number of formal relations in the ethnic community.

Aspects of the parent-child conflicts as they appear in the Greek family were presented earlier with evidence that the fathers are still exercising their patriarchal prerogatives over the children. But it is also evident that the children are chafing under the constraints. Interviews with the fathers revealed that they have lost ground in their effort to maintain the traditional inclusive controls, more so than have the Polish fathers. It will be remembered, for example, that most of the Greek parents have yielded their claims on their children's earnings. This is explicitly conceded in the assertion of one Greek father: "The younger generation has different ideas. In some places where there is a big community, so that all live together, it's different. But here they are so mixed up that the children get different ideas. It will change a lot in another generation. The children go to school and get American ideas. They are a lot more independent and want to have their own way about things." There is a significant intimation here that the Yankee City Greek community is not large enough to maintain ecological, group cohesion.

The priest of the Yankee City Greek church takes an even more defeatist view: "The older generation [P^1] is disregarded. The younger ones call the older ones 'old fashioned' and pay no attention to them. Some time there will be no Greeks [here], for the next generation will be Americans." This judgment of the priest is overly colored by the children's attitude, especially to the Greek school, and by their "sampling" attendance at different Protestant churches.

To the inquiry whether many of the young Greek children went to the church, one Greek father made this report: "No, not many. That's the trouble with them. All they want is a good time. They don't stop and think. They read magazines, go to movies. If I was President, I'd close all the movies. That's not good for the children, they read these magazines, love stories and all that. The Bible says the world is coming to an end some day, and that's the way it is. I think it's coming now; everything is going wrong."

Another Greek father focused his antagonism elsewhere: "With regard to the younger generation, having gone to the public schools and such things, they have succeeded in being assimilated into the worst parts of American civilization."

Finally there is the description by a young married P^2 Greek woman of the conflict between her brother and her father. The brother, already adult when the parents arrived in Yankee City, is also P^2. "Our brother came to this country when he was sixteen, and soon he wanted us to come too. When we did arrive he was already twenty-five. That is an important age, between sixteen and twenty-five, and he was very much changed. He couldn't understand us, and we couldn't understand him. The worst thing was the fighting between my father and my brother. My father was the old Greek type; my brother wanted new things. Mother was getting the worst of it. She didn't know whether to take my father's side or my brother's. Always they were quareling. Of course it was terribly hard for my father; he suffered terribly. Now he is more liberal, but it took him twelve years. The relationship between my father and mother is now more of companionship. He is afraid to be left alone without her." That the conflict has "broken" the father is apparent in the concluding remarks.

Among the Armenians, who are a slightly older group in the city than the Greeks, a special factor enters parent-child relations. The Armenian group is part Protestant and part Gregorian or Eastern Orthodox in church affiliations. The community system, divided by several internal dichotomies, lacks integration. Because of this fact and because of its articulation with Yankee City

churches, the P¹ Armenian generation has assumed extensive relations, especially of the associational type, with Yankee City
society. The personalities of the members of this generation have
changed more than those of the P¹ generation of any other ethnic
group except the Irish. They have therefore sanctioned the personality changes of their children and have accordingly somewhat relaxed their controls, except in one sphere, the relations of
the sexes. The conflict between parents and children is confined
to this one issue.

In the Jewish family is found a further development of the
parent-child relation. First the Jewish P¹ parent is extremely
ambitious for his children. Whereas among the Greeks and Poles
less than half of the children finish high school (being withdrawn
at the legal working age of sixteen), it is unusual for a Jewish
child not to finish high school. A school official said: "The Jewish
parent is anxious for the child to speak English, go to school
without exception, and is always willing to coöperate. Jews do
not become problems. I have not prosecuted in Juvenile Court a
single Jew. The trouble with the young Jew is the swell-headed
attitude." Many of these F¹ Jews continue with professional training and, as stated earlier, a high proportion of them leave the
families for larger opportunities than are offered by the Yankee
City economic system.

As a result, the Jewish P¹ parents make no attempt to confine
or constrict the extra-familial relations of their children except
those of marriageable daughters with Gentile boys. But within
the home, the children are expected to conform with certain of the
traditional modes. Here issues frequently arise which are sources
of argument and friction. For example, an investigator reported:
"On the Jewish Sabbath, which includes Friday evening, it is
sacrilege to have any form of entertainment in the home. The
children, however, not sharing this sentiment, want the radio
played for certain favorite programs. In every Jewish home the
issue has arisen, and after persistent nagging and threatening to
go elsewhere on the part of the children, all but one family capitulated. . . . The Misses Cohen smoke regularly when they are
not in the home and when they are not in public places. At home
the only time they will accept a cigarette is when their parents
are not at home. When Miss Margaret Cohen told her mother
once that she did smoke, her mother absolutely refused to believe
that she would. I may mention another incident similar to this.

At the Gold home, Miss Ruth Gold was offered a cigarette in the living room. She said, 'Yes, thanks,' and reached for it, then slapped her mouth, saying 'Oh, my God, did my mother hear that?' "

There was an interview with the parents of the Misses Cohen in the family living room. Mr. Cohen was discussing a synagogue matter when Mrs. Cohen commented on an article she was reading in the Jewish daily newspaper about a father who slapped his daughter when he found her smoking a cigarette. "Well, he was wrong for slapping her, anyway. She was a grown girl, and slapping her, that kills the girl's respect for herself and her parent. The father was wrong, but why should girls smoke? I don't think it is nice; it's not becoming. Does it make a girl any more attractive or charming or pretty? I don't think so. I don't like it. A man is a man, but a woman is different." Mr. Cohen joined in: "Yeh, in America the women try to become men. They smoke, they work, they wear pants and knickers. This is all against the Torah, which says that man should not wear women's clothes and woman should not wear men's clothes. Ei, America, America, an upside-down world. I don't understand it, that's all."

This is the focus of the conflict between the generations. In spite of the contraction of the Jewish parent's controls over his child, the personality differences between them still exist; and with these, the child's judgment of the parents as "old fashioned."

Between one P[1] Jewish father and his children there was extreme bitterness on this score: "Children are not worth while. What do you get out of them? Once you used to get respect and honor at least. Here they throw you away. You become a back number. My daughter had a birthday party last Sunday, and she had some friends up. You know where we stayed? In the kitchen, until I got disgusted and said to my wife, 'Let's go to bed.' That was about eleven o'clock. What time they went to bed, I don't know. But do you think in Europe you would leave a girl alone with a boy? Never, on your life! But you see, I am still a young man with pep and enjoyment, and already I am a back number. So where will I be ten years from now?

"I like them when they are small, but when they get seven or eight or nine years old, they begin to get their own ideas and they don't respect you any more. And it's gotten so they make me nervous. I feel jumpy and bad—because they get me so mad. Now I sat down with my daughter to talk to her like a pal. She is graduating from high school. So I said to her, 'You may not get a job, so you'd better be looking for your chances.' She laughed and she said, 'I'm only nineteen, and I've got six years yet.' But you can't talk to her. I can see that she thinks I don't understand her. All right, she has different ideas, but I'm her father, and I'm interested. But you can't even talk to them. And if I should tell them what to do, they would look at me as if I belonged in an insane asylum. What good would it do for me to say to them, 'Don't do so-and-so'? None! They would say everybody does it and so can they. Can you answer that? No, and you don't want them to think you are crazy. So I have to let them do anything they want, provided it is decent.

"In Russia the Jewish children would give their lives for their parents, so devoted were they, but here the children may respect their parents, but haven't that reverence of the old country. My wife asked my daughter the other day to wash some of her own hose, and she said it was too hard. I told her that in Russia to wash something in the winter, you had to walk a half mile to the river, break through the ice, and wash your clothes that way, and here all they know is comforts.

"Two years ago, my eldest son, a smart kid, graduated from high school. I thought maybe he should go to work, but he said he wanted to become a lawyer. Of course, as a clerk here he could only get $15 a week, but say, that's a help. Not that I object to more education or that I don't want him to be a lawyer, but I am just showing that a parent's word doesn't mean anything any more."

The bitterness of this father at the loss of his children's respect and over his inability to be a father even in American terms, as well as his efforts to act the minimal role, have reacted on the attitude of his children, one of whom said: "Oh, he gets me sick. Every time I have some friends up to the house, he wants to sit with my mother in the parlor. You know what that does to a crowd of young people. What have we in common with them? Nothing. So then they sit in the kitchen, with the door open, so they can hear everything that goes on. Peeking on us! As if we can't be trusted, or need watch dogs. Besides, at every little thing I do, he preaches to me. Not that he forbids me to do it, mind you. He has more sense than that. But simply he's always telling me how they used to do things in Russia. Well, that's all very interesting, but this happens to be the United States of America, not Russia, and the twentieth century, not the nineteenth. His body may be here, but his mind is still in Russia and the nineteenth century.

And it'll never be any other place. He thinks I don't respect him. Well, he's right, and you can see my reasons."

Among the French-Canadian and Irish families the P^1 generation is advanced in age, with the result that the subadult children in both groups are predominantly F^2 and F^3, their parents F^1 and F^2 respectively. Between these generations there is little trace of the conflicts found between the P^1 generation and their children. As in the case of the husband-wife relation, the Catholic Church is a powerful buttress to the family structure. Through the subordination of the child to the church, his subordination to the parent is kept almost inviolate. Not only has the child an important place in the church, denied to children of other churches, but through the parochial school the child is progressively indoctrinated with attitudes of reverence for and obedience to authority, whether it be of the priest, the parent, or the civil officers. Further, in the church associations the child's play is regulated by the church authorities, in the persons of the curates and the nuns, and is organized around the sacred symbols of the church. Hence the expansion of the child's personality is kept within the framework of the authoritative church. Also, the child's absorption of the American logics is accompanied by a parallel absorption of what we might call the Catholic logics, keeping the breach between the generations far narrower than in the groups already considered. Further, the church, being sensitive to the particular social system in which it is embedded, absorbs the shocks of transition by sanctioning those changes which might lead to conflict between parent and child.

The authoritarian values provided the Catholic family by the church are suggested by a churchman:[26]

The Christian home is based upon an absolute respect for law and order. The walls of the Christian home are solidified by religion. The atmosphere of the Christian home is purified by morality. The cross of Christ is on its walls. The day opens and closes with prayer. The model of the Nazarene home is ever before it. Obedience to God and the State and the Church is the cardinal principle of its activities.

Because of obedience the Christian home is a nation in miniature. There can be no valid nor virtuous citizenship where there is neither authority nor obedience to authority. Authority is the right which

26. Curran, *op. cit.*, pp. 61–63.

an individual or an organization possesses to compel the obedience and coöperation of those in whose interest the authority is held and exercised. . . .

How important a prop the church is to the parent is revealed by one F[1] Irish mother discussing her two young children, aged four and five: "You just have to keep the children well behaved. If you do not, then when they get to be sixteen, how can you control them? You have to start early, and now is the time. Each night in my prayers I always pray that they may grow to be good men and women. That's all I can do. I don't care if they are nobody, just so they are good. You cannot put them into a bandbox and not let them out. That doesn't teach them the world. Yet it is awful when you cannot control other people's children. You never can tell about their children. I do the best I can, that's all, and pray. And of course the church backs us right up. If it were not for the church, we could do nothing."

Second, the church emphasizes the important role of the mother in the orientation and training of the child. "The moral education of the child," the church holds, "should begin at the mother's knee." Since the mother, especially in an industrial society, is close to the child for longer periods of the day than is the father, this explicit investiture of authority in the mother adds another circumscribing control to the behavior of the child.

That the Irish and French-Canadian parents have been in large degree successful in maintaining their controls is evidenced by interviews. Contrast the conflict of the Jewish parent and daughter already recorded with this comment of a French-Canadian P[1] father about his daughter: "My Anita is a good girl, thoughtful and a hard worker. She doesn't run around like a lot of them do. It makes the parents happy to have a daughter like that." Or a native's report about an Irish family with four unmarried sons, all over forty: "They say they've never been to the movies since they've been in town. The old man won't let them spend the money and they are all grown men." Similarly, a P[2] French Canadian, now a father, asserted: "There were fourteen of us kids, and my father told us to be in the house at nine o'clock every night, and if we weren't in at that time we'd get our tails kicked. We got in, by God, every one of us."

But among the Irish, at least, there has been a slow movement away from orientation to symbols of Ireland. For example, one old Irish spinster of the F[1] generation observed: "I am afraid that we are getting farther away from the Irish strain. You know, to be 'Irish' is to be old fashioned. To be gladly 'Irish' is to be a little queer. The new generation are not strongly attached to Erin. They won't deny that they are Irish, but it is an incidental matter to them. . . ."

Another Irish woman of the F[1] generation remarked: "In the old days the priest was greatly reverenced. The new crop of children have their own opinions. It's the spirit of the age. They don't stop to understand. Everything with them is go, go, go. They don't take anything serious. They know everything there is to be known before they are out of high school." But most of these children are removed from Ireland by two and three generations, and this lady's comparison might equally well have been made by a native of her age about the new generations of native children.

Finally, an aged F[1] Irishman commented: "The young people don't keep up their Irish. They don't tolerate it. A great many young people don't know what county in Ireland their parents or grandparents came from."

The conflict over behavior controls in the parent-child relations, so striking in the newest ethnic groups, has been almost eliminated among the Irish, and among the French Canadians in lesser degree, by the intermediating influence of the Catholic Church. The antagonisms between parent and child by reason of their different personality orientation, dramatized in extreme form among the Jews, are almost absent among the Irish, because the subadult children have native-born parents whose personalities are almost completely oriented to the American social system. These parents, however, maintain a slender symbolic relation to "Irishness" in the form of recognition of their Irish descent. Their children incur their disapproval, to judge from informants, because they fail to acknowledge even this minimal relation. The personalities of these children, in the complete sense, are American Catholic. Assimilation has worked itself out in the Irish F[2] generation, only two generations removed from Ireland. The American social system is not, strictly speaking, a "melting pot" which fuses its diverse ethnic elements into a new amalgam, as was once popularly believed, but is rather a system which performs the transmutation of diverse ethnic elements into elements almost homogeneous with its own.

VII

THE CHURCH

1. *Nationalistic Background of the Ethnic Church*

IN this study we are concerned first with ethnic groups articulated to two distinct church systems which have in common certain cosmological representations "revealed" in the Old and New Testaments; they are centered around the symbol of Christ and are called Christian. A third church system, that of the Jews, is based upon the cosmological system defined principally in the Old Testament alone. The Christian church systems referred to are the Roman Catholic and Eastern Catholic; they are distinguished from each other in the following details: (1) interpretation of the Christian cosmology and moral law; (2) symbolic and ritualistic representations; and (3) internal organization of relations.

Neither of the two Christian church systems in their complete extension is exclusively identified with a particular national social system. For example, among the countries represented by immigrant groups in Yankee City, Southern Ireland, French Canada, Italy, and Poland are articulated to the Roman Catholic Church; and Armenia, Greece, and Russia to the Eastern Catholic Church.

While both the Roman and Eastern Catholic Church systems transcend national lines in terms of their content, within each country the church was (and is) a subsystem of the national social system. Both extended church systems were formally organized in recognition of this fact. The body of control offices, e.g., the priesthood, was recruited for the church subsystem from each country's citizens and was organized into an inclusive national hierarchy, independent in the Eastern Catholic Church, subordinate in the Roman Catholic Church to the Papacy. Within the Eastern Catholic or Eastern Orthodox Church system, there are recognized the Greek Orthodox Church, the Russian Orthodox Church, and the Armenian Apostolic Church, each with its own patriarchs, bishops, etc., and each autocephalous and autonomous. Within the national subsystems of the extended Roman Catholic Church, national differences are frequently and explicitly recognized in reference to: (1) the national saints within the church's hierarchy of saints; (2) the traditions of the national church; and (3) the national aspects of the national church's priesthood.

A speech by an Irish priest before an Irish-American nationalistic association illustrates: "God has been good to us. Our patron saints, Patrick and Brigid, have watched over us. It has not been done thus with every nation. Many a brilliant volume of Church history, blazoned with the names of Saints, purpled with the blood of martyrs, has closed with the sad record of defection and decay. Not so with us. We can go back through the early history of the Irish Church, when her sanctity and learning were a theme of praise."

The national church, then, is a subsystem within two different systems: (1) the national social system of the country in which it appears; and (2) the extended church system.

It is necessary to establish the nature of the relation of the church to the national society of which it was a part. In the first place, the reader will recall that many of the countries represented by groups in Yankee City were without formal national or political status in the nineteenth century. They were still subordinate "minorities" within larger political entities. Their one semblance of national organization, in fact, appeared in the only organized subsystem of the group—the church. The typical consequences of this fact may be gathered from the literature on the Greeks, Armenians, and Jews.

Greece, for example, had no political identity from 1453 to 1823, when it was under the dominion of the Turkish Empire. Nevertheless, during these four centuries Greece centered its own concept of nationality about the Greek Orthodox Church. As a recent observer relates:[1]

During all the long years of Ottoman subjection, the Greeks, no matter how scattered or oppressed by their Moslem conquerors, clung with tenacity and fervor not less than that of the Hebrews to their own history, religion, language, and learning. . . . Even under Ottoman domination, every little Greek community in Asia Minor, Thrace, Macedonia, the Aegean Islands, or the Greek peninsula had its Orthodox Church, presided over by a priest whose patriotic ardor for the "Great Idea" of Greek unity under a free govern-

1. E. G. Mears, *Greece Today* (Stanford University, Stanford University Press, 1929), p. 230.

ment has finally triumphed in the independent united Greece of today.

Another writer,[2] in referring to the secular functions of the Patriarch of the Greek Church under the Turks, adds:

[These] gave a status of double dignity and authority to the patriarch as the head of the Greek race as well as the church. He held a position similar to that of the Jewish high priest under the Romans.

This helped the Greeks to keep their language, customs, rites and traditions as a race in the midst of trying circumstances. They feel they owe it to the influence of their church. Church and race being identified, the Greek Church has become the symbol of nationality in the estimation of the Greek people. The threads of religion and nationality are so woven that it becomes difficult, if not impossible, to separate them. The one cannot be touched without affecting the other. Many religious observances, customs, festivals, usages are rather national affairs.

Mears,[3] commenting further on the persistence of this nationalistic aspect of the Greek Church, adds this footnote:

So closely identified were the church and nationality in those days, that during the Second Balkan War of 1913–1914, when both Greece and Bulgaria were claiming Macedonia, each country attempted, as a matter of course, to prove how many of its citizens lived there by counting the number of adherents to the Greek and the Bulgarian Orthodox Churches, respectively.

Greece regained its independence in 1823, and while the Greek Church thereby lost many of its political control functions, the identification of the church with the nation persisted as strongly as ever through the nineteenth century.

The Armenians, however, were not freed of Turkish domination until after World War I. The organization of national functions and attitudes around the Armenian Church was even more strongly developed than in the case of the Greek Church. The Armenian Church had acquired, as had no other national subsystem of the Eastern Church, the secular function of exercising political

2. J. P. Xenides, *The Greeks in America*, pp. 61–62.
3. *Op. cit.*, p. 231.

as well as religious control. As one writer[4] states: "Ever since the Armenians lost their independence they were known as a religious community in the Turkish empire, and their patriarch as the representative of the whole people."

The church hierarchy discharged certain of the administrative functions of the Armenian group. The ecclesiastical Assembly of 1906 had its purposes defined by the Catholicos or Patriarch who called and led the assembly:[5] "To adopt measures for improving the Armenian schools; for regulating and increasing the revenues of the church; and to draw up a constitution for the administration of church and community affairs."

At the Versailles peace conference the Armenian delegate was "the diplomatic representative of His Holiness, the Catholicos, the supreme head of the Armenian Church and the Armenian nation." [6]

Most significant was the fact that the agency of political rapprochement between the Turkish government and the Armenian social system was the Armenian Church. Elections of the church were subject to ratification by the Sultan. For example, the Armenian Constitution of 1860, approved by the Sultan, states: "The Armenian patriarch is the head of his nation, and in particular circumstances, the medium of execution of the orders of the [Turkish] government."

In other words, like the Greeks under the Turks, so also the Armenians under the Turks, the Irish and the French Canadians under the English, the Poles under the Russians, were each a national minority deprived of nationality by the political domination of a conquering group. Because each of these groups differed also in its church subsystem from that of the dominating society, and because, at least since the Napoleonic edicts, European minorities were allowed religious liberty, each tended to organize itself as a nationality around its church. Thus there were national churches like the Irish Catholic, the Armenian Apostolic, the Polish Catholic, the Greek Orthodox, at a time when there were no Ireland, Armenia, Poland, and Greece in the political sense.

Given these facts, the intense attachment of these minorities to their church can be more readily understood. Moreover, these churches were in all instances the instruments for keeping at

---

4. M. C. Gabrielian, *Armenia, A Martyr Nation* (New York, F. H. Revell Co., 1918), p. 158.

5. K. S. Papazian, *Patriotism Perverted* (Boston, Baikar Press, 1934), p. 33.

6. M. V. Malcolm, *The Armenians in America,* p. 119.

white heat the group's resolve to free itself from subjugation and the moving forces in the actual events which led to final winning of freedom and national autonomy. That this was true of Greece is suggested by Burgess:[7] "The greatest day of all the year is the Greek Independence Day . . . commemorating that great day in 1821 when Archbishop Germanus first raised the standard of the Cross for freedom."

It is understandable, then, that immigrant groups from these several countries, moving into Yankee City and finding themselves again a minority, should each turn to re-create that church which in other times and circumstances had served to keep alive the national group identity. With certain significant exceptions, each established a church following a pattern which had served it for hundreds of years as its first formal institution in Yankee City. The church was the first line of defense behind which these immigrants could organize themselves and with which they could preserve their group, i.e., system, identity.

What is probably the highest development of the national aspects of a church, however, is to be found among the Jews. Since the Exile imposed on the Jews by the Romans, and their dispersion through the Western World, the Jews have had neither the political system nor the ecological locus essential to nationality. The Mishna and the Talmud, codifications of traditional law based upon the Old Testament, emerged during the Exile to regulate and maintain the disparate Jewish communities in all their traditional cohesive solidarity. This was accomplished by the proscription, with sacred sanction, of almost every form of behavior impelled under the new circumstances, and represented a development which had begun during the earlier exile to Babylonia in the fifth century B.C. Like the Priests' Code of the earlier period, the new codes aimed at the codification of the scattered Jewish society by legislating behavioral modes which would differentiate and exclude the Jews from all minimal external relations. Moore[8] writes with reference to the influence of these codes: "Of all the religions which at the beginning of the Christian era flourished in the Roman and Parthian empires, only Judaism has survived . . . because it succeeded in achieving a unity of belief and observance among Jews in all their wide dispersion then and since. . . .

---

7. Thomas Burgess, *Greeks in America*, p. 87.

8. George Foot Moore, *Judaism* (Cambridge, Harvard University Press, 1927), I, 110–111.

[The synagogue of Israel] might with good right have taken to itself the title catholic (universal) Judaism. . . ."

The communal synagogue which arose definitively in the Exile to replace the Temple at Jerusalem "was not primarily a house of worship," to quote Moore,[9] but "a place where the common prayers were said together and where the Scripture was read, interpreted and expounded—a place of religious instruction and edification.

Thus for the former political system with Palestine as its basis, the Jews substituted an elaborate legalistic system, sanctified as the revealed will of God, its study ritualized as the most important part of synagogue services. Into the system were drawn all the former national sentiments. Hence the Jews remained a nation in effect in spite of their dispersion. Explicitly their concept of themselves as a nation persists undiminished into the twentieth century, as will be observed among the Yankee City Jews.

2. *Development of the Ethnic Church Structures*

SINCE the ethnic personality type itself is an aspect of the national social system which conditioned it, the community system of the Yankee City ethnics would necessarily tend to reproduce certain elements of the original societies. Since, furthermore, the church subsystem is the repository of the sacred values as well as of the national attitudes of the original society, and since these were assertive aspects of the ethnic personality, it was inevitable that the first formally organized structure of the ethnic community system in Yankee City should be the church. In all three of its representational aspects, as well as in its relational organization, this church structure was an extension and reproduction of the formal church system. It was the only structure that, at least in the beginning, was a pure reproduction of a structural type characteristic of the national society. Subsequent structures which appeared in the community system reflected the fact that the changing personalities in the group were mixtures of ethnic and American elements. These later structures, for example, the association, had no direct antecedents in the society of the homeland. The church structure alone linked the community with the national social system. The associations and schools which later emerged in the ethnic community were structural fences newly contrived to keep the ethnic individual articulated to the church

9. *Idem*, p. 114.

and the community while keeping him from straying too far out into the Yankee City social system.

From the end of the eighteenth century on, Yankee City had a handful of resident Catholic families—chiefly French refugees who had either fled the revolution of 1789 or who had come via the West Indies. A very few were Irish Catholics. The following quotation[10] gives an account of the latter's early history:

The first visit of a Catholic priest to Yankee City took place between the years of 1792 and 1796. This priest was probably Father Bleyer. His visits were made annually. Bishop Cheverus was consecrated for the newly erected See of Boston in 1808. The religious services were held at that time in the house of Captain John Nile, whose wife was a French lady, a Catholic. Father Wiley of Cambridge, who was ordained in 1827, preached there. He celebrated Mass at intervals until 1840 in the house of Mr. Patrick Nealy and in other Catholic residences.

In 1839 Father James Brown offered the Holy Sacrifice in Yankee City. He was then on his way to Europe, worn out with labor, as pastor of Portland, Maine, from 1826 to 1838.

There were ten [Irish] Catholic families in Yankee City in 1841. The French residents seem to have entirely disappeared before that time, and the few Catholic families here then were of the Southern Irish stock who ever since have been numerically the major element in the church here. The first regular pastor was appointed during that year. He was Reverend Michael Connolly, the resident pastor of Suffolk. His visits at first were quarterly, then monthly. He celebrated Mass in private houses until 1844, when the vestry of the Old East Church was bought and moved to land already purchased near Lower street [in trust for the use and benefit of the Roman Catholic Religious Society in Yankee City]. The first resident pastor was Reverend James O'Neil, afterwards pastor of Springfield. He received his appointment to Yankee City in the Spring of 1848. The appointment of a resident pastor of Yankee City always had an important air in local Catholic history. It was so in this case.

In 1849 Father Hannon succeeded to the pastorate, and under him the parish reached full status with the building of a new church edifice in 1851. An informant reported that the land (in

10. A composite of two sources: a Catholic newspaper in Boston and a program of an anniversary of the Yankee City Irish church.

Zone III) on which the church was built had to be acquired through the subterfuge of an out-of-town agent, for, had the native owners known its intended use, they would never have agreed to the sale. The Boston Catholic newspaper stated:

It was during the pastorate of his successor, Reverend Hannon, that land was bought on Grey Street at the cost of $1,800 for the purpose of erecting a church, the pioneer chapel having become comparatively small for the growing congregation. The cornerstone of this new church was impeccably laid by Bishop Fitzpatrick, assisted by twenty clergymen, on Tuesday, April 27, 1852. The sermon was delivered by the venerable and well-remembered Jesuit Father McElroy. The dedication took place St. Patrick's Day the next year; the same prelate officiated.

It is significant that the church should be dedicated on the day celebrating the national patron saint of Ireland, representing again the fusion of national and church symbols in the church of the Yankee City Irish community.

The subsequent developments of the church under the succeeding pastor are recounted as follows:

It is not always that a zealous priest and a generous people can show in work accomplished so visible a truth of unseasoned labor as in Father Nealing and his parishioners. And what are the works accomplished? The erection of a monument to the departed pastor, Father Hannon, the purchase of a chapel for Sunday School and society purposes, and of land for school purposes in 1873, the building of a bell tower and spire and the purchasing of a burial ground in 1874; the remodeling of the church entrance in 1877; the erection of a fine school building in 1880; the building of a new parochial residence in 1891, the old one having been destroyed by fire; the erection of a parochial hall in 1882; and the purchasing and remodeling of the Bliss Estate for contact purposes; the introduction into the diocese of the Sisters of Charity of Nazareth, encouraging and keeping order; the incorporation in 1884 of the school, convent, and parochial residence under the title of the Saint Mary Educational Association (incorporated under the Laws of the State) and of the church and cemetery under that of the St. Mary Society of Yankee City; the purchase of the Leads Estate for a convent, the former one being inadequate for the greater number of sisters needed in the ever-growing school; and in the midst of all the vital star in the constellation of noteworthy deeds, the consecration in 1879 of the church, remodeled, readorned, and free from all incumbrance of debt. These are some of the events that speak more forcibly than words do for the zeal of Father Nealing and the generosity of his flock.

The religious behaviors of the Irish group, then, were in the first phase centered entirely around the sporadic visits of the priests sent as representatives of the extended church hierarchy. As the group grew, these visits occurred more regularly. In the second phase, worship was given a locus in a chapel, although the priest was still a visiting rather than a resident pastor. In the third phase and with the appointment of a resident pastor by the diocese, the group was organized into a parish, housed since 1853 in a regular church edifice. Thereafter the church structure expanded its functions, acquiring progressively a parish (priests') residence, a cemetery, a parochial school, a parochial hall for "society," i.e., associational, purposes, and finally achieving integration into two corporate organizations under the charter from the state. Today the community system of the Irish is still the inclusive parish, its school, and a complex associational system directly articulated with the church structure.

Since the priest is the necessary intermediary for ritualistic behaviors directed toward the sacred symbols, there could not have emerged a church structure without the agency of a priest. Since also the Roman Catholic priest was an instrument of the extended church system, specifically of its hierarchal organization, this hierarchy was directly responsible for the emergence and organization of the church structure. The Roman Catholic Church system embraced the Irish group of Yankee City, organizing the group as a component subsystem. The implications of this transcendent aspect of the extended church system for the Irish community system will be analyzed presently.

The French Canadians, also Roman Catholics, began their influx in the 'eighties and by 1893 were represented by fifty-five families. The church structure of the Irish community system, the Church of St. Mary, performed ritual ministrations to all Roman Catholics within the Yankee City area.

The French Canadians were absorbed into the Church of St. Mary without being absorbed into the Irish community system. In 1894, when the French Canadians numbered about sixty families, the church hierarchy recognized ethnic differences by appointing a French-Canadian curate who was to minister to the French Canadians as assistant to the Irish pastor of St. Mary's. Thus, within the single church structure related to the Irish community system, there appeared a French-Canadian congregation served by a French-Canadian priest.

By 1903 the French-Canadian group numbered 127 family units, and in that year the controlling officers of the diocese organized a separate French-Canadian church structure and recognized a second parish in the city on the basis of ethnic distinction. The church, named for the French St. Pierre, was provided with a church building and a resident French-Canadian pastor. Since that time the Church of St. Pierre has expanded to embrace almost the entire French-Canadian community system.

It is significant that until the group numbered about a hundred families, neither the Irish nor French Canadians were organized into parishes. The Irish achieved organization in 1848 with close to a hundred families, the French Canadians in 1903 with 127 families. This factor of number is also important in subsequent ethnic groups.

The Italians were the next Roman Catholic group to appear in Yankee City. The number of families increased slowly, from nine in 1893 to ninety-two in 1933. Before 1933 they were far too few in number for the diocese to recognize and organize the group as a separate parish. Furthermore, by 1933 the F generation was predominant in the composition of the Italian group; and this group by that date had moved too far toward identification with the Yankee City system to be organized around a national-church structure. Hence the Italian group is still nominally articulated to the Church of St. Mary, as were the French Canadians in their first phase. A contributing factor has been the split of the Italians into North and South Italian subgroups with few relations other than those of antagonism between them. This fact, together with their small numbers, has militated against the organization of a formal structure in the Italian group. Except through the informal clique relations within each subgroup, the Italians in Yankee City present no community system of their own.

The Poles are the most recent Yankee City Roman Catholic group. They also were strongly attached to the national church subsystem in the homeland. It was only by the second half of the 1920's that the Poles were numerically strong enough to be organized into a community church structure. The Catholic Church hierarchy, however, has always maintained the policy that each church structure in the system must be completely self-support-ing. Except for funds distributed to the diocese offices, each par-ish is financially self-determining. The low wages of the Yankee City textile industry, in which the Poles were principally occu-pied, and the later national depression made it impossible for the Poles to finance an independent church. They are still related ritualistically to the Church of St. Mary but, on the whole, in-effectively.

The Russian Jews first appeared in 1893 with fourteen fam-ilies. In the souvenir book distributed at a benefit affair to raise funds for a new synagogue edifice, the history of the Yankee City Congregation Beth Israel is recounted:

The congregation Beth Israel dates its organization back to August 3, 1896, with the following charter members . . . [list of fourteen names]. At first, due to its meager membership, the congregation met in private homes . . . but with characteristic vision they soon established a little synagogue [in a store loft on Wharf Square]. About twenty-seven years ago [1907] a fairly large building [on the upper edge of Zone I] was purchased and made into a synagogue. This served its purpose well as a House of Worship and a center of Jewish Life.

The Jewish group, then, like the Irish, shows three phases in the organization of a church structure marked by these loci as centers of worship: (1) private homes; (2) temporary and make-shift quarters; and (3) synagogue structure. About a decade elapsed between the first and third phases, both among the Irish and among the Jews. In the case of the French Canadians, there was somewhat more than a decade interval between the group's appearance in the city and the formation of a community church structure.

Although there were fourteen families in the Jewish group when the congregation was formally organized under a state char-ter in 1896, worship actually began, according to the testimony of the only surviving charter member, in private homes about 1890 when there were eleven adult male Jews in the city. When the synagogue edifice was purchased in 1907, there were about thirty-five families in the group.

A determinant in this early appearance of a congregation among the Jews is that public worship is not only enjoined but is explicitly predicated in the Law upon adequate numbers—a minimum of ten worshipers, called a *minyan*, being necessary for public worship. In explanation of this edict, Moore[11] says of post-Exilic Judaism: "Judaism thus made religion in every sphere a personal relation between the individual man and God . . . a relation . . . not in isolation but in the fellowship of the religious community, and ideally, of the whole Jewish people. . . . Judaism became in the full sense a personal religion without ceasing to be a national religion."

One of the P[1] elders of the Yankee City Jews, discussing what they do when they haven't a minyan said, "Well, we have certain individual prayers, but the prayers of the congregation we cannot give unless there are ten. In fact, the more there are, the more effective these prayers are. It is like a parade; you know, the bigger the parade, the more impressive it is. And so if the congregation is bigger, then God takes the prayers better." He then quoted in Hebrew from Proverbs: "The glory of the King is the multitude of the people."

From these facts, and from the fact also that in worship no priestly intermediation is necessary, the Jews in Yankee City could form a congregation just as soon as they had a minyan.

The Greeks were represented in Yankee City in 1903 and 1913 by seven and by five families respectively and in 1923, by thirty-three families. In 1921 they organized themselves into a congregation which in 1923 met regularly in a chapel provided by a native Episcopalian church. The first priest was secured in 1924, and he tells the story: "In the earlier days the Greeks always wanted a church, and they used to have services every so often. When I first came, the Greeks held services in the Episcopalian chapel with the priest brought over for the day from Boston. Then they thought it all over and decided they wanted a church building of their own. Later, this church building came up for sale, and we bought it."

Because of insufficient numbers it took the Greeks about two decades to form a community church structure but only three years more to acquire a church edifice, at a time when the group consisted of about thirty families. The Jews numbered thirty-five families when the synagogue building was purchased. Like the Irish and the Jews, the Greeks went through the preliminary, makeshift phase of church organization, during which services were centered in a Protestant chapel.

The Armenians present a rather anomalous church situation.

11. *Op. cit.,* I, 121.

The national church in the homeland was the Armenian Apostolic, which was independent, yet related representationally to the other national subsystems of the Eastern Orthodox Church. For the past century, however, an American Mission group has been actively engaged in Armenia in "reforming" the Armenian adherents of the Apostolic Church along Protestant—specifically, Congregational—lines. By the outbreak of World War I some 150,000 Armenians had been converted.

Among the Armenian immigrants to Yankee City were members of both churches, the Apostolic families outnumbering the Congregational about two to one. This division has militated against the appearance of a single church structure in the Armenian community system, even though in 1933 the group totaled sixty-eight families.

In 1933 there were thirty-six Armenian families organized into a rudimentary Apostolic church housed (as were the Greeks until 1927) in the Episcopalian chapel and meeting sporadically as an Apostolic priest happened to visit the city. However, a committee has very recently been formed to raise funds toward the purchase of a church edifice. The Apostolic church, then, is in the embryonic phase which the Greeks displayed between 1921 and 1923.

The Congregational subgroup among the Armenians in 1933 totaled fifteen families. (Seventeen families had no church affiliations recorded.) The Congregational Armenian families were originally welcomed into the native Congregational church but withdrew to form a church which meets regularly in the vestry of the Congregational church.

The Russians, numbering about thirty families in 1933 and affected by the same industrial circumstances as the Poles, have made no effort whatsoever to organize a Russian Orthodox church. As with the Poles, when ritualization of crises becomes necessary, priests of their national church system are secured from neighboring cities.

3. *Sacred Symbols in the Ethnic Church Structures*

THE internal aspects of the separate church structures and the changes which have occurred in each will be analyzed with special attention to the Irish, Jewish, and Greek churches as representatives of three distinct structural types. The analysis will distinguish between the *form* of these structures, by which is meant the organization of the relations within these structures, and their *content*, or what we have called their representational aspects,

Ethnic Group	Phase I *Informal*	Phase II *Rudimentary Structure*	Phase III *Complete Structure*
Irish	1800(?)– 10(?) Families Itinerant priests Worship in homes	1841– 50(?) Families "Regular" pastor—periodic visits Worship in chapel	1848– 100 Families Resident pastor Permanent church edifice (1853)
French Canadians	1883– 13 Families Worship in Irish church	1894– 60 Families French-Canadian curate associated with Irish church	1903– 127 Families Resident pastor Permanent church edifice
Jews	1890– 11 Families Worship in homes	1896– 14 Families Congregation formed Worship in a store loft	1907– 35 Families Permanent synagogue edifice
Greeks	1903– 7 Families Worship in homes	1921– 30 Families Congregation formed Worship in Protestant chapel	1924– 35 Families Resident pastor Permanent church edifice
Armenians	1903– 13 Families 1. Apostolic—worship in homes 2. Congregational—worship in Protestant chapel	1923–1933 36 Families 1. Apostolic—worship in Protestant chapel 2. Congregational (15 families) worship in Protestant chapel	
Italians	1893–1933 92 Families Worship in Irish church		
Poles	1913–1933 154 Families Worship in Irish church Worship in Polish churches in neighboring cities		
Russians	1913–1933 35 Families Worship in Russian churches in neighboring cities		

TABLE 5

Development of Ethnic Church Structures

ideal, symbolic, and ritualistic. The form of the church structures will be analyzed in some detail, their content only in terms of significant changes which have taken place.

All churches are based upon the fundamental relation of the group to a transcendental, cosmological principle such as that suggested by the term God. Church systems differ in their conception of the nature of this principle, consequently in its symbolic representations, and in prescriptions as to the behavioral modes by which an individual may establish his relation with this principle. Transgression of these modes—and, by extension, of most behavioral modes of the social system with which the cosmological system is associated—endangers this relation. Hence the source of the system of moral law which defines the modes of behavior is the primary cosmological principle (or principles).

Churches differ, however, not only in the formal aspects of their symbolic representations but in the degree to which these symbols become intermediaries in the man-God relation. For example, in the synagogue the principal symbols are the Holy Ark and the Scroll bearing the Mosaic Code known as the Torah. These serve to convert a profane edifice into a House of God. The Scroll, in addition, serves the Reader, generally a layman, who leads the congregation in reading aloud. This reading aloud from the Torah Scroll is the principal form of worship in the synagogue service. By reading the text of the Law in concert with the rest of the congregation, each individual Jew establishes direct communication with God, who is held the author of the Law. The Torah, therefore, is the symbolic intermediary between the Jewish worshiper and his God. Reading the Torah even in the privacy of one's home is an act of worship, although it has not the same efficacy, as a Jewish informant who was quoted above declared, as in the group congregation.

For the Christian churches, Christ is the mediating symbol. In the Protestant denominations, communication with God in prayer is effected by verbal appeal "in the name of Christ."

In the Catholic churches, both Roman and Eastern, however, such direct prayer is secondary to communication with God through the symbol of Christ. The rites of Communion and Mass center on the symbols of bread and wine, representing the "body and blood of Christ." By Communion, the church declares, "the soul is united to God." Transubstantiation of the bread and wine, moreover, can only be effected by a priest who is the representative of Christ, since the church itself is also the "body of Christ."

Similarly, the priest is the agent of Christ in conferring the other sacraments by which the soul is joined through the sanctity of Christ to that of God. In the synagogue no social personality such as the priest exists, and authority and controls reside in the congregation itself. After the conclusion of the investigation a rabbi appeared in the Yankee City synagogue, but the rabbi's role is judicial, advisory, and instructional, not that of ritual intermediary.

The keystone in both the Irish Catholic and Greek Church structures is the office of priest. In sacred functions the power and prestige of both priests are nearly alike; both priests are indispensable in linking the community to the sacred order of their respective church systems. In their profane functions, their authority differs enormously—for instance, in control over the affairs of the church structure—since the Roman Catholic Church system is hierocratic, i.e., ruled by priests, whereas the independent national Eastern Orthodox Church systems are democratic, i.e., ruled by the community.

Zankov[12] writes of the Eastern Orthodox Church:

The laity . . . participate as an active force in all phases of church life; through the Parish Council they direct all the not purely spiritual or liturgical affairs of the parish. . . . It elects the holders of the offices from the priest up to the Patriarch [the head of the national church]. In various forms they participate in the supreme governing bodies, both of the diocese and of the whole Church.

Control of the Greek church in Yankee City resides in the community itself and is delegated to elected officers and committees; the church edifice is the property of the community; and the priest is a salaried employee of the community. Whatever secular authority the priest may have is indirectly derived from his relation to the sacred aspects of the community system.

The priest in the Irish Catholic church on the other hand is not subordinate to the Irish community in any respect. He derives his secular authority, not from the local community but from the authority passed down to him from the papacy itself through the diocese bishop. He is an officer in the Roman Catholic government and is responsible to it alone. This government is self-perpetuating and in the direction of its affairs is independent of the

12. Stefan Zankov, *The Eastern Orthodox Church,* translated by D. A. Lowrie, (London, Student Christian Movement, 1929), pp. 90–91.

laity. It is a supersystem transcending its parish components. The Irish church is controlled not from "below," as in the Greek church, but from "above." The church edifice is the property of the diocese officers, not of the community. The priest is paid directly from rents collected for seats in the edifice, i.e., as the agent of the property owner, rather than as a salaried employee. He cannot be "fired" by the community as Greek priests have been. Therefore the pastor of the Irish church, by virtue of complete concentration of authority in his office, is the director of all secular aspects of his church structure, which has been proliferated to embrace almost the entire Irish community system. The Greek priest has power to direct nothing beyond the church ritual. Hence Rolfus[13] can say of the Roman Catholic priests that they are "governors, guardians, watchmen, lawgivers, dispensers of grace."

But even in the exercise of their sacred function, differences exist in the statuses of Roman Catholic and Greek priests. Rolfus[14] calls the Roman Catholic priests "guardian angels upon earth," and adds, "a power is given to them which no angel is privileged to possess." Of the Eastern Orthodox priesthood, Zankov[15] asserts:

. . . the clergy are the servants of God in the most holy things. . . . Still, this service in no wise lifts them to a higher order, in which they are changed to another kind of person . . . the priests are only servants, unworthy and sinful, among the most sinful of God's servants . . . and are not the "proprietors" of the gifts of grace . . . are not cut off from the intimate life of the people. They marry and participate in all the important events of popular life.

This difference in sacerdotal power is suggested in the words used by the two priests in the rite of baptism. The Roman Catholic, at the close of the ceremony, pronounces the words, "I baptize . . ."; the Orthodox priest uses the passive tense: "The servant of God, X [the child], is baptized." In the former instance authority for conferring grace resides in the office of the priest, whereas in the latter instance authority resides, not in the priest, but in the ritual itself.

13. H. Rolfus, D. C., *Explanation of the Holy Sacraments*, p. 33.
14. *Idem*, p. 258.
15. *Op. cit.*, pp. 89–90.

The sections that follow will analyze the positions of the Roman Catholic and Eastern Orthodox clergy from data gathered from the priests of the Irish and Greek churches. Their sacred functions will be examined and also their secular roles in their respective communities, the attitudes and evaluations attached to them by their parishioners, their relations to the larger society of Yankee City, and the changes that are observable in each of these aspects of the priest's status.

4. *The Irish Church*

THE functions of the priests of the Irish church can be enumerated as follows: (1) administration of all sacraments and rituals; (2) supervision of the family structures through the confessional and by periodic visits to all homes in the parish; (3) administration of the finances and property of the church structure; (4) supervision of the moral training of children in the parochial and Sunday schools; and (5) supervision of the leisure of all parishioners in the church associations. One Yankee City curate, asked about the relation of the priest to the parishioners, replied: "You know there are seven sacraments, starting with baptism and ending with death. That means the priest is in constant contact with the individual from birth until death, at baptism, confessional, communion, etc., so that the individual is never separated from the church and the priest."

Another priest says: "We come in contact with all phases of life. I buried a man this morning. This afternoon a woman asked our help for a husband who is unmanageable. We baptize children, marry them later; we comfort the dying and console the people in grief. And in our confessionals we have the deepest insight into the lives of our people."

Both ritually and informally, the priest, as the instrument of the church, is in touch with the "flock" at every crisis in the life cycle. Through the confessional the priest is aware of the most detailed and intimate facts concerning every parishioner. With no areas of the community system closed to him, the priest is in a position of extraordinary power in that system. As one Protestant woman married to a Catholic admits: "The Catholic church knows everything about the family, even its work and its income. The Protestant church knows little."

One incident illustrates the significance of the confessional as an instrument of control. The Irish priest discovered through the

confessions of the Catholic boys that they were being taught by a
doctor in one of the high-school clubs what the priest called "the
profane facts of life." The subject of sex, according to church
doctrine, is profane, and its teaching is prohibited. The priest
immediately formed a club for the Catholic high-school boys, and
under his orders all Catholic boys withdrew from the high-school
club.

The priests are accordingly in a position to define norms of
everyday social behavior for the church's members. A further
illustration is contained in the following excerpt from a priest's
sermon at a Mission Service for male adults of the church:

The Catholic church has never demanded anything but temperance
from its people. It has commended abstinence and indicates that a
man who doesn't take a drink may become a saint, and then again
he is also just as intemperate as a man who drinks to excess. In this
connection, if you can take a drink and not get drunk, or if you
take many drinks and not get drunk, it is all right to drink; but if
you take one drink and it makes you drunk, you shouldn't drink.
In the eyes of God you are committing a sin. The thing to do is to be
temperate. Just this afternoon I was walking down the street and I
passed a man of the community who had five children. He was so
drunk that he was wobbling from one side of the sidewalk to the
other. Just about this time school was dismissed, and one of the
young sons of this man saw his father going down the street. One
of the boys poked him and said, "Isn't that drunken man your
father?" What would you think if your boy should come out and
see you staggering down the street? There is no getting around it.
Every son thinks his father the greatest man in the world and every
son has that right.

It is significant that the priest, in making the point, literally
"drives it home" by appealing to the male's status of father to
his sons.

Through his function of ritual mediator and through his role
as moral guide and "father" to his "children," the priest is in
the position of having extraordinary influence on the community.
The reflex of these functions of the priest may be found in the
Irish community's expressed attitudes toward its priests.

The various publications issued by the community on important
anniversary occasions generally include a history, not of the Irish
community, but of the "Catholic Church in Yankee City." Ex-

amination of these short historical accounts reveals that they are inevitably organized around the pastorates of the various priests who have succeeded each other in the church structure.

At Father Hannon's death in 1871, the Yankee City *Herald* printed an article describing the funeral, from which the following is taken: "Thus was buried a good man and a good pastor, one whose influence on his people is admitted by people of all sects to have been beneficial to them and for the interest of the community in which he and they lived." At the Golden Jubilee celebration of the Church of St. Mary's dedication, held in 1893, one speaker spoke of Father Hannon as "a saint."

Accounts written of Father Hannon's successors stress the priest's function in guiding members of his church and in conciliating native antagonisms by his "Godly example." Thus of one pastor it was said: "He advanced the cause of religion a great deal not only by his zeal for the spiritual welfare of his flock but also by doing much to disarm non-Catholic prejudices, which were very deep-seated at that time."

A Yankee City *Herald* article dated 1880, which had an honored place in the scrapbook of one old Irish lady, relates the behavior of the community at the return of their pastor from a vacation:

A large number of the parishioners of the Church of St. Mary crowded the Parochial hall last evening to welcome their pastor on his return from the south. . . . The happy faces of the people manifested the pleasure they felt at their pastor's return and enjoyment they experienced from the entertainment. As Father Nealing . . . entered the hall the whole concourse arose to their feet. The beautiful sound of "Home again" with the words appropriate to the occasion greeted the pastor as he took his place on the stage. This was followed by a beautiful address delivered by Master James Michael, one of the Parochial school boys, who presented the pastor in the name of the parents and children with a basket of flowers enclosing $300 in gold, as a small token of the high esteem in which he was held. Father Nealing feelingly responded.

Between 1848 and 1930, a period of eighty-two years, the Irish church had only three pastors. The fourth died in 1933. Referring to the third pastor of the church, one Irish woman declared: "We feel very close to our priests, but Father OBrien, you know, was my special favorite. He was lovely. He called us by our first names, even while passing, from across the street. He was everything to everybody—absolutely the pastor. A simple, sweet soul. Every flag was at half mast when he died in 1930."

5. *The Greek Church*

THE general Greek Church organization has been defined as of the democratic type. Zankov[16] elaborates:

The Constantinople patriarchate . . . gave rise to the idea of and model for the broad and active participation of the laity in the life and management of the Church . . . all orthodox churches represent free communions. Within the bounds of the oecumenical-orthodox rules of doctrine, regulation and cult, every separate orthodox church is free in its inner life and management. . . . And in spite of this independence they cling closely and firmly together . . . bound together by the bonds of faith and love and by their mystic appurtenance to one body of Christ.

Whereas the Roman Catholic Church is integrated both symbolically and formally, with its priestly hierarchy providing the sinews of the extended church system, the Orthodox Church system, while an integrated entity symbolically, is in organization atomistic. This deviation between symbolic and formal organization expresses itself in a division of functions within a church structure. While the Orthodox priest is the guardian of the symbols and the ritualistic mediator for the community, the community itself is in control of the nonsacred aspects of the church structure.

Before undertaking the examination of the position of the priest, however, the operations of this democratic type of organization in the Yankee City Greek church will be analyzed.

A Greek informant commented on the fact that the Yankee City church has the same organization as the church system in Greece: "When I was in Greece, they had an elected church committee, just as they do here. The committee would go around to the people to collect money to support the church and would take care of the church affairs. The local church here is just like they had there."

As this informant suggests, the Greek church of Yankee City is directed by a committee elected democratically by the male adults of the community who are also all church members. He

16. *Op. cit.*, pp. 24, 25.

added, "We are a corporation and our constitution is on file at the State House." The committee is in the position of board of directors of the church for the community, and the church itself receives recognition of its legal status from the American society.

Under the charter granted by the state, the communal committee is recognized as the controlling directorate of the church structure, in contrast with the Roman Catholic churches, whose charters assign that function to the diocese officers. The Greek democratic organization is sanctioned both by the original structural pattern and by the American legal system.

The committee, our informants tell us, is elected annually. Nominations are made in the following way: "Several weeks before election the old committee posts a paper in the coffee house, and anyone who wants to run for an office puts his name down and what office he wants, and then on the first of June they hold the election. We have a rule that we have to have at least twenty men running for office, that is, two for each position."

The committee has ten members, differentiated as follows: "Four are officers, three are on the church committee, and three on the school committee. Well, the three on the church committee attend to small affairs, collect the money, and turn it over to the treasurer of the whole committee. They can't spend any money without a meeting of the whole committee—at least, they can't spend over $50. The president of the committee cannot spend over $100 as a necessary thing without a meeting of the whole committee to vote on it. About all the three members of the school committee and the church committee do is to collect funds and attend to small details, fixing up the place, etc., which they can do without a meeting of the whole committee."

That is, the committee is composed of four officers who are responsible to the community and two administrative subcommittees in charge of the routine and minor details of the church and school. These subcommittees are responsible to the officers, but on all matters of importance the entire committee must make the decision. The affairs directed by the committee include: (1) collecting and handling church funds; (2) acquiring and maintaining the church building; (3) hiring and paying the priest; (4) hiring and paying the Greek school teacher; and (5) arranging church and school picnics.

In all such matters the committee's decision is authoritative and final. For instance, its decision, in the interest of economy, to discharge the school teacher and have the priest assume the duties of the Afternoon School withstood the objections of almost the entire community. Later, the community won out, however. Ultimate power lies with the church members, for they can turn out an unpopular committee at the next annual election, but while the committee is in office its decisions are beyond appeal. There is only one occasion on which a church matter is referred beyond the committee directly to the entire membership, i.e., to the adult males in the community: a three-fourths vote of the entire membership is necessary if an incumbent priest is to be dismissed.

Twenty-three male adults filled the thirty places on the committee in the years 1931, 1932, and 1933. In age they ranged from thirty to sixty years, with almost equal distribution among the three brackets, 30 to 39, 40 to 49, and 50 to 60 years. They were divided between the P^1 and P^2 generations: fourteen were of the P^1 generation, and nine were P^2. All but one were married. By occupation fifteen were shoe workers, seven hand-craftsmen, and only one a merchant. Distribution among the class strata was as follows: lower-lower, twelve; upper-lower, ten; and lower-middle, one. Only half were members of the Greek-American Progressive Association. Only seven of the twenty-three were naturalized voters. Twelve were from Greece and eleven from Asia Minor. Three were Welfare cases and three others had minor crime records.

It would seem that neither age nor ethnic generation is a selective factor for election to the committee. However, marriage, in view of the large number of bachelors in the community, is a factor since the family is the unit of the community and only adult males who are the heads of families appear eligible for the church committee. Neither occupation nor class strata appear to be effective selective factors, since the lowest in both systems predominate. Birthplace is not a factor. Even crime and Welfare records do not prohibit election. The secretary of the committee for the three years was "on Welfare" throughout that period.

These facts indicate that members of the committee come for the most part from among those Greeks who have not yet moved, in any important degree, into external relations in the Yankee City system. Only eleven of the members cited, in fact, had even gone so far as to enter the Greek-American Progressive Association. Eight of the twenty-three committee members were comparative newcomers to the Yankee City Greek community, having arrived only during the past decade. One Greek arrived in 1931 and by 1933 was on the committee. Of considerable significance is the fact that, with the single exception noted, none of the Greek merchants, who are the economic leaders of the Greek community, was represented. Again, with a single conspicuous exception, officers of the G.A.P.A. over the same three-year period failed to become members of the committee.

It would appear that the essential factor in the selection of committee representatives is not mobility by American standards but fixity by Greek standards; it is not articulation with American society but more or less complete identification with the Greek community. (Newcomers moved quickly to identify themselves with the local Greek community.) This explains the fact that on those occasions when representatives of the Yankee City society wish to organize the Greek community around some American crisis or into some American ritual, contact is made, not through the president of the church committee, who more than any other lay member of the group represents the whole community, but through the priest.

To explain why individuals low in the American status scale are predominant on the committee, we have said that for service on that body strong articulation with the ancestral tradition is a requisite. What, then, of the nine P^2 males on the committee? Analysis of this group shows that all but one married P^1 wives; only two were in the G.A.P.A.; none was in open (native) associations; four were of the lower-lower class, and four of the upper-lower. Even the P^2 committee members, therefore, are among the more fixed members of their generation.

But something more than cultural fixity is involved. Twenty-three individuals filled thirty offices over a period of three years, or, on an average, eight of every ten committee members in any one year had not served before, and only two were carry-overs from the year before. In 1932 all ten members elected to the committee were without previous service. This is a significantly high turnover for offices which have functions as important for the community as those of the church committee.

Said one Greek, an ex-committeeman, after the 1932 election: "Yes, it is a good thing to let somebody else have it a while. One of the new committee members was not very active in church work, which was one reason we put him on. Two of the other fellows were the same way. Some people always complain. You work hard, and you give dances and parties and you collect the money and tend to the bills, and people say, 'Oh, that's easy,' and you think you haven't done anything. Then they see all the money coming in, and then they say that there's some crooked work somewhere and somebody's making a lot of money. Three fellows on the new committee are like that. We want them to see just how hard the work is." There is considerable drafting of candidates, then, as well as the volunteering of service described by the informant quoted earlier. A Greek who had been president of the committee said: "In the offices of the committee, we switch around a bit every year and let other people do it a while. If someone doesn't think things are running right, we elect them so they can see how it is."

This seems to suggest that drafting candidates for the committee is first of all a device for absorbing the inactive and silencing the antagonistic, and that, since the responsibilities are considered arduous, the offices are a community duty which should be shared in rotation. Both of these factors, which are unusual in positions of importance and prestige, were correlated with the period of the American depression and of financial crisis for the Yankee City Greek church. The committee was in an exposed position since the fate of the local church was in its hands and it received criticism from all sides. One informant stated this explicitly: "One time the priest asked me why I wouldn't serve on the committee, and I told him that anybody that gets on the committee, people don't like him or something. You know how it is, if you have an office, just like the President of the United States or anybody else, people always say things about you."

The fact that inactive and carping individuals could be drafted indicates that they were compelled by the structure to go through with their challenges to the church's administration. Furthermore, the 1932 committee was so effectively "put on the spot" that it carried out certain necessary changes which offended the whole community, as we shall see in discussing the priest-teacher controversy.

This analysis of the committee's composition covers a crisis period during which the church and the community were in a dangerous position. The reaction was to spread responsibility as widely as possible, which accounts for the large turnover on the committee, and as deeply as possible, which accounts for the representation of those organized around the inner community system rather than the American. The crisis also accounts for the fact that, whereas men had served five and six years on the committee prior to 1931, sixteen of the twenty-three committeemen between

1931 and 1933 served only one term; and it accounts for the recurrent theme among the informants: "Let somebody else do it a while."

There is one other function of the committee which must be considered. It will be remembered that earlier we said that the church committee is divided into three subgroups: officers, church subcommittee, and school subcommittee. The third of these groups supervises the Afternoon School. However, there is also a Sunday School, taught by the priest, for Greek children of adolescent age. The Sunday School is not under the control of the school subcommittee but is directed by a special Sunday School committee.

The priest described this committee: "There is an adult Sunday School committee, consisting of the president of the church, two members of the church committee, and three other church members, not committee members, making six in all on the adult Sunday School committee. The committee serves from October till October. The Sunday School has a vacation during the summer months from the time of its annual picnic until October, so the committee serves through the active year of the Sunday School. However, the church committee serves from June to June. There is an overlapping of the time of the committees, and at the present time there are committee members still on the Sunday School committee who are no longer on the church committee. In October the new president of the church committee will take his position on the Sunday School committee, and two other members of the new church committee will be selected to serve with him."

The list of the Sunday School committee included the name of only one man who was not a church committee member, and he happened to be the teacher of the Afternoon School. Why the Sunday School should nominally not be the province of the school subcommittee and should have a formally separate supervisory committee is not clear. In effect the Sunday School is also the charge of the church committee.

Concerning the sacred organization of the Greek church, the secretary of the church committee stated: "The Greek Church in America has its actual head in Constantinople, but there is a bishop in New York who administers all of North and South America. All the churches throughout the world have consistent policies, the same services, and all. Whenever any changes are made, they notify them all and all abide by the changes."

The priest supplemented this information: "Until ten years

ago [1921] the Greek Church in the United States was still in the mission stage, and it wasn't until that time that a hierarchy was established here with an archbishop and various bishops."

The relations of the Greek community to the bishop were described by a church committee member: "When a community wants to get a priest, they organize the church and write to the bishop in New York for permission. He sends a priest there. If they do not like the priest, they have to have a meeting with seventy-five out of one hundred members present, and must vote that they want a new priest. Then they notify the bishop and he sends them another one and investigates the conditions."

Thus the bishop serves the individual Greek communities as a clearing house for priests, or really as an employment agency. The bishop has slight authority in the administration of the affairs of the separate community churches, except in matters of ritual and dogma in which he is the agent between the Mother Church in Constantinople and the priest in the Yankee City church. Zankov[17] states essentially the same facts:

. . . The organization and authority . . . [are] other than worldly and formally juridical, having rather a preponderantly spiritual and mystic character.

The highest authority of the Orthodox Church is the Church itself, the whole community of the Church.

The Orthodox Church . . . is in no wise a hierocratic Church. . . . The Bishops are set over priests in liturgical and disciplinary matters but in no autocratic sense of that word.

The following is a vivid picture of the function and status of the priest in rural Greece:[18]

The condition of the ordinary Greek priest is, as a rule, one of abject and dismal poverty. Being unpaid by the State, he has to live as best he can, and support his wife and family—for he is a married man— on the fees which he receives from his flock for baptisms, marriages, and funerals, and which are usually paid in kind after arrangement with the parties concerned, and on presents at Easter. In the country he may be seen tilling his field, scarcely, if at all, distinguishable, in culture or wealth, from the poorest peasant of the village. He is not allowed to keep a shop; but his son is not infrequently the proprietor of the local inn or general store, and he may often be seen

17. *Op. cit.,* pp. 86–89.
18. W. Miller, *Greek Life in Town and Country,* pp. 62, 63.

there fraternizing with other men of the hamlet on equal terms for he enjoys no social superiority whatever by virtue of his cloth.

But it is not to be inferred that this status is without sanction in the church dogma. Zankov[19], himself high in the church hierarchy, has already been quoted to this effect: ". . . . the priests are only servants, unworthy and sinful, among the most sinful of God's servants—[and] are not the 'proprietors' of the gifts of grace."

The Greek priest is a man among men, but one who by special training and ordination at the hands of the bishop is designated to effect communication for the community through symbolic and ritualistic representations to God. He is the community's ambassador to the realm of the sacred church; but beyond the circle of the church he is a human being, earthly by nature and existence. This duality of the priestly character is expressed in the attitude of the Greeks as described by Burgess:[20] "And although they [the Greeks] may sometimes despise the *man* for his lack of education or his worldly-mindedness, they nevertheless respect the *priest* and treat him with the proper marks of courtesy, as doffing their hats, or rising when he enters the room." Thus the Greeks distinguish between the profane human in the priest and the sacred functions he performs in his office.

Because of the deep-rooted Greek tradition of democratic organization, the priest has no formal control; but by reason of the divine function with which he is vested, he has considerable informal influence if he cares to exercise it.

What happens to the priest when he comes to minister to the Greeks organized in community systems within the American social field? Almost immediately he begins to change his personality by the mere fact that he dispenses with the priestly clothes of Greece and adopts the dress of the Roman Catholic priests. Xenides'[21] report accords with the observed dress behaviors of the Yankee City Greek priests: "Almost all of the clergymen of the Greek Church in America have adopted clerical clothes and collar, and trim the beard and hair. In Greece they wear long robes with loose sleeves, preacher's high hat, and have long hair and beards, in accordance with the Nazarite rule in the Old Testament."

19. *Op. cit.*, pp. 86, 87.
20. *Op. cit.*, p. 108.
21. *Op. cit.*, p. 124.

Of the general status of the Greek priests among the Greek communities of America, Burgess[22] says:

He [the priest] has not power as far as the written constitution goes. Thus, we find a most anomalous condition in the Greek Churches in America. It works out sometimes like the worst side of the vestry system of the Episcopal Church parishes, without the legal rights of the rector. . . . So the Greek priest is hired and often "fired" by a parish committee composed usually of poorly educated peasants . . . and thus, the poor priests sent out by the Holy Synod in response to the cry for spiritual help, sometimes find themselves as office boys at the mercy of their employers.

This was written before an archbishop was established for the Americans. While the archbishop has changed the situation considerably by enforcing the three-fourths-vote rule on the dismissal of a priest, nevertheless, the fact stands that because of the independence of each Greek community and its autonomy with respect to its own church affairs, the priest remains in a subordinate position. For example, in Yankee City the Greek church committee, to the complete exclusion of the priest, administers the church for the community.

An expression of the priest's point of view was given in a statement of the Greek priest who had been in Yankee City during the years 1924 to 1932: "The church here is a corporation under the laws of the state—a corporation which was drawn up about the time I came, which has a president and other officers. The officers change every year. In other cities the priest is very often the presiding officer, but I feel that this is a bad plan. I never attend their meetings and don't interfere in any way. Such is the policy of my church. It is, you know, most democratic, and a great deal of the government is left entirely to the members. I would rather not interfere with them. In fact, I wouldn't do it for twice my present salary [$2,400 per annum]. The laymen are often constrained if the priest is present, and they do not express themselves as freely as they do without him."

What is obvious here is that since he lacks authority the priest could only further subordinate himself by forcing himself into the affairs of the committee. This Yankee City priest says, in effect, that he prefers to maintain his dignity by keeping at a distance from the committee, and appeals to church policy for

22. *Op. cit.,* pp. 57, 58.

sanction of his attitude. Arriving in the community after the corporation papers had been drawn, he was helpless to challenge the committee's authority as Greek priests in other communities have done, and resorted to a secondary sanction—that of refraining from inhibiting the free action and speech of the committee members. This suggests that the priest has worked out a rather pointed defense of his anomalous position of ritual leader of the church with no voice in its affairs. Equally defensive is his statement in another interview that the acquisition of the present church edifice was "my work."

A similar defensiveness was noted in a succeeding Greek priest who, as teacher in the Sunday School, set up a children's Sunday School committee. In describing the affairs of this committee in considerable detail, he said: "Of course, you understand that I am over the committee. I lead them all."

An indication of the value placed upon the priest's "hands off" policy is suggested in the following comment of a Yankee City Greek: "The priest is a good man and doesn't try to play politics the way other priests do. He doesn't interfere with members outside of the church. The church has been here some eight years, and he has been in it all the time. The man before him tried to play politics. He is a good man and doesn't do that."

The basic core of priestly functions includes conducting the church services around the ritual calendar of the year, performing all rites of passage, preparing and giving the Communion, hearing confessions, and officiating at ceremonies for the dead. But the priest is not free to perform these functions whenever he may choose, for as an officer of the church committee told us: "Couples from here who want to be married, the Greek priest in another city can't marry them unless they have a letter from the president of our committee saying that it's all right. If he'd marry them without permission, he'd lose his job. He couldn't come down here to hold a funeral or anything without permission."

A priest, then, is a priest to a particular community and to no other. Furthermore, he can discharge his office only with the sanction of the church committee.

For his services the community pays the priest a stipulated salary, which is another subordinating factor. He stands to the community in the relation of employee to employer.

Beyond the regular ceremonies in the ritual calendar performed for the community as a whole, there are certain special ceremonies around the rites of passage which are performed with the family as the special focus. Since such rites do not invoke the sacred for the community but only for the family (although the community may furnish participating spectators), the family so benefited is obligated to remunerate the priest for his special services. One Yankee City Greek told us that on the occasion of his marriage he gave the priest $15. Another Greek said: "The priest gets lots of tips. If I have a child christened, or a funeral, or a marriage, there are always tips to the priest of $5 or $10."

Besides the functions strictly related to the community and to the family, the priest in his office links the Yankee City Greek community with the world-wide Greek Orthodox hierarchy and the other Greek communities which it serves. This is suggested in the following clipping from the Yankee City *Herald*:

The Reverend A——, pastor of the local Greek Church, left this afternoon for Boston, whence . . . he will leave for New York this afternoon by steamboat to represent the clerical association of the Boston diocese at the installation of the new archbishop of the Greek Orthodox Archdiocese of North and South America, which will take place at the Greek Cathedral of St. Eleftherios of New York City Tuesday evening at eight. The Reverend A—— is secretary of the clerical association of the Boston diocese.

Finally, there is the priest's traditional function of "shepherd to his flock." The Yankee City Greek concept of this function is explicitly stated by a Greek informant: "My idea is that the priest should be the same to everybody. I pay my dollar, you pay your dollar [monthly church dues], the other people each pay their dollar. There isn't any one person who gives a hundred, and another five, but they are all the same, and he should treat them all alike. It is like we are the children and he the father. He should not do things for one and not for the other.

"B—— is a smart man and knows what he should do. He goes around and calls on everybody. He is friendly and just the same to everyone. He'd come by here and see me and say, 'Hi, John, how's the business, how's everything?' Then he'd go on down the street and with everyone else he'd be just the same way, friendly to them all. But if I start talking about somebody, he wouldn't pay any attention to me. He'd say 'Yes, I think it is going to be nice weather. It looks like rain.' But he wouldn't listen to what I was saying. He didn't gossip about people. He was a good man, knew his business."

Another Greek said of the same priest: "When you didn't go to church, B—— would come around in a nice way and talk to you so you would feel ashamed, and feel you just had to go. Not only that we had to go, but we wanted to go. I certainly hate to see B—— go, because we got along fine with him."

There is also the illuminating incident, already referred to in another context, of a P^2 unmarried Greek who had a tailoring shop on one of the main business streets and was still in the lower class. Apparently innocent of the proprieties of class, this young Greek bought a second-hand Lincoln car, which he drove about the city. Immediately he found his business declining. His usurpation of a value symbol identified with a higher class was offensive especially to the natives, from the highest stratum to the lowest. The society's reaction was to withdraw from the offender, thus isolating him until he had separated himself from the symbol. In this predicament the young Greek sought the paternal advice of the priest. Of course, the priest counseled that he give up the car, which he did.

In spite of his paternal relation to the community, the priest is never referred to by the title "Father," but simply by his surname. This is in contrast to the behaviors of the Roman Catholics to their priests.

The following are the three original functions of the priestly office:

1. To relate the community to the national society's sacred ideology.

2. To relate the community spatially to the social structure of the nation through the church hierarchy.

3. To relate the community to the national society's norms by keeping the members from deviating from these norms. It was in this realm that the priest was said to be "influential in Greece."

However, in Yankee City the first Greek priest, A——, appears to have extended his personality and functions far beyond the traditional limits.

The community in Greece was organized as a system of structures, which were components of the larger Greek social system. One of these was the church structure, in which the priest was the ritual leader. The other structures, such as the public schools, the local political unit and its offices, etc., were controlled by other specialized functionaries.

The situation of the Greeks in Yankee City presented certain anomalies. They did not reproduce the community organization of Greece because they could not. Basically they were parts of the American social system, to which they had to articulate themselves in several different subsystems. While they were in the process of effecting articulation, moreover, they were beginning to construct their own embryonic community system around the nucleus of the family. This system evolved slowly and by accretions of different types of structures. First, there were the coffee houses, established in the Yankee City Greek community even before World War I. Then, a full decade later, came the establishment of the church. The committee elected to organize the church constituted the first formal crystallization of the community system. A church building was bought which was of considerable status value, and the group then had the ultimate sacred symbol of community. Subsequently the Afternoon and Sunday Schools and the junior and senior branches of the G.A.P.A. were organized.

Reverend A—— was the only personality in the community who could tie together these structural components of the system for these reasons: (1) He, more than anyone else, was the human symbol of the Greek Orthodox Church system, which was synonymous, it will be remembered, with the Greek national social system and to which the local community, in spatial separation from the latter, assigned high value. (2) His ritual functions in the crises of the family life cycle tended to identify him with the family, the age grades, and the whole Greek community system.

Therefore, although removed from control of the nonsacred affairs of the different parts of the system, formally the priest integrated these discrete parts in his own person. Thus the annual Church and Sunday School picnics were given community sanction by his presence and by the sacred rituals he performed at the beginning of each. The officers of the G.A.P.A. and G.A.P.A. Juniors were blessed by the priest at their public installation; and at the G.A.P.A. Ball the priest was one of the guests of honor. Likewise, although having no direct connection with the Afternoon School, the priest was the focus of its graduation exercises. Finally, the priest's frequent presence at the coffee house lent it sanction, although informally.

So, from the original threefold function of the priest which derived from his office, there evolved a much wider function, that of giving inner integration and sanction to a community system that was an exile component of the parent system. Not only did the priest tie the community externally to the other American-Greek communities and to the larger society in Greece, but symbolically, in his office, he linked the inner parts of the local Greek community itself. The priest provided the church and the community system with its inner operating unity. As ritual leader of the church he became the secular leader of the community. This greatly extended function existed in spite of the fact that he had no direct control over nonsacred aspects of the church structure and in mundane matters was subordinate to the church committee.

Just as the Greek community system needed internal integration, so did it require articulation to the society of Yankee City.

In his dual capacity of pastor to his flock and leader of his community, the Greek priest was invited by the Yankee City Community Welfare Service, a private charitable organization serving the whole city, to join its board of directors. He was active in the general affairs of the organization thereafter and was specifically the agent between it and the needy among the Greeks. When an unemployed Greek required help, the priest would contact the secretary of the organization, give her the facts in the case, and quietly convey the assistance to the distressed family. If on rare occasions a Greek applied directly to the Welfare Service, the secretary would consult the priest before taking action. The priest thereby became identified not only with the Greek community but with Yankee City society as well.

This function of the priest for the Yankee City polity grew rapidly.

In 1930, at the time of the winter unemployment crisis, when an executive committee of the Yankee City Chamber of Commerce and various welfare agencies of the city were organized, and a committee of town notables was created to handle the various organizations of the town with a view to obtaining aid for the unemployed, the Reverend A—— was picked to carry the unemployment appeal to the Greek population. A somewhat similar incident occurred during the time of the national Red Cross drive, when the Reverend A—— was assigned to handle the collection of Red Cross subscriptions and donations among the Greek population. Similarly, on the occasion of the tuberculosis tests at the various public schools which were carried on at the Welfare house, the Reverend A—— took active part in the work. On the occasion of the tercentenary convention in 1930 when each of the various organizations in the city was called upon to take part in a parade, this priest was called upon to marshal the Greeks for their part of the ceremonial. Thus it can be said that when Yankee City as a whole seeks a point of contact with the Greek community as a whole and needs a mechanism to bring about the coöperation of the Greek community with the large American community, A——— is the man picked to act as liaison officer.

This accord between the priest and the Yankee City society probably explains why it was he who reported to the police and to the newspaper that petting parties were being held in the yard of the Greek church and threatened prosecution of the offenders, even though supervision of the church building was in the hands only of the church committee. Through his dual identification with the Greek community and the society of Yankee City, he was logically the one to convey the community protests of the Greeks to the law-enforcing agencies of the city.

Even more interesting is the fact that this priest was not only the liaison agent between the Greek group and Yankee City but on one occasion acted as leader for all ethnic groups. When the Evening Americanization School, conducted to teach ethnic adults the English language in preparation for American citizenship, was discontinued by the city, the priest was provoked to the point of contacting the leaders of the other ethnic groups. A protest meeting was held and the school was reopened. This indicates that the leaders of the meeting, among whom the Greek priest was prominent, had sufficient prestige in the eyes of the city to have their protest acknowledged and acted upon.

The important position of this priest in Yankee City may be measured by the fact that when the church committee found it necessary to make a drastic cut in his salary, which he refused to accept, full notice of his transfer to Portland, Maine, was chronicled in the news columns of the local paper, together with expansive praise in the editorial column. Twenty-seven column inches were devoted to him in all, divided among four different issues of the daily.

An editorial, judging from its tone and its lack of general verbal stereotypes, was a genuine expression of appreciation. It commended specifically his interpretation of the Greek Church system to Yankee City in terms of the American system of ideal representations; his numerous external relations with the Yankee City system and his reticulation of the Greek community with the Yankee City social system, e.g., "the Greek church took its proper place among the influences for good in this community [Yankee City]"; his tolerance in accepting the religious representations of the Yankee City church subsystem, e.g., "his lack of dogmatism" and his "kindness to adherents of other religions."

The editorial is revealing in its expression of what Yankee City desires of its ethnic communities: "He interpreted the Greek church as a beneficent American institution ready to take up its burdens in no spirit of seclusion." The key word here is "seclusion." Yankee City verbally, at least, approves of the ethnic communities within its social system as long as they accept and acknowledge the American representations, and participate fully "in their proper place" in the system. It does not approve "seclusion" of the ethnic groups, i.e., within the internal relations of their community system alone.

Priest B—— arrived in October, 1931, eight months before the election of a new church committee. In the face of falling income and fixed church expenses, including salaries of the priest and the teacher of the Greek Afternoon School, the committee realistically decided to discharge the teacher and have the priest, who taught the Sunday School, also teach the Afternoon School. Although the matter touched the pocketbooks of every family in the community, an almost unanimous protest was immediately raised.

CHART VII

RELIGIOUS AND CULTURAL SYMBOLS IN THE COMMUNITY
SYSTEM

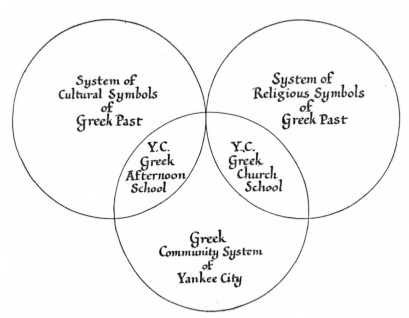

Some members suggested that the salaries of both priest ($1,500) and teacher ($900) should be cut and both men retained; some wanted to increase the salary of the priest and have him serve as teacher too; and a few wanted to retain the teacher and let the priest go, closing the church.

Objections were made to having the priest teach the Afternoon School because (1) he would not retain the respect of the children due to a priest, (2) he would not have sufficient time, (3) priests are not trained to teach school. These objections illustrate the disparity in personality type between a priest in Greece and a priest in Yankee City. Traditionally priests in Greece were poorly educated and not equipped to teach school, whereas the Yankee City priest had had a four-year college course.

Although the Greek Church system is associated specifically with the Greek nation, its Christian representations have not that specific association and are "catholic." The cultural system, however, is specifically Greek, antedates the church, and has an inordinate value to the Greek, since it is acknowledged as the source of the European and American cultural systems. To the Greek in Yankee City the structure within which that cultural tradition is transmitted, and the teacher associated with it, would appear more important than the priest himself.

Priest B—— had acquired new prestige both by his important position in the Greek community system and by his important relations in the Yankee City system. On this particular issue of teaching Greek culture, the Greeks were insisting that the priest maintain his traditional status, but they could not state their remonstrance in terms of status, first, because the priest's status was now changed, and second, to have referred to him in terms of his former status would have been to detract from him as a symbol of the Greek community, and consequently from the community itself. Hence they centered their objections around the functions of teaching itself.

6. *The Jewish Congregation*

IN the church structures already discussed principal emphasis was placed on their formal aspects (i.e., the organization of internal relations and controls) as these are centered in the office of priest. The content of these structures, by which is meant the three defined classes of representations, ideal, symbolic, and ritualistic, was treated summarily because it exhibited few, although significant, changes.

This examination of the synagogue structure of the Yankee City Jewish community will be concerned not so much with the synagogue form as with its changing content.

The congregation of the synagogue is a voluntary association of ten or more adult Jewish males, who are organized to the end of relating themselves as a group to the sacred symbols of the God principle. The synagogue is a structure characterized by a congregation, a complex of symbols, and an edifice.

The principal nonsacred function of the congregation is maintenance of the synagogue. To direct the performance of this and secondary functions, the congregation designates by secret popular vote a board of officers from among its own numbers.

The functions of the synagogue in Russia were essentially those which it had acquired in the Middle Ages.[23] The congregation was not only an autonomous religious association but also the secular, political subsystem of the community system. That

23. These are described by Wirth (Louis Wirth, *The Ghetto,* Chicago, The University of Chicago Press, 1928, pp. 53–55). "The synagogue had three traditional functions. It was, of course, first of all, a Beth Hattefilah, a 'house of prayer,' in the widest sense of that term. Here not only was the scene of the routine services and ritual, but here too gathered the Jews for those more spontaneous prayers in time of crises, when death threatened a member of the community, or when enemies assailed the gates of the ghetto, or when disease or pestilence swept the country, or when their political fate was in the balance.

"The synagogue was also a Beth Hammidrash, a 'house of study.' The association between school and synagogue in the Jewish community has always been close. Before and after the services the Jews studied in the synagogue, read, and argued about the 'Law' and the commentaries of the rabbis. The rabbis were generally not only the religious but also the intellectual leaders of the community, and learning has always been a primary duty and a mark of distinction for every Jew. Here, at the synagogue, moreover, was the meeting place for strangers, who brought news from the world without, and here one gathered such knowledge of conditions of affairs in foreign lands from wandering students, scholars, and merchants as the medieval world afforded. In the synagogue centered those currents of thought that gave the Jewish medieval life some of its distinctiveness, in strange contrast to the intellectual stagnation in the world outside.

"The synagogue was, finally, a Beth Hakkenseth, a 'house of assembly.' In the synagogue centered all those activities that were vital in the life of the community and held it together. The synagogue was the administrative center of the ghetto and at the same time the community center. Most of the public announcements that concerned the entire community were made there, and through the synagogue the secular authorities were able to reach the Jews. Here taxes were assessed and such functions as were left to the Jewish community itself by their civil or ecclesiastical overlords, such as local regulations, passed and proclaimed. The synagogue officers had important judicial functions which they sometimes exercised with the assistance of the secular government. In the synagogue centered the educational, the philanthropic, and much of the recreational life of the community. The synagogue organization remained for several centuries a highly integrated and undifferentiated unit, and thus strengthened its hold on the community."

it could be both derives from the fact that under the Law most aspects of the community system, as of individual behavior, were the subjects of sacred prescription.

In the synagogue structure the rabbi had no differentiated ritualistic functions. Rather he was a scholar who was learned in the literature of the Law. He was a judge who interpreted the Law and gave his decision when questions as to its applications arose in the community. In fact, the Law is itself a codified corpus of decisions of scholars since the second century of the era, these decisions representing applications of the revealed Scriptures, written and oral, to the new circumstances of Exile. But the judgments of the rabbi were advisory only, unenforceable except by authority of the prestige attached to his position and by the community's sanction of that prestige.

The synagogue structure in Yankee City underwent a radical change in the course of this investigation. This change will be described in two separate phases.

The Yankee City congregation has few of the secondary functions of its prototype in Russia. Charity is dispensed by the women's associations. The Hebrew school is administered by a school committee. The congregation has its roster of officers, who merely manage the financial affairs and supervise maintenance of the synagogue building. It possesses in no sense the definitive controls of the congregation that existed in the Jewish communities of Russia.

No rabbi was attached to the synagogue (until the close of the research). This, however, makes no decisive structural difference since a rabbi, even in Russia, is something of a luxury, acquired only when the congregation is large enough to afford one. At few times during the course of the investigation were any attitudes expressed reflecting an awareness of this lack as serious.

The synagogue building, in addition to being a house of worship and a house of study for the adult men, provides a place for the classes of the Hebrew school. It is also the focus of an informal association of the older men in the congregation, as well as the meeting place of their formal association, the Independent Order of B'rith Moses. None of the other formal associations in the community uses it at any time.

It has two other traditional functions. In the building there is maintained a "travelers' room" for itinerant Jews passing through the city, but this is supervised and paid for by the P[1] women's association and not by the congregation itself. The second function is the upkeep of the "Mikveh," where married women are traditionally required to take a bath of purification following menstruation before renewing intercourse.

The most obvious evidence of the changes in the synagogue structure was in attendance. The congregation is traditionally expected, although not required, to gather thrice daily in the synagogue for prayer—at sunrise, at noon, and at sunset. In the first period of the investigation only about fifteen men were found who observed this mode regularly, and these were all men in their sixties and seventies. Even at the more sacred Sabbath services, attendance consisted of about twenty men and thirty women, again confined with few exceptions to the older age groups. Observation of the Sabbath at least is required of all males over eighteen and considered desirable for all females over eighteen, an age group numbering close to three hundred. Yet hardly 15 per cent of the men joined the congregation in the important Sabbath services, and the other 85 per cent made few, if any, appearances at the synagogue, except at the high holidays of Yom Kippur and Rosh Hashana, the most sacred days in the ritual calendar of the Jews.

Only about twenty-five of the men "belonged" to the congregation itself. The rest contributed to the synagogue's support by payment of a seat tax at the high holidays. An informant told us that at business meetings of the congregation "only five or six men were present."

A P^1 male, in his forties, said: "The synagogue isn't important. Well, I usually go into Boston for the big observances such as Passover and New Year's."

Asked whether the Jewish community observed the religious holidays, a P^2 woman answered: "Just the high holidays. I can remember when I was a kid. A holiday was a holiday then. They meant family reunions. Now people go to New Hampshire [resorts] and places like that for the holidays."

The contraction of the functions of the congregation and its membership and the defection of all but the oldest in the community from the important religious observances not only reflect the decline of the synagogue structure but are symptomatic of far deeper changes in the group.

To analyze these changes, religious behaviors must be examined in terms of generations. The P^1 generation can be divided into "elder" and "younger" subclasses. Only the elder P^1 generation males, who in 1932 numbered fifteen, attend the synagogue daily. These are almost unbendingly orthodox and observe the Law to the letter. With few exceptions they remain bearded. On the Sabbath they refrain abstemiously from any tabooed activity such as making fire, handling money, riding, writing, smoking cigarettes, etc. Several incidents illuminate the extreme degree to which this generation observes the Law. An F¹ girl, whose parents are in the elder P¹ class, relates: "Last Sukkoth [a minor holiday] it was raining pitchforks, and since on holidays you cannot carry even a handkerchief, not to speak of an umbrella, my father couldn't go to the *shul* [synagogue] without getting soaked to the skin because the shul was so far. And it was the first time in years and years that he hadn't been to shul on Sukkoth. And he said to me then that he felt as if his life had ended."

An elderly P¹ woman, an officer of the female association that discharges most of the charity functions for the community, indignantly turned away a middle-aged itinerant Jew who had come on a Saturday to her home for fare to the next city, with the words: "Even if we could, we wouldn't give you money. How can you come to ask for money to travel today? Today is Shabas [Sabbath]." The double offense of the supplicant was the intent to travel on the Sabbath and the handling of money on that day.

In a family which has the reputation of being the most pious in the community, the issue of playing the radio on the Sabbath arose and was reported by a daughter: "You know we're the only house, the only Jewish house in Yankee City, that does not play the radio on Friday nights and Saturdays. You can't imagine how hard we fought with our father in order to let us play the radio. In all the other houses they play the radio at that time, but no matter how much we argued, my father simply would not give in. He says that when you turn on the radio or you pick up the telephone, a light goes on either in the radio tube, or on the switchboard, and so you are making fire. You can't imagine how holy the Sabbath is to my father, but gee, it makes it awfully quiet and boring." It is significant that this father extends the edict against making fire to the advanced technology and that on this point all the other elder P¹ fathers have capitulated to the demands of their children, who obviously do not share their parents' attitudes as to the Sabbath.

The younger P¹ generation has rarely been observed to attend the daily synagogue services and is only occasionally seen at the Sabbath services. Some are members of the congregation. All attend to business on Saturday, write, drive, handle money, etc. To these, Saturday is not a day of rest but a work day, and since many are merchants, it is the busiest work day of the week. On the other hand, in the observation of the dietary laws this group remains conformist.

The P² generation exhibits a further departure from the traditional religious practices. No member makes an appearance at the synagogue except on the high holidays, and through 1932 not one was a member of the congregation. It is this generation which first exhibits a critical attitude toward the sacred prescriptions.

For example, at a point in the Rosh Hashana services the rights to ritual privileges, such as leading the reading of certain portions of the sacred text, are auctioned off to the highest bidders. One P² man said: "You know, they ought to dispense with this sort of thing, auctioning in a house of worship. Of course the main purpose of selling these privileges is to get income by which to run the synagogue, but there are much better and more respectable methods than this one here. I don't like it."

On the same occasion another P² male broke off in the course of his reading to expostulate: "Now here's a section that is repeated over and over again; in fact, this section, which lists all of the possible sins which an individual can commit, is repeated seven times, twice at the services last night and five times today. Now they could really shorten the services by cutting out so much of the repetition. Half of these readings is a repetition of what has already been said."

Finally, it is this generation which has broken with the dietary laws such as prohibiting the use of pork and mixing meat and milk foods, or the dishes and utensils in which each is prepared or served. The P² wives will deny that they do not maintain what is known as a "kosher home," but reports from the P¹ women indicate otherwise. One of the latter, who is atypical for reasons she indicates, uses strong terms with respect to these young wives: "This business of keeping a house kosher is a joke. The old ones are strict, but the younger ones are hypocritical. Some may tell their husbands that they are keeping kosher, but they are not. I know that one of my neighbors borrowed a pan from a Gentile neighbor in which to fry bacon.

"Many of them have one set of dishes for both milk foods and for meat foods, and if they have two sets, they wash them at the same time; and what is more, they mix butter with meat. All of this is hypocritical. I believe that if you do it, you should do it right or not at all. Now I do not keep kosher at all. Personally, I don't think it is a disgrace if you keep your home entirely kosher or if you don't keep it at all. But what I do object to is those that try to make others believe that they keep their home kosher and really do not. I come from an orthodox family. But when I was a girl, I went to the city, to Vilna. I listened to lectures, and I became interested in the Socialist movement. I began reading and lost my old orthodox ideas; and when I came here, of course, I became still less orthodox."

The wives of the P^2 generation have broken with the dietary prohibitions but cannot bring themselves openly to exhibit or admit the fact. This describes the relation of this generation to the entire Jewish religious system.

The F^1 generation cannot be accused of being hypocritical. An F^1 boy, eighteen years old, said, "I go to shul on New Year's [high holidays] but that's all. I don't know what it's all about." On the Day of Atonement, Yom Kippur, the most serious and portentous holy day in the year, these young Jews will stay home from school or work, by the constraint of the parents, but in many cases do not go to the synagogue. Those that do stand on the walk chatting with their friends and displaying their new holiday attire.

The critical attitude to the religious representations observed in the P^2 generation reaches a frank skepticism among the F^1 generation. One of them in a discussion of the afterlife, the existence of which is declared in the tradition, said: "If you can prove it to me, I will believe it." Another characterized Judaism as "old-fashioned and meaningless."

In summary, in 1932 the elder P^1 generation was unswervingly attached to the Jewish religious system; the younger P^1 generation was still attached but had abandoned—out of necessity, as will be demonstrated—certain of the essential modes. The P^2 generation had broken away from the system, although it maintained minimal ties. The F^1 generation had broken almost completely from the system. This classification tends to accord with the following, offered by an elder P^1 Jew: "There are four kinds of Jews: (1) those who go to the shul every day; (2) those who go only on Shabas; (3) those who only go on Yom Kippur; and (4) those who don't go at all. About ten to twelve go every day now, about twenty go on Saturday, and on Yom Kippur almost everybody goes."

A P^2 generation Jew made a dual classification on the basis of age and, implicitly, of generation: "There were really two types of Jews who came over—the older, religious Jew and the younger Jew, who came and threw everything over because he suffered so much for religion here."

What are the factors determining the progressive defection of successive generations of Jews from their religious system in a process apparently nearly completed among the children of immigrants themselves? In the religious systems already examined, there were no comparable defections even among the F^3 generation.

The answer to the question seems to lie in a certain unique aspect of the Judaistic religious system. Post-Exilic Judaism may be characterized as a defensive religion, defensive in the sense that it was directed to maintaining cohesion among the scattered parts of Jewish society. This means, at bottom, that its purpose was to preserve that society in spite of its lack of territorial place, to keep its communal components from being absorbed by the societies in which they were embedded. To accomplish their end, the *Hakimim* ("the learned") of the early post-Exilic period, who were the prototypes of the rabbis, set to interpreting and adapting the Scriptures and the oral tradition in the light of the contemporary situation. Their writings, legalistic in spirit, comprise an extensive literature which is codified in the Mishna and the Talmud. These codes define the behavioral modes down to the minutest point; an example frequently cited is the discussion as to whether an egg should be opened at its round or at its pointed end. In effect, this literature represents a common law, whose prescriptions arose from the body of decisions and interpretations and which became established by precedent. No one of the scholars was accepted as or pretended to be the authority, but the accumulated exegeses, when codified, indicated the weight of their collective interpretations.

This legal corpus was characterized by the fact that its sanctions, like those of earlier codes down to the Mosaic, were not only sacred but divine; for the Law was the revelation and the will of God. Moore[24] therefore classes Judaism as a "nomistic" religion, which he defines as one in which the divine law embraces not only what we call the principles of religion but their manifold application to all man's relations to God and to his fellow men. ". . . the infraction of even the seemingly most trivial prescription may be

24. *Op. cit.,* I, 235.

followed by incommensurable consequences, for it is not the trivial rule that is transgressed or neglected but the unitary law of God which is broken."

The effect of the Law was the ritualization and sanctification of the behaviors of the individual Jew, hence of his internal relations to the Jewish community, with the result of withdrawing him from any but superficial relations with non-Jews. In a sense, the Law tended to keep the community centripetal and exclusive. As has often been said, it set a "wall about Jewish life." As a concrete illustration we may take the circumscribing effects of the dietary laws. First, a Jew may not eat certain foods; and second, even those foods which are approved he may not consume unless they have been prepared and served according to rigorously defined modes, which only Jews observe. A Jew thereby is kept from sitting at any board except that of another Jew. Since eating at another's board reflects and facilitates an intimacy of relation, a wide range of possible relations with non-Jews is removed. The dietary laws are one element in an extensive system of law which is similarly isolating.

Throughout the centuries of the Exile the dispersed Jewish groups maintained their exclusive, circumscribed community systems solid and intact. Yet here among the Yankee City Jews in the year 1932, the religious subsystem of their community is apparently in a state of disintegration.

The primary factor, seen especially in the failure of the younger members of the P^1 generation to attend Sabbath services, is economic. The Jewish Sabbath falls on Saturday. In Russia the Jews, comprising an important part of the merchant class, maintained their own work rhythm in the week, and non-Jews had to adapt themselves to it. On Saturday their shops were closed, whereas on Sunday they were "open for business."

The work rhythm of the American week, however, is Christian. Sunday is the Sabbath, and Saturday is a work day, the most important day in the week. This rhythm the Jews are powerless to resist. They must accept it or lose out in the competitive race. The elder P^1 men have refused to compromise by maintaining themselves as junk peddlers. Since they almost monopolize the field in the city, by unanimous agreement they observe the Jewish Sabbath and avoid the competitive handicap. As one of these put it: "There isn't big money in peddling, but I wanted to be religiously independent."

What happened when one of these Jewish peddlers became a

merchant is reported by a younger P[1] Jew: "Mr. Wexler was in the junk business and observed the Sabbath strictly. He changed his business to a variety store and now he lets his sons work on Saturday and doesn't enter the store himself, although competition forces him to keep it open."

Of others like himself, who have no mature children to use in their stores, this P[1] Jew said: "The men here would like to observe the Sabbath, but competition forces them to keep their places open. Those who are in strictly Jewish businesses as junk dealers can and do observe the Sabbath, but competition forces the others to keep their places open."

An F[1] girl, daughter of one of the elder P[1] generation men, was asked why her father let her work on Saturday. "Well, what can he do?" she answered. "He doesn't like it, but he decided a long time ago that he couldn't do anything about it, so now he doesn't even think about it any more. After all, it's impossible to get a job when you don't work on Saturday, so we work whether he likes it or not. Anyway, now he doesn't mind it any more."

One elder P[1] Jew was asked about the Sabbath synagogue attendance and replied: "On the Shabas people are busy, they work, they have businesses and they can't come. In Europe the Jew wouldn't open his business on Saturday if he knew he could make a million dollars. The *Goyim* [Gentiles] knew that the Shabas was holy to the Jews. But here the Jews keep businesses open. They can't help it. So what's left of the Shabas? Yet you have to work." And he continued, describing the effects of this fact: "In America the Shabas is lifeless. In *der Heim* [Russia] it was beautiful. When the family sat down to the table on Friday night, even the poorest became rich. The Shabas came like a great renowned guest. Everybody was excited; it was a real holiday. The candles shone and were blest and the meal was the best of the week. Even the poor families that had only *milchichs* [milk foods] during the week always had meat on Friday. After the meal, the father and the rest of the family would sit around the table and sing songs and tell stories. Everything was so happy and beautiful. The next day on Saturday everybody went to shul. Saturday was no different than Yom Kippur. Everybody came in their best clothes, and everybody prayed with their whole hearts. The shul was always packed. After shul, we used to take a walk and come back for dinner and after dinner we laid down for a sleep until supper time; and when it was dark and the Shabas was over, it was a little gloomy, just as if the guest had left. Things were not so shiny and lovely any more. They were dull and everydayish, and one could hardly wait until the next Shabas. You counted your days by it.

"But here in America, what does the Shabas mean? Nothing, worse than nothing. Take even our own family. My wife and I both observe the Shabas. We don't work, we don't ride, we don't talk on the phone, and we hold it as it should be. All right. But the children have to work, so already there are in the family two strings pulling against each other, and if they work they also do other things they shouldn't do, and already is the Shabas broken in this house. It is not a living real thing, but is a dead corpse. It is missing the fire, the beauty, the sincerity. The meaning is gone. Ah, things were different in der Heim. Yeh, America is a new world. It makes me sad." If even in this strictly orthodox family the Sabbath is "dead," then indeed, as the traditional holy festival of the week, it is no less dead in the entire Jewish community system.

The destructive influence of the economic factor on the observance of the Sabbath is, however, only one manifestation of a more far-reaching phenomenon. In all other aspects of the Jewish community, the process of change is one of a replacement of traditionally Jewish elements by American elements. In the religious system of the Jews there is no such replacement. The Jews are not dropping their religious behaviors, relations, and representations under the influence of the American religious system. There are no indications that they are becoming Christian. Even the F^1 generation can only be said to be irreligious.

The basic fact is that the isolating function of the Judaistic religious system has collapsed under the powerful attraction of the American class system. Heretofore, in their post-Exilic history, except in the Greece of Philo's time, in Spain before the Inquisition, and in Germany from the second half of the nineteenth century to 1933, Jewish communities have not had the opportunity to rise in the social scale of the society in which they were situated. Western Europe until Napoleon and Eastern Europe until World War I used almost as powerful measures to keep Christians excluded from the company of Jews as did the Jews.

Between the two sets of circumscriptions, the Jews maintained their ghetto or ghetto-like systems through centuries. But through those centuries the Jew was also circumscribed and confined economically, for which he often compensated by pushing into neglected or newly developed areas of the economic system, thereby improving his status. Illustrations are provided by the Jews in Spain in the Middle Ages, and in pre-Hitler Germany.

In Yankee City the class system is open, and the Russian Jews climb its strata faster than any other ethnic group in the city—faster even than those groups that have been in the city one or two generations longer.

But rising in the class system demands conformity with the standards and modes at the system's various levels. Given the choice of conforming with the behavioral modes prescribed by the sacred Law or with those demanded by the Yankee City class system, only the P[1] elders have accepted the former. They alone wear beards—beards were a factor in antagonism in Yankee City even in the earlier years of the Jewish community.[25] These Jews alone, with the exceptions of the man who became a grocer, have remained junk peddlers, even though there isn't "big money" in it, in order to observe the Sabbath. All of them have remained in the upper-lower class, while the younger P[1], P[2], and F[1] generations are predominantly in the lower-middle class. The latter, to facilitate economic and class mobility, have progressively sloughed off the traditional behavioral modes, until in the F[1] generation little remains.

The P[1] Jews, elder and younger, explicitly recognize this factor. One of the latter said: "In the cities the Jews live compactly. They influence each other and keep each other Jews. Here in the small town we have the Gentile influence very strong and we live loosely and are assimilating. I don't believe in the future of the Jews in America. Today we are religionless, and although in the past we were scattered, we had our religion. But today we don't have it any more. The influence has been of the whole stream of life. We have tried to assimilate ourselves to them and their customs and ways. The differences in Jewish life here and in Russia are great. I say there is hardly any Jewish life here, that we live very little as Jews. There we lived really as Jews. And the differences that occur are in every branch of our life."

An elder P[1] generation Jew said, "No, here it is not like in the old country where religion was the whole life, where, on the high holidays, everybody came and stayed for the entire day. Why, I remember when I was a young boy, and I was sick. It was on a holiday and everybody was going to shul. I was sleeping, and my father, *alava sholom* [may his soul rest in peace], let me sleep. When I woke up and found everybody gone, I cried my eyes out

25. Incidents of beard pulling are reported by informants.

because I had not gone to shul. Even though I was sick, I went to shul anyway, and I remember how guilty and shameful I felt when I came into the shul late. Does anybody here feel that way? No. Why? Because there, the religion was the whole life. Here, it is nothing at all. There, a boy was brought up from his earliest days in the sacredest and holiest of religions. Here, he is taught little or nothing, and even the boy's own parents are not good examples. So how can you expect the children to be?"

To repeat the remarks of an elder P[1] Jew, partially quoted elsewhere: "In Europe the Goyim were a low class of *mujiks* [peasants] who were crude and ignorant and used to imitate the Jews. Here in America, however, the Jews imitate the Goyim. They are educated and have money, so now in the temples they take off their hats like in church. In the Mishna it is written that musical instruments must not be brought into the shul. In the reform temples they have organs like in church. So there you are; we copy the *Goy* inside the shul and outside the shul. That's why the home, the Shabas, the shul, are so changed. We are imitating someone else and forgetting that we are Jews."

An upper-middle-class P[2] Jew speaking for his generation said: "Here there are the younger Jews, whose parents are pious but who believe that if you do as the Christians do, things would be much easier. Therefore he drops his religion, wipes away the Jewishness from him."

But given the fact that the Jewish community system, once relatively closed and centripetal, is now open and centrifugally oriented to the Yankee City class system, does this altogether explain the disintegration of its religious subsystem? Admittedly it does not. The final factors responsible are a certain aspect of the religious system itself and a wide intellectual current running through Western societies.

Judaism, we have said, is a unitary system of legislation sanctioned and revealed by God. Transgression of the minutest edict is a sin and an offense to God. The moment that one edict is questioned, the authority of the entire system is challenged. As an elder P[1] Jew quoted above put it: "If they [the children] have to work [on the Sabbath], they also do other things they shouldn't do." A single note of skepticism may shatter an entire theological system. In the Jewish F[1] generation the Judaistic system is seen completely shattered. In the P[2] generation it is very nearly shattered.

A P[2] Jew describes the process: "When I first came over when

I was eighteen, I was as religious as anybody. I didn't do anything I wasn't supposed to do. But I had to get a job, and the only job I could get, I had to work on Saturday. So what could I do? The first Saturday I worked I felt as if I was committing an awful sin. The next Saturday was bad, but not as bad as the first. So, little by little, I got used to it. And now it doesn't bother me in the least. But that was only the beginning. Soon, because some boys made fun of me, I ate my first ham sandwich. The first bite I tried to swallow, but it wouldn't go down. I tried again, and still it wouldn't go down. The third time it slid down. I was sick all day. But I got over it, and now I like it. So I didn't go to shul on Saturday, I ate *trehf*, and I thought to myself: 'What's the use? If I've sinned so much, there's no use being a hypocrite.' So I gave up my ideas about trying to be orthodox and my ideas about sin. I did what was necessary and what I wanted to, and that was that. I may be a poor Jew, but say, I'm honest. Still I'm a Jew. I go to shul on Rosh Hashana and Yom Kippur and go to the Passover *seder* [feast] at my in-laws. This isn't much, but say, it is better than nothing."

The second factor is the general current of religious skepticism which dates from the second half of the nineteenth century and has swept through Western Europe and the United States, affecting vitally the Protestant churches. In no case was it made explicit by a Yankee City Jew, although it was reflected in the remark of the F[1] high-school boy who said, apropos of immortality: "If you can prove it to me, I will believe it."

This was the state of affairs in the Jewish community when in the summer months of 1932 three of the elder P[1] generation men died, reducing the daily congregation close to the minimum of ten. During and immediately after the high holidays in September, the community suddenly galvanized itself into a burst of organized action. In a period of a few weeks, through a series of mass meetings, close to $10,000 was raised within the community itself, and a church edifice, vacated by the merger of two Protestant churches, was purchased outright.

Let us consider the wider context of this phenomenon. The year was 1932, the second of the "Great Depression"; the Jews had lost heavily on their property and were all gloomy about business. The Hebrew school committee had just met and decided that it could no longer continue paying the teacher his salary unless he was willing to take a sizable reduction in pay. In these circumstances, and with one synagogue building more than adequate to accommodate the entire adult group, not to speak of the bare handful of old men who were daily worshipers, the community could arouse itself to the point of pouring out more than $100 per family, on the average, in order to purchase a new synagogue edifice.

The incident appears to be incongruous and completely non-logical. Several pertinent facts must be presented in order to prove how socio-logical were these extreme measures.

The synagogue edifice then being occupied had been bought in 1907, when the Jews were concentrated in residential Section I-A, and was located in the upper part of that section. It was a plain frame building, fronting on a narrow, unpaved alley-like street. Families of new ethnic groups lived all around it. The attitudes of all but the elder P^1 men toward this synagogue building were derisive. One P^2 woman said: "I attend the synagogue only on the high holidays. It's an ugly place to go." An F^1 boy, asked why he didn't attend synagogue services, replied: "The synagogue is dirty and the services are dull."

A P^2 man remarked at greater length: "The community will not stay in the present synagogue because it is below their dignity. They are ashamed of themselves to bring their own children to it. The present building was acquired twenty years ago, when the Jews were all 'greenhorns' and once belonged to the Salvation Army [lower class]. The reason that the synagogue is below the dignity of the Jewish community is the fact that it is situated in an old, plain house, on the second floor, with very bad furnishings, and is in the very poorest section of town."

The newspaper article announcing the purchase of the vacant church, however, offered the explanation that "the present building has been outgrown and a structure that is larger was wanted."

The new edifice is in Section II-B of the city's residential structure, close to Zone III, on a paved, tree-shaded street whose residents are predominantly middle-class natives. One of the speakers at the dedication of the building as a synagogue spoke of it as being "in a desirable section of the city . . . one that will make every Jew proud."

In the *Herald* article announcing the dedication, the remodeling of the church interior was described, with this addendum: "In making the changes, the Jewish people took care to follow the old architecture of the building. They believe they have one of the most beautiful places of worship in the city."

In the period immediately before the 1932 high holidays, the community was in a state of dysphoria, or collective melancholia, over the status of the synagogue structure. Interviews that touched on religion inevitably struck the note indicated below. One younger P[1] Jew said: "You ask about the ritual observances. Actually very few of the Jews observe the ritual, and, in all, no more than ten hold observance at all strictly. But I think that the Jews will maintain themselves in America because my faith takes precedence over logic. I feel that there will always be Jews."

An elder P[1] Jew said, "Sometimes we haven't even got enough men for a minyan, and we have to run out into the street to pull in somebody to make ten. Who knows what will happen to the Jews in America? But it says in the Bible that 990 Jews out of a thousand may be lost, but if only ten out of the thousand remain, God is satisfied. But always when the Jew was about to be assimilated, for example, in Babylonia, always when things were too good something happened. They were driven out and this made the Jews come together again. The Jew must always be reminded by suffering and, let me tell you, it will happen in America. You will see."

Both of these Jews despair of the future, since, as another informant expressed it: "If you take away religion from the Jew, there is nothing left for him by which he can be a Jew." That is, the disintegration of the synagogue structure implies ultimate disintegration of the community system. In view of these facts, one Jew had recourse to faith over logic, and the other cited Jewish history to prove that the Jews have persisted, notwithstanding that they were often "about to be assimilated." The implication that "things were too good" seems to point to class mobility as also a factor in the present situation. The elder P[1] Jew's historical statement, "always . . . something happened," proved prophetic only a month later.

From this general condition of dysphoria, the "drive" to secure the new building put the entire community into a condition of euphoria. In the interest of the "United Jewish Community," a mass meeting was held to plan for a new synagogue. The Jewish community turned out en masse, the investigator reporting that "every family was represented, with only one exception, namely, the one considered intellectual." Close to $6,000 was either paid or pledged on this occasion alone, the contributions ranging from $250 from the fathers to $5 and $10 from adolescents and single dollar bills from children as young as five.

Typical comments made by adults to the investigator at the

close of the meeting were: "This is the happiest day of my life. It's grand." "This is a new chapter in the history of the Yankee City Jews. The spirit was simply wonderful." "Everybody pledged more than they could pay. Especially in times like this, how people can scrape together the money for the new shul I don't know." A Jewish ex-resident of the city who was at the meeting said: "The community is certainly not normal now. Everybody is enthusiastic, inspired."

During the meeting a younger P[1] male arose to suggest "that Gentiles [of Yankee City] be approached for subscriptions." The suggestion was almost unanimously voted down, and the consensus of opinion after the meeting was expressed by the president of the Jewish Ladies' Aid Society when she said derisively: "It should not have been even mentioned." This attitude reflects an extreme tightening of the internal relations of the community around the internal crisis so that reference to the group's external relations was incongruous and not even to be "mentioned."

How these internal relations of the community system were all focused around the synagogue may be gathered from the fact that almost every adult above the age of twenty-five was represented on the various subcommittees working under the building committee.

Similarly, in the process of remodeling the building in order to convert it into a synagogue, many of the men volunteered their labor in order to avoid spending money for hired help. These were thanked publicly at a meeting by the president of the congregation.

Most striking of all, however, was the mobilization of the community associations. The Jewish Ladies' Aid Society started "the ball rolling" in the fund-raising campaign by giving the first donation—$1,000. Speaking for all the associations, an officer of the Junior Hadassah declared: "Now all organizations will be one—the shul. The Junior Hadassah will not have a chance to raise any money for itself. All contributions and all affairs will be for the shul. We won't make our quota [annual contribution to the national office] of $236. We will just hold affairs and turn over our profits to the shul fund."

Finally, we may quote from an interview with a member of the building committee: "We have never at any time in the last twenty-five years gotten all the Jews in the town to agree about anything. The new synagogue is something that all agree about. Every Jew in Yankee City has pledged money to it. And a number of Gentiles offered money. We tried to sidetrack it, since the Jewish community felt that they themselves should pay for it. If they make a sacrifice themselves, they would enjoy it better. They thought it was wrong to take Christian money.

"We took down young fellows who hang around the corners and showed them the new building, told them of our plans for the community center. They were all willing to work and were enthusiastic. They had worked for the Y.M.C.A., why shouldn't they do it for themselves? It woke up the entire Jewish community; it gave them something to look forward to. You know, the day of the meeting there were thirty-five people there to help clean up, even the older people." And he concluded: "Yes, everything is revolving around the synagogue. Everybody is working for it."

To understand this phenomenon, we must again turn to our generation classification. In the first place, it should be stated that the campaign, from first to last, was engineered not by the older P^1 men who had been the effective congregation, but by the P^2 and younger P^1 men who had not been members of the congregation and whose only articulation to the synagogue had been manifested on the high holidays.

The beginnings of the affair were described by the chairman of the building committee, who is of the P^2 generation and in the upper-middle class: "Recently this place on Jefferson Street came on the market. The first day of Rosh Hashana five of us [three P^2 and two younger P^1 men] went down to look at it, and from then on the thing grew. A committee was appointed with full authority and began negotiations. We wanted to know if the community was behind us, so we turned in a report not to buy the building because of the obstacles, and the moment we did this they all wanted it; in fact, the same group which was opposed to it before were now all for it. We said that we have no money and the people all said that the Jews are ready to give the money.

"We got the old men to turn their power over to the younger men so that we could reorganize things, elected officers, and we took in fifty-five new members [into the congregation] in one night. At our meetings there have been Jews who were never in a synagogue before."

The new officers of the congregation included five P^2, five younger P^1, and two elder P^1 men. At the time of this election, the members of the congregation had reached a new high of eighty, only twelve of whom were of the elder P^1 generation. But what were these younger men doing leading a campaign for a new synagogue building when some of them "were never in a synagogue before"? This question, in the course of intensive interviewing, was put in a less direct form to these very men. Their answers are illuminating.

One younger P[1] man replied: "We hope that the new shul will enthuse the younger people so they will come [to the synagogue] willingly." Another of this generation said: "A lot of us are not orthodox, but we all want the new shul. It will be a community center, plenty big, in a good neighborhood, and respectable. The middle-aged Jews are afraid of the younger generation, and are therefore taking [the synagogue] into their own hands."

These individuals seemed to say that the purpose of the community effort was to articulate the F[1] generation to the synagogue structure, but since the largest part (65 per cent) of this generation is still subadult and ineligible for membership in the congregation, there must be more to the situation than these answers reveal.

A few informants came closer to the truth in their replies. One P[2] Jew asserted: "The older people began to pass away and the younger people began to feel the responsibility, especially in the last few weeks."

In essence, therefore, a basic aspect of the phenomenon is the community crisis of age-grade movement. The elder P[1] generation, alone represented in the congregation, served to maintain the synagogue structure and to articulate the community with the extended religious system which is identified with the whole Jewish society. The dying out of these men carried the threat of extinction of the synagogue structure. This implied that the community would be severed first from the larger Jewish society; second, from its extended religious system; and third, from its traditional past. It would mean the collapse of the community as a Jewish community.

Under this threat, as several informants actually expressed it, of being left adrift and lost, the pressure of the community system compelled the age grades below the elder P[1] generation, i.e., the younger P[1] and P[2], to move up into the synagogue structure in order to keep it active in the community system. Every man in the younger P[1] and P[2] generations joined the congregation, fifty-five of them in one night.

The frequent emphasis upon bringing the F[1] generation into the synagogue fits into this interpretation. In any movement of an age-grade system, the lower age grades must be carried along.

In this instance, unless the F^1 generations, who had dropped the traditional religious behaviors almost altogether, were somehow related to the synagogue structure, they would fail to move into the structure when the present younger P^1 and P^2 generations passed away. Therefore, it was necessary not only for the adults below the elder P^1 generation to establish relations, somewhat less formal, to the synagogue structure. When the men interviewed said, "We must bring our children into the synagogue," they meant in effect, "We must bring our children into the synagogue *along with us.*"

There is a sentence in the souvenir program issued at a benefit affair for the Synagogue Fund which reads: "They [the Yankee City Jews] realized that they were building not only for the present, but for posterity."

It was symbolic that, at the dedicatory ceremonies of the new building, the four-year-old grandson of one of the leading P^1 elders was chosen to kindle the perpetual light which hangs above the Holy Ark in every synagogue.

Another highly important element of this age-grade movement, the attitude of the P^1 elders to their displacement from control positions in the synagogue structure, will be considered later in this chapter.

What is the relevance of the history of the new synagogue building to the movement of the age-grade generation system? The answer lies in the functions of both the old and new buildings as status symbols. The older building, in a lower-class area, was associated with the phase of the Jewish community when it was concentrated in this area and was largely lower class in status. By 1932, however, the Jewish group was residentially scattered, largely in Zone II, and the younger P^1 and P^2 generations were, with few exceptions, in the middle class. If these young adults were to move into the community synagogue structure, it was necessary that it be housed in an edifice that had adequate status value. The original building definitely lacked that value. It was therefore necessary to secure a new building, and this was found in the Protestant church building in the upper part of Section II-B. In the souvenir program already mentioned the need is expressed in somewhat rhetorical terms: "Even as a child outgrows its clothes, and the sleeves of its garments become too short, and the buttons will no longer fasten and keep the body warm and healthy—even so did the Jewish people of Yankee City outgrow their spiritual garment. There soon arose a demand for a larger, finer, and more noble edifice. Something greater was needed to keep the body of the community functioning properly."

Purchase and remodeling involved an outlay of close to $10,000, which for the size of the group and the condition of the times was a prodigious amount. Yet given the absolute necessity for movement of the younger adults into the synagogue structure and also the need for a structure that represented an adequate status symbol, the community worked itself up to the highest pitch of euphoria in order to acquire the new building and facilitate the age-grade movement into the synagogue structure.

The status value of the new building was important in relating the F^1 generation to the synagogue structure, as the chairman of the mass meeting stated in his speech: "The old people depended on the old building, but the young people were not interested. They came only on the high holidays and they would say, 'you are in the worst section of town,' and so they stayed away."

This seems to ascribe the religious desuetude of the F^1 generation entirely to the status value of the old synagogue building, a condition which, if corrected, would restore the religious orientation of this youngest generation. The behaviors of the Jews, however, indicate that their reason is less simple than this. Throughout the entire affair, their plans were directed to converting the new building not only into a house of worship but also—and explicitly—into a "community center," principally for the F^1 generation. One Jewish informant said: "We are only working for the shul because of the young people, in order to bring them in somehow, by giving them a nice place where they can dance and play." Providing recreational facilities has often been described in Jewish circles as "bringing the Jewish young people into the synagogue through the back door."

An expression of the recreational function of the synagogue is found in the following enthusiastic remarks of an officer of one of the F^1 associations: "You know, we, the Junior Hadassah, had our dance there [in the new synagogue], and it was a grand feeling. This auditorium and building was our own; we felt at home in it. It wasn't as if it were at the Masonic Temple, where we rent the hall and know that it is ours only for the evening. In the shul it is as if we are in our own home."

An entirely new development for the community, whose weddings had heretofore been held in Boston, is reported in the following: "Did you hear about the wedding that we had? It was the first wedding we had here in the shul and believe me, everybody was excited and thrilled. I think absolutely everybody in the community came."

Regarding the age-grade aspect of the situation as it affected the elder P men, it was immediately evident that the attitudes of some were ambivalent and that others were guardedly hostile, explicitly to the purchase of the new building, and implicitly to their displacement from the control offices in the congregation. One of them, a merchant who still lives in Section I-A, as do most of the elder P[1] families, said: "Ach, I don't know what to think of the new shul. What good is it? It's too far away. Here it is near, but there it is far. It takes a half hour to get there. You stay an hour, so that means two hours, and I can't take two hours. I have to open the store in the morning. We have to live, you know, so I won't be able to go. And the same thing with the others [P[1] elders]. So if they don't come every day, what good is the new shul?"

His statement, "I won't be able to go," in the face of his past behaviors in attending the synagogue daily seems to be an empty threat of withdrawal from the synagogue. Since the opening of the new synagogue, in fact, his attendance has been as regular as before.

"The new shul will bring in the young people—yes, to dance, to play cards. Put in a swimming pool and maybe they'll come. What good is it if they don't believe? In Europe when I was a boy the shul, *davening* [prayer], and the Sabbath was a holy thing. Here the boys laugh at it. It doesn't mean anything to them. If they don't believe, they won't come to the shul."

Another of the elder P[1] generation made this remonstrance: "We haven't many going to shul now. Why do we need a new shul? This one is big enough and good enough."

At one point after the new building was purchased, a few of these elders threatened secession on an issue of seating arrangements. An informant reports: "Mr. Leiber got sore and tried to get a group together to form a separate congregation in the old building. When the young men heard this—they are very smart—they went to the old building and took out the Torah [the Holy Scroll of the Law without which a synagogue is profane], which could have stayed a while, and everything else. That is, they stripped the building of all its holiness and therefore it was no longer a shul."

This antagonistic attitude on the part of the elder P[1] men must be considered in connection with their behaviors in contributing to the synagogue fund to the limit of their means and their verbal recognition of the community crisis. Their hostility is a corollary of the age-grade movement, which pushed them out of control of the synagogue structure.

However, this movement pushed them not only out but up, as seen in the attitudes of the younger men who treated the elders, for all the latter's antagonisms, solicitously, in a manner analogous to that used toward the "dying fathers" of Chinese society. For example, at the first mass meeting, contributions from two P^1 elders evoked this remark from the P^2 chairman: "I am happy to say that the older people are with us. Mr. Berg gives $50. Here is another contribution from the older generation that we are afraid about satisfying. One hundred dollars from Mr. Marcus." In the course of his address that evening the chairman said: "To the older men, I want to assure that we do not intend to disturb the ways of your worship. We want you to continue as you have in the past in your religious life."

More especially is this solicitous attitude seen in the compromises of the new synagogue officers on issues of "liberalizing" the synagogue. Not only were the younger men predicating their entrance into the synagogue structure on the acquisition of an edifice with adequate status value, but, in the beginning at least, they were determined to change the synagogue services from the strictly orthodox modes of the past to what are known generally in American Jewish communities as "conservative" services. The latter are characterized by omission of daily services, although this is optional; celebration of the Sabbath on Friday night instead of Saturday mornings; reading important parts of the service, such as the benedictions, in both Hebrew and English; sermons, when there is a rabbi, in English; and seating the congregation without regard to sex.

Before the community mobilization took place, a P^2 Jew's remarks indicated the direction these younger men were taking: "The orthodox synagogue has had no influence at all on the young people. You see, religion must be modernized to be accepted. I don't believe personally in going to the other extreme of Reform; but I believe that liberal Judaism can be a great influence. If you take way religion from the Jew, there is nothing left for him by which he can be a Jew. The Nationalists feel that the Jewish nation in Palestine alone will keep the Jew. But even with the Jewish state, the Jew in the Diaspora must have religion. Without it he loses all of his Jewishness. Judaism has applicability in modern times. But I mean liberal Judaism. It happens that because I am in an orthodox community I have to belong to the orthodox synagogue. But it's all very halfhearted. It's only lately that orthodoxy has come to a standstill. We have stopped fitting ourselves to the environment and to modern times, which orthodoxy in the past has always done before. The Catholic Church in America has adapted itself—has fitted itself to conditions—and it is one of the strongest religious bodies in the country. Jewish orthodoxy will not yield one iota, although in the past it has always adapted itself, else it could not have lived as long as it has. The Judaism of Babylonia was altogether different from that of Russia. I cannot explain why orthodoxy no longer adapts itself. Orthodoxy at present is a European orthodoxy, whereas American liberal Judaism is really an adapted form of orthodoxy.

"Martin Luther, just as Moses Mendelssohn, attempted to modernize and to bring religion into the common language of the people. The young people of today need the Bible in the language that they can understand. Of course Reformed Judaism has gone too far, has become an ethical culture society, rather than a religion. I have the most respect and veneration in the world for the Reformed rabbis; they are great scholars. But I cannot accept Reformed Judaism. It is too Christianized."

Here is seen a clear instance of the change of content in a church structure. For the changes proposed, while not altering the fundamental representations of Jewish orthodoxy, reflect the changing elements in the personalities of these younger Jews, especially those of the P^2 generation. By adaptation of Judaism "to the environment and to modern times," the informant means adaptation to his type of personality, which, containing American elements to an important degree, has radically moved away from Orthodox Judaism. For this type of personality to return to the synagogue it has left, the synagogue must be altered to "fit" that personality. It must be "liberalized": it must relax its unbending, rigorous prescription of behavior after an ancient pattern in a social system that can make no place for such a pattern. Evidence from the informants is that the movement of the P^2 social personality toward the American type has not proceeded so far as to eliminate its fundamental orientation to the Judaistic religious system.

It is noteworthy that the movement of the P^2 Jews, who had been so markedly dissociated from it, into the synagogue structure was justified by their relations to the American social system. For example, a P^2 upper-middle-class Jew, a leader in the campaign, after discussing how the younger Jews had thrown over their Jewishness, said: "The young men have found out that even to have the Christians like us, we should go to the synagogue. A Jew who is an honest Jew and takes an interest in his synagogue, that is, in his community, is really liked better by the Gentiles. A Christian who is a customer of mine told me that he would have more faith in one who was an observing Jew than in one who denied his religion." This is a man who, previous to the community's "drive" for a new synagogue building, had been described as being "removed from the shul and the community."

These remarks refer to personality development in ethnic communities generally and specifically to its second and third phases as presented in the previous chapter. After having dissociated themselves from their community system and oriented themselves instead to the American social system, a process designated as the second phase, the P^2 personalities have returned to their community and synagogue.

In spite of the determination of the younger men to change the new synagogue structure to conform with their own personality pattern, they did so only in certain significant details. The evidence indicates that they were constrained by consideration for the P^1 elders. Throughout the speeches and press notices during the campaign, no mention was made of reforms in the direction of what is called Conservative Judaism. However, cautious reference was made to "semi-orthodoxy," "liberal orthodoxy," and "modern orthodoxy." The larger view of the younger men, however, is revealed in the remark of one P^2 Jew: "The older people, of course, are strict, but the younger ones are liberal. However, the new congregation is not going to be liberal because the younger people still have their parents and they [the parents] cannot break away from their practices. But when the old people die they will change the synagogue to the liberal ritual."

Nevertheless, certain members of the P^2 generation were frankly impatient with the congregation officers at delaying "liberalization" out of regard for the older men. One P^2 woman said petulantly: "I don't see why they insist on keeping the synagogue orthodox when almost everybody except the old are liberal."

On the issue of the seating arrangements of the sexes the P^2 men, under the prodding of their wives, pushed through a compromise reform, described in the last chapter. This one detail especially illustrates the correlation between changing personality and changes in the content of a religious system. This single reform expresses a change in the evaluation, status, and participation of the women in the synagogue cult.

In the controversy over the seating arrangement, the younger P^1 men among the executive committee (officers and directors) sided with the P^2 men, although the latter were the more active. During the first Yom Kippur after the dedication of the new synagogue the large middle section, reserved for family units, was almost empty except for P^2 families. These, of course, are far outnumbered in the group by P^1 families. The younger P^1 families, with only two exceptions, separated to sit in the outer male and female sections which were well filled. In other words, the younger P^1 parents, although in many instances sympathetic with the P^2 generation on the seating issue, actually behaved in conformity with the strict letter of the Law.

That the new synagogue is serving its functions and has brought in those who had been outside is indicated in the investigator's report: "Attendance at the new synagogue, on the high holidays, I was told, was 100 per cent, which I confirmed in Yom Kippur. There were approximately five hundred present at the *Kol Nidre* services on Yom Kippur eve, including many out-of-town relatives and friends. Whereas formerly local families went to their relatives in other cities for the high holidays, the new synagogue has reversed this movement. The average attendance at Sabbath services is about 125, which contrasts with the average of thirty in 1932."

7. Summary

THE two Christian church structures, here described and analyzed in certain limited, selected aspects, reveal for all their changes that, compared to the other structures in their respective community systems, they have been the most resistant in the interaction of social systems. Those changes that were observed were not induced by the conformative pressures of the religious subsystem of the American society but have come indirectly through changes in the patterns of their component family structures and personality systems.

The Irish Church has shifted in its national orientation until today it may be said to be an American Catholic Church rather than Irish Catholic. Its concessions to alterations in the family structure have not been made through its own agency but under the legislation of the extended church. Its principal direction of change, however, has been in proliferation of associational auxiliaries, to be described in a following chapter.

The Greek community and its church especially are of too recent development to admit generalizations. Nevertheless, the Greek Church illustrates the general integrative function performed by a church structure for its community system, together with the correlated rise in the traditional status and expansion of functions of the priest associated with the church. The church structure stands in somewhat the same position to its community in Yankee City that the national church subsystem did to the national society when the latter had been deprived of formal nationhood by a dominating political entity.

The impact of American society directly on the Jewish personality, however, was seen to shake the Yankee City synagogue structure to its foundations. The crisis, upon the death of the P^1 elders and the movement of the younger men into their position, served to reorganize the structure on a pattern far more harmonious with its American context. The rigid orthodox mold, which has been little changed in fifteen hundred years, in Yankee City has been broken down and been reassembled to fit the changing Jewish personality.

The ethnic groups in Yankee City are within a social system that demands conformity on all its sectors, and secures it both by its positive prizes of class mobility and by its negative constraints on the deviant within it. The church structure to an ethnic group threatened with loss of identity serves more than any other structure to organize the group as a community system. No clearer demonstration of this fact is needed than that presented by the differences between the Protestant North Irish in Yankee City and the Catholic South Irish. From the fact that the 1930 United States Census figures for Yankee City list about one hundred of the former as being either foreign born or native born of foreign-born parents, i.e., P and F^1 generations, and from other evidence also, it may be assumed that there are several hundred additional North Irish in the city who are of the F^2 and F^3 generations. The known hundred North Irish originally presented few differences from the South Irish beyond their church orientations. Yet the North Irish, even those who were adult immigrants, are undifferentiated from the native population, whereas the South Irish, through their Catholic Church structure, present themselves in a highly organized community system with the Yankee City social system. Within that community system, moreover, are members of the F^3 generation whose great-grandparents were migrants to Yankee City almost a century ago. P^1 North Irish have been directly assimilated by Yankee City. F^2 South Irish only now are close to assimilation.

VIII

LANGUAGE AND THE SCHOOL

IN this chapter we shall be concerned with the ethnic school—
that structure in the ethnic community which had as its original function the organization and orientation of the ethnic
filial generations to the linguistic, historical, and religious aspects
of the ancestral society.

1. *Generation Shifts in Language Usage*

LANGUAGE, that system of defined and meaningful verbal forms
which is the medium of social relations, is an absolute necessity
of a social system. But it is not only the medium of social relations at any given moment of time; it is also the medium by which
the cultural forms of a society are transmitted from one point in
time to another. It is indispensable for the persistence of a social
system. It is the abiding framework by which a society appears as
the "concrescence," to use Whitehead's term,[1] of its past. Language, therefore, is inextricably interwoven with the social system of which it is part. Hence, it is of importance in the ethnic
community systems of Yankee City. Before considering the structural form of the ethnic schools, instrumental agencies in the
maintenance of ethnic languages, special attention will first be
given to the linguistic aspects of these systems.

Among the most recent ethnic groups, the Poles and the Russians, the P[1] wives have known little if any English. As already
noted in the analysis of the husband-wife relation in the family
structure of these communities, the wives are as yet strongly
bound to the home and, with few exceptions, rarely venture out of
it even for purchases at the Polish or Russian stores. The P[1] men
use the native tongue exclusively in their relations with each
other, although in their external relations those who are of the
pre-1918 migrations use a passable, broken English. Post-1918
arrivals know only enough English to "get by" in the factories,
which often is not enough to carry on a conversation for purposes
of an interview.[2]

1. A. N. Whitehead, *Adventure of Ideas* (New York, The Macmillan Co., 1932),
pp. 303, 304.
2. Parenthetically, it may be said that the close relations between the Polish

The investigator reported of a Russian storekeeper: "He regards Polish as almost as much his mother tongue as Russian." A questionnaire distributed among the school children of Yankee City included one question relating to ethnic language which a number of children, Russian as well as Polish, answered with "Polish and Russian." The P^1 generation in these two groups each uses its native tongue predominantly, the language of the related group second, and English a weak third.

The factors for the linguistic differentiation between the P^1 generation and the F^1 generation have already been reviewed in the analysis of the parent-child relation. Specific manifestations of this differentiation may be considered here.

The pre-adolescents of the F^1 Polish and Russian groups speak English with almost as much ease as they do the parental tongue. Before the age of thirteen or fourteen, the F^1 child's personality has not diverged sufficiently from the ethnic pattern to provoke any reaction against the ethnic language. A clear dichotomy is made between the internal relations and the external relations and the language that goes with each. How far it may carry is revealed by a young F^1 Polish mother who said: "The rising third generation [F^2] is interesting. Of course, Polish is a hard tongue, and I don't understand all of it myself. I know only the short words. My boy is five and not in school yet. But he won't speak Polish to me; but he does speak Polish to my mother, who can't talk American. He says that I am an American and so is his daddy [who is a native], so why should he speak anything but American to us."

As the F^1 child's personality develops toward greater orientation to the external relations, a reaction sets in against the ethnic language, provoking antagonisms in the parents. For example, a Polish father said, "Yes, my children still speak Polish. But when they grow up they forget it. I have a son seventeen who doesn't speak it or understand more than half of it, and he used to do both good."

It is this element which seems to account for the failure of a number of school children to answer questions in the school questionnaire as to ethnic languages spoken by them. In large part these were children in high school, often having younger brothers and sisters who had no compunction about writing the answer. A

and Russian groups, to be described later, have language as their principal basis. They are familiar with each other's language, the Poles especially being acquainted with Russian, for the reason stated by an informant: "Our tongue was not allowed to be taught in Poland. Everyone had to know Russian."

few high-school students, in whose homes Polish and Russian are spoken exclusively, even went so far as to answer "none" to the question.

From the fact that this generation development has reached a further stage among the Greeks, and from the fact that the Greek language is associated with a longer cultural tradition, the Greeks are more explicit and more defensive in the expression of their conflicting attitudes to the problems of duality of language. Through their language modern Greeks feel themselves immediate kin of Homer, Pythagoras, Hippocrates, and Plato. The intensity of this feeling of kinship with Greek culture is made explicit in the following statement of a Yankee City P[1] Greek who was discussing the reasons for sending his children to the local Greek school: "I want my children to say, 'We are Greek, and our fathers were Greek,' even though they have been in this country one, or two, or three generations. It doesn't matter to me after I'm dead, but I'd like to know that they'll always say it. So I want my children to know the language, so they can know something about the history and philosophy."

Another Greek declared: "The Greek people are interested in education. They want the children to learn the Greek language. A person who can't be a good Greek can't be a good American. While we have the schools we want them to know the language, to know what they come from. If they understand the language, then they can understand the philosophy and all the Greek ideas." To be a "bad" Greek, in other words, is to be a "bad" American, and orientation to both cultural traditions apparently is held to be a virtue in both systems.

The defensive aspect is expressed in the remarks of a Greek informant: "You must know other languages. Since the children know Greek anyhow, why not keep it up? When certain Americans say 'Why keep your language? This is one flag, one country, and one language,' they're crazy!"

This conflict sets the problem for the Greek immigrant in Yankee City. Within the relations defined by the Greek community of which he is a part, he remains linguistically a Greek. Within the family circle and at the coffee house he speaks Greek. Closed meetings of the Greek American Progressive Association and services of the church are conducted in Greek. The newspapers and books he reads, which coördinate all the relations he has in these structures, are in Greek. But the moment he steps out of these closed-community relations, he steps into another order

of relations which are organized around other than Greek representations, and within which communication is effected through
the English language. The life of the Yankee City Greek consists
of a shuttling back and forth between his internal Greek relations
and his external American relations.

Therefore, the Greek must learn English as the language of
the society which surrounds his closed community system, and he
becomes bilingual. But the P^1 individual acquires English by the
slow and painful method of the foreign visitor, picking up the
basic words and filling out the vocabulary through increasing
contacts with the host society. Even so, there is little probability
that English can for him supplant or even challenge the Greek
language. Greek is inseparably a part of his personality; and his
basic relations are centered in the closed Greek community structure where only the Greek language is spoken.

How these internal relations influence the bilingual disposition
of the P^1 Greek is suggested in the following excerpt: "After I
came to Yankee City I studied hard and learned to talk English,
and I passed my citizenship exams with high marks. But after I
was married I forgot some of my English, for then I talked Greek
at home and did not use English as much, and so my English was
poorer than it was before I was married." This individual arrived
in this country in 1910 and his wife followed ten years later. Their
family relations tended to pull the husband back to a proportionately greater use of Greek.

Bilingualism is one manifestation of the dual social situation
which every ethnic personality attempts somehow to integrate.
But the two systems are not composed of comparable elements,
and the best the ethnic can do is to move from one linguistic system to the other. For example, the Greek just quoted, when told
that there were Poles who had been here almost as long as he had
who could not speak English, replied: "Greeks over here want to
learn American. They are ashamed to speak Greek out loud on
the streets and in public; they may talk Greek at home or with
their friends, but not among strangers. Other people like the
Poles never learn any as they talk their own language everywhere, even on the streets, and don't try to learn."

The trucks carrying Sunday School children to their annual
picnic carried signs which were printed in both Greek and English. At the important Greek-American Progressive Association
Ball, which many prominent American guests attended, the ceremonial speeches were all in English with the exception of that of

the deputy governor of the G.A.P.A. who, after defensively apologetic remarks in English, spoke in Greek. In the memorial services at the Greek graves, the Greek priest first gives the prayers in Greek, then repeats them in English. The issue becomes especially clear in a Greek informant's apology for the fact that the play by the Greeks for the Relief Fund show was not performed in English. His explanation was: "The actors do not speak English well enough."

Here is observed the feeling that not only should the Greeks be able to speak English in their external relations but in their participation in American rituals they should speak it relatively well. This is again brought out in an interview with a Greek immediately following the arrival of the new priest of the local Greek church. "The new priest doesn't speak any English. He's been over only four or five years, and speaks very little English. But he ought to be able to understand it and talk it. Now tomorrow he'll have to say some prayers at the Memorial Day rites at the American cemetery. To come in contact with people he ought to be able to give them in English, but to do it, he'll have to have them translated, because he can't do it himself."

For all their loyalty to the mother tongue, the Greeks feel that at least they must not isolate themselves linguistically from the American society. There is compulsion to accept English as a necessary *modus operandi* for achieving accord with the host society. Conflict therefore arises between the use of the two languages.

We have seen that in most cases the attempt is made to resolve the conflict by defining distinct social spheres for each language. This, however, only serves to accentuate the conflict by creating a sharp dichotomy between the two social systems—the internal Greek and the external American. The futility of this dichotomy is shown in the illustrations given above of crossing between the two systems. When Americans participate in Greek rituals, when Greeks participate in American rituals such as Memorial Day, and when Greek rituals, such as the picnic, take place in the "open," the conflict is pointed, and the only resolution is to be apologetic and defensive.

However, there is a more general effort of the Greeks to resolve the problem by stating it in intellectual terms and by emphasizing the educational value of multilingualism. There is, for example, the statement of the Greek coffee-shop owner: "I like for my children to learn the Greek language. Some people don't care, but I think it's nice for them to talk Greek just like I do and my parents do, and it helps them in school. Sometimes you see Americans that learn to speak Greek. They have to know some language in school. It's always better to know more than one language."

The teacher of the Greek school, educated in Greece, carried this reasoning one step further when he said: "I am very proud that all the Greek children here can speak at least two languages and lots of them more. In our home country nearly all educated Greek who go through what compares to your high school can speak four or five languages." Here the two levels of thought are fused by extending bilingualism to the traditions of Greece.

On another occasion, however, this same teacher in defending the teaching of Greek to the Greek children showed the conflict more ingenuously when speaking of the benefits to the Greek children of learning to read and write Greek. He explained that a number of words in English come from the Greek language and went over a list of them. He then looked through a newspaper, pointing to the words which are derived from the Greek. He said it helps the children to know Greek since it increases their English vocabulary.

The foregoing demonstrates that in the minds of the P generation Greeks the linguistic issue resolves itself into two essential conflicts: (1) the compulsion to adopt English, yet the inability to accept or master it completely because they are still largely oriented to the internal Greek system; and (2) the compulsion to impose the Greek language upon the children, yet their inability to do so because the P generation themselves are part, ultimately, of the external American system. Hence the P generation are defensive in their attitudes toward the English language and even more defensive in their attitudes toward their own Greek speech.

What are the consequences of the linguistic conflict upon the F generation Greeks? Certain factors in the situation are altered. The Greek language, defensively imposed by the parents, is the language of the child's home and of the Greek school. English, however, is the child's language in the public schools and in his play relations with other children, both American and Greek.

Therefore, the young child, like his parents, uses Greek speech for closed and English for open relations. This is the testimony of a young P^2 Greek mother about her seven-year-old daughter: "This thing about speaking Greek. Poppy won't speak Greek except when she is alone with the family, never in cars, or when there are other children, or when there are English-speaking people around. So we have arranged that we speak Greek at home and English when we are out with people where English is spoken."

A Greek father of pre-adolescent children reveals something of the processes involved in the bilingual behavior of his children: "I have a little girl who hasn't gone to school yet, but she talks English just as well as she does Greek. She learned them just about the same time. Whenever she is out playing with other little children she hears them talking English, and then she hears the older children speaking English around the home a bit, and she learns very fast. My older children too learned to speak English almost as soon as they learned to speak Greek. They speak Greek at home and speak English when they are away from home. Of course, they never hear Greek when they are out on the streets with other children or when they go to school, but a lot of the women can't speak much English so they have to talk Greek in the home. My children, if you speak to them in Greek, they'll answer in Greek. If you speak to them in English, they'll answer in English." In other words, the pre-adolescent child is conditioned by different sets of factors, each of which predisposes him to act in one of two different linguistic ways. These frames of reference are:

1. *The social system.* An internal Greek relation is associated with the Greek language, and an external American relation is associated with English. Introduction into one or the other of these systems will elicit the language appropriate to it, almost automatically, and the child can shift effortlessly from one language to the other with the shifts in framework.

2. *The linguistic framework.* Whether in an internal relation or an external relation, the use of either Greek or English as a linguistic framework will elicit in the child a response to fit the linguistic framework established. In essence, the linguistic framework is torn out of its system context and set up in another; that is, a young child addressed by an American in Greek will generally respond in Greek, and if a Greek addresses him in English, his response will be in English. Because of the incongruities of frameworks, the situation is socially artificial, hence more or less unsettling, and considerable effort is required of the child to adapt himself.

That there may be explosive consequences from this mixing of frameworks is illustrated by the following account of a P² Greek mother: "Annie didn't speak any English until she was about three years old. Once we took her to play with a little boy, and he hit her over the head. His mother was surprised. She said he never hit other children over the head, she couldn't understand it. It was because Annie couldn't understand him when he was speaking English. All she knew was, 'No, no,' and she said it so much that it got on his nerves, and he hit her.''

The bilingual disposition obtains for the child while he is still young and firmly anchored to the family structure. During this state he maintains the same dichotomy of social systems as does his parent. But as he rises in public school and his proficiency in English develops, he is increasingly exposed to American symbols. As he extends his external relations in wider and wider circles, the orientation of his personality is progressively shifted from the ancestral Greek system to the American system. There can be no question that his orientation would shift in time completely to the American system were it not for the restraint of his family and the Greek community, exercised through its school, church, and associations.

This process is clearly indicated in the child's linguistic behavior. The parent's attachment, of course, is basically and irrevocably to the Greek language; English is superimposed upon him only to the extent of his necessary minimum participation in the open American society. The child, on the other hand, through school and play influences, attaches himself strongly to English. His family and the Greek school press the Greek language upon him, but only after he has already broken through the Greek linguistic system into the English system. He enters the Greek school at the age of seven or eight and is formally taught the elements of the Greek language. However, he has already been in the Yankee City public school a year or two, and with the widened external relations opened by his participation in that important American structure, the emphasis on the respective languages has begun to shift. The Greek school has the function of keeping the child rooted to the Greek language while this development is taking place. As the child develops, his use of English extends, and however fixed in number his internal Greek relations remain, his use of Greek diminishes as his use of English increases. The artificiality and incongruity of the ancestral language in the American context grow upon him. At first this is expressed in his unwillingness to continue in the Greek school which he is constrained by his parents to attend. He completes the work of the Greek school after five years, or at about the same time that he leaves grammar school to enter high school. It is at this point that he breaks out in open revolt against the Greek language.

For example, a Greek father admits the following of his two sons who are in high school: "The trouble is they don't want to use the Greek language. If I ask my boys to read me something in Greek, they don't want to do it. If I want to write a letter in Greek to the old country, they won't hardly do it. Children don't like to use the language. If I ask them to write something in English, that is all right." In what is still a strongly patriarchal family, these boys resist the parental dictates that they read or write Greek.

A Greek mother, of the P^2 generation, can be more sympathetic with the F generation's linguistic antagonisms: "So many children hate Greece, the name of Greece, everything Greek, because they have been made to learn Greek. Then, when they grow up, they give it up entirely. The English language is their mother language. It comes first. We try to be an example for other families; we don't force the children to speak Greek."

Among the Jews the linguistic situation is at once more complex and developed. To understand its complexity it is necessary to refer to the linguistic history of the Jews.

Hebrew was the language of the Israelites at the time they settled in Canaan and Palestine *circa* 1400 B.C., although it is not clear whether they brought it with them from the northeast or borrowed it from the Canaanites. There is no question that throughout the thousand years of their tenancy of Palestine, Hebrew remained both the spoken and written language. It ceased to be a colloquial language, however, after the fifth century B.C., when it gave way to Aramaic. After the beginning of the Diaspora, and with the spread of Islam in the seventh and eighth centuries, the Jews replaced Aramaic with Arabic. In the twelfth century Arabic in turn gave way to the then emerging Romance languages, especially Spanish. In Germany of that time, the Jews spoke the same German as the Christians. And in the succeeding centuries, when they were segregated in ghettos, the old forms of Middle High German were preserved but many Hebrew words were added. The conglomerate finally became set in a modified Hebrew alphabet. It was this "jargon," as it was explicitly called, which was carried by the German Jews in their migration, from the thirteenth century on, into the Polish kingdom. In Russia, also, the Jews spoke Yiddish. But it was a profane language, and the low esteem in which it was held is suggested by the Jews' own refusal to consider it a language and their insistence upon calling it a "jargon." Not until the middle of the nineteenth century with the appearance of a written literature in that tongue has the name "Yiddish" been used to any great extent. On the other hand, Hebrew remains the *Loshen Kadish*, the Sacred Language, read in the synagogue liturgies and in the familial festivals, and taught the boys in the *Chedarim* or schools. Any male above the age of thirteen not able to read and write Hebrew would have been stamped either an idiot or a heathen. To the two languages, the spoken Yiddish and the written Hebrew, most Jews added Polish or Russian. The Jews in the Russian Empire were trilingual: there was the language spoken exclusively in the external relations with the Russian social system; there was the profane "jargon" used exclusively in their internal relations; and there was the sacred language used only ritualistically in the synagogue, in the family structures, and in the school structures.

The steadfastness of Hebrew throughout all the changes in the spoken tongue has served, first, to keep the Jew bound to the long cultural tradition framed and preserved in the continuity of Hebrew as the ritual, literary, and scholastic language. Throughout the wide dispersion of the Jews since early in the Christian era, Hebrew and the sacred cultural tradition which it framed remained the integrative basis for a social system which lacked the fundamental basis of a single geographical locus.

This recognition of the importance of Hebrew appears throughout the enormous Jewish literature on Jewish society. A modern writer[3] states:

Without the Hebrew language we will become severed from the great tree which is life unto those that cling to it. Hellenistic Judaism is the only one in history which dared to make the experiment of dispensing with the Sacred Language. The result was death. It withered away and terminated in total and wholesale apostasy from Judaism. Let us not deceive ourselves. There is no future in this country for Judaism that resists either the English or the Hebrew language.

What then is the linguistic usage of the Yankee City Jews? Polish and Russian have been dropped altogether, as shown in the investigator's report: "I have not heard a single instance of the use of Polish or Russian. The P[1] generation Jews admit they

3. Solomon Shechter, *Studies in Judaism*, quoted by J. H. Hertz in *A Book of Jewish* (New York, Block Printing Co., 1926), p. 15.

understand one or both but never speak them. Common language has not produced relations between the Jews and the local Poles or Russians as it has between these two latter groups. The few relations found between the Jews on one side and the Poles and Russians on the other are purely economic ones occurring in the Jewish stores, and for these English is used. On rare occasions the Jewish storekeeper may introduce a Polish phrase, and the Poles will respond in kind. Both will be amused but the talk will continue in English." In the context of Russian-Polish society the Jew used Polish in his relations with Poles; in the American context he uses English. The P^2 generation Jew, on the other hand, does not understand either Polish or Russian. He was still a child when he migrated, and the little he knew of these languages was quickly forgotten after arrival in Yankee City.

The English language, which among the P^1 generation replaces Polish or Russian as the medium of exchange relations, is used with varying facility and thick accent. The women are not as developed in their command of English as are the men although, with the exception of a few aged among them, they can all carry on conversations without difficulty. Communication in the P^1 generation's internal relations continues primarily in Yiddish, onto which have been grafted many English words.

Children of P^1 parents, to judge from their answers to the school questionnaire, all understand Yiddish. They have rarely, however, been heard to use it. Generally the P^1 parents speak to the children in Yiddish only, and the children respond in English, even in extended discussions. In a considerable number of cases, however, Yiddish has broken down completely between parent and child, and only English is used. The parents, however, continue to converse with each other in Yiddish.

Thus, in the Jewish P^1 family, the husband-wife relation is characterized by Yiddish exclusively, although in the parent-child relation Yiddish and English occur in conjunction or English appears alone. This family structure is completely bilingual and there is a different linguistic orientation of the two generations.

English has penetrated deeply into even the P^1 family, but apparently without the strains and antagonisms noted in the other ethnic groups. The F^1 child will flare up, as did one Jewish boy, at the parent's use of Yiddish in an American context. But this is directed not so much at Yiddish as at the parent who does not observe the distinction between internal and external relations. Of the Jewish children who filled out the school questionnaire, not one of those in high school failed to answer the question with respect to language spoken. This is in contrast to the number of Greek and Polish children who refused to answer the question at all.

The essential situation, then, is that while the children of P¹ Jewish parents consistently use English in both their external and internal relations, they are not actively antagonistic, as are the Greek and Polish children, to their parents' language. The responsible factor is that the Jewish parents do not place such critical value on Yiddish as do the P¹ parents in other ethnic groups on their ethnic language. Their attitude is still that Yiddish is a jargon, and they have made no organized attempt to perpetuate it by imposing it on their children in the community school, where emphasis is placed almost exclusively on Hebrew. The parent has not resisted the child's orientation to English and has in many cases come to adopt English in his speech with the children. English not only has come to replace Polish or Russian as the language of external relations but is in process of replacing Yiddish in the internal relations of the P¹ generation and its offspring.

English is not in any sense a competitive language to Hebrew as it is to the ethnic languages of the other groups. Hebrew, at least until its recent revival in the Jewish communities of Palestine, was not conceived as a language of ordinary speech but one to be read, to be studied, and to be spoken only in ritualistic intercourse with God and the sacred symbols of the synagogue. It is in Hebrew, not in Yiddish, that the society's traditions are represented. In the community Hebrew school the parents have made provision for the children's acquisition of the Hebrew language and literature but no provision, as will be seen in the analysis of the school's curriculum, for Yiddish. With this basic orientation to Hebrew, therefore, the displacement of Yiddish by English has few of the implications that displacement of the ethnic language has for the other groups. The defection from the ethnic language by the Polish and Greek children implied their defection from the traditions of the parents and their social system. The Yankee City Jews, on the other hand, so long as their children remain anchored to Hebrew, do not take their shift from Yiddish to English as a critical matter. Hence the Jewish parents exhibit little of the defensiveness and the children few of the antagonisms that were observed among the other groups toward the ethnic language.

The Hebrew anchorage, however, is most important. A P^2 Jewish mother remarked: "My son attends the Hebrew school. Almost all the children here do. It's a good thing. We don't speak Jewish at all in my house, and I'd like my son to know something about his own people from the Hebrew school."

With the P^2 generation parents, Yiddish disappears from the family altogether, and English is used in its place. The P^2 mother just quoted is typical. Although most of the P^2 parents have been through the Yankee City schools, their English is marked by a varying accent which in no case, however, is as extreme as that of the P^1 generation. Their retention of Yiddish is usually complete, but the only occasions on which they use it are community meetings attended by the P^1 elders or in conversations with the latter. With their wives and children, conversation is all English. Here is a significant contrast between the linguistic behaviors of the P^2 generation and those of the F^1 generation in their common relations with the P^1 generation.

Since in the P^2 home only English is spoken, the result is that, whereas the F^1 child could understand Yiddish but would not speak it, the child of P^2 parents is capable of neither. In an F^1 association of young adult females, affiliated with a national Zionist organization, an officer reported: "We tried a Jewish meeting last night and only seven girls showed up, so we couldn't hold it. Three girls went to the show and came when the meeting was almost over. Can you imagine such nerve? One of them, the Berg girl, said snippily, 'Well, why should I come up to the meeting? I can't speak Jewish; I can't even understand it.' " The seven girls who made their appearance were all daughters of P^1 parents. Those absent were all the daughters of P^2 parents.

A further and significant change on the P^2 generation level is the marked weakening of Hebrew. It is to be remembered that this group, in contrast with the P^1 generation, migrated while still children, and thus their prescribed Hebrew education was cut short. All that remains of it in many instances is the ability to read Hebrew, but the meanings of the words are forgotten. This is by no means general, for there are others of the P^2 men who know their Hebrew as well as some of the P^1 men.

In summary, the Jewish parental generations and the filial generation show a greater development in their linguistic behaviors than do the corresponding generations in the ethnic groups thus far reviewed. The Jews are trilingual and can keep Hebrew from fatal competition with English. They do not exhibit the conflict which accompanied the linguistic orientations of the other ethnic groups.

The French Canadians are an older group in Yankee City than are the Jews, and the progressing dominance of English over the ethnic tongue observed among the preceding groups here reaches its culmination.

A factor governing the situation in the French-Canadian groups is that only 20 per cent of the parents of children of grammar school age are P^1. In other words, the parents in this group are now predominantly of the F^1 and F^2 generations, a fact which has predictable consequences for the linguistic behaviors of their children. A qualifying condition is that the French-Canadian school, unlike those of the groups previously discussed, does not supplement the public schools and seek the orientation of the child to only the three categories of ethnic representations, but is a full-time parochial school that functions to orient the child to both French-Canadian and American representations. Instead of the child's being offered each representational system in separate and competing school structures, the public and the ethnic, his personality is organized around both systems within one school structure. The French-Canadian parochial school may therefore be expected to restrain more effectively the defections of progressive generations from the French language. This expectancy is partially negated, however, by the fact that of the two-hundred-odd French-Canadian families with children between the ages of six and fourteen only one fourth send their children to the French-Canadian parochial school; 11 per cent send them to the Irish parochial school; and the rest to the public schools.

The linguistic orientations of successive F generations of French Canadians may be determined more accurately from the results of the school questionnaire which was distributed in every one of the public schools and in the Irish parochial school. Permission was denied only in the French-Canadian schools. However, in the public and Irish schools French-Canadian children from one hundred families returned the questionnaires. Although the sample is small, the trend is clear.

The following table is compiled from the responses to the question, "What language other than English do you speak?" Children who are the offspring of a marriage between a French Canadian and either an Irish ethnic or a native are distinguished from the children of wholly French-Canadian marriages by an "x" following the generation designation. Generation is computed on the basis of the generation of the French-Canadian parent.

Child's Generation	No. of Families Whose Children Speak French	No. of Families Whose Children Do Not Speak French	Total
F^1	12	6	18
F^1_x	1	13	14
F^2	14	17	31
F^2_x	1	23	24
F^3	0	3	3
F^3_x	0	10	10

The figures are, of course, inconclusive in themselves since the sample covers only those French Canadians in the public and Irish schools. Those fifty families having children in the French-Canadian school are almost evenly divided between the F^1 and F^2 generations, and it may reasonably be expected that they all speak French. Of the forty-eight "mixed" families, the children of only two speak French.

The linguistic shifts suggested in the table are confirmed in the expressed attitudes of the French Canadians. For example, one P^1 elder said, "You know it is awfully hard to get the children to talk French. Look at my little granddaughter out there. She is playing with those children from across the street, and they are all talking English. Whenever they go out to play with other children they talk English and they pick it up and even want to talk it at home. Then they hear the older children talking it, and they learn it quicker than they learn French. Then in the homes the parents often talk English. Even if the parents only talk French the children will want to talk English. In lots of homes the children never hear French at all. Some of them never hear or speak any French except when they are in the parochial school."

A P^2 French Canadian asserted: "The children should speak French. It is a great pity that they don't. Very often when they are young they speak it very well. For instance, I have a younger brother who came out of Canada at thirteen and then lost all his French. Today he can't speak it at all." But later he says: "I think everyone ought to know more than one language. Indeed, if everyone knew English, we would all be brothers, and there would be no nationality. Language barriers keep one from understanding the other fellow and from understanding their habits and customs which may be just as good, or even better, than your own. I don't draw any lines between any races, creeds, or nationalities." He significantly fixes on English as the language of his choice for universalization.

An older P[1] French Canadian likewise approved of English on more utilitarian grounds: "The French parochial school doesn't teach much French. It's not like the Greek school where all they teach is Greek. It's better that the children learn English well; they have to know English to get along in business here."

The Sister Superior of the French-Canadian school declared more pointedly: "There are some members of the church who don't send their children to the school. Some say they live too far to send their children to the parochial school. Others say it is difficult for their children to learn French. I notice that those who say it is too difficult for children to learn French are the families where they don't speak it at home and are not interested in it. Many of the children don't hear French except at school. We find we have difficulty making the children speak it on the playground."

The parents who no longer speak French are not likely to send their children to the French-Canadian school. Among those children who go, the use of French is restricted to the relation with the Sister teacher. The curriculum of the school is in large part American. The French language appears here almost as the equivalent of the foreign language requirement in the public high schools. French, therefore, is approaching the status of a "foreign" language among the French Canadians. None of the F[3] generation children in the public schools is able to speak it. The pastor of the French-Canadian church recognizes the situation but is little disturbed by it: "The Americans are now thinking better of the Canadians, though they're beginning to laugh at the second generation which has forgotten its French tongue."

Some of the Irish were bilingual in Ireland, speaking English and Gaelic. The latter was dropped by the P generation, except among the women, almost upon arrival in Yankee City and persisted only in the "brogue." The only trace of the use of Gaelic in Yankee City has been found in a genealogical notebook of an Irish spinster, now dead, in an item referring to a family who came to the city directly after the Civil War: "At home the Irish language was spoken but the children rarely spoke it, using the English which they knew so well. Mrs. H—— lived to the good old age of ninety-seven and spoke the Irish language up to the time of her death."

The attitudes of the Irish today to ethnic languages are typified in the following words of an octogenarian F[1] Irishman: "The Irish are not like other foreigners because the other foreigners always take pains to have their children learn the language of the homeland. For example, the French, the Italians, or Armenians, and Greeks, and Poles all speak their language at home, and what little English they do get they get in school. Among the Irish the children are not taught the Irish language. The Irish were frank, honest spoken, and they don't secrete anything, as these foreigners here now do, speaking in their own language to each other, and you can't tell whether they are planning to kill you or what they are going to do. An Irishman always had a brogue, but you could understand him."

Contrast this with the urbane attitude of the editorial appearing in the local newspaper which concludes: "Americans have long been laggards in the matter of language. Cultured men and women of Europe and the Orient have put us to shame by knowing and speaking easily one, two or more foreign languages in addition to their native tongue. It will be good for Americans to know more of the languages and literature of other peoples."

2. *The Catholic Parochial Schools*

Transmission of the ancestral language is but one of three functions of the ethnic school structures. Equally important is the orientation of the F generations to two other cultural aspects of each community system, the religious symbols and the national symbols. These schools also function to orient the child to the American social system. This is developed to only a slight degree in the communities newest in the city and to a high degree in the parochial schools of the two oldest Roman Catholic groups. Two school types can be distinguished on the basis of curriculum: (1) The parochial—with a full curriculum paralleling that of the public schools *plus* courses oriented to the ethnic linguistic, religious, and national symbols. This is a full-time school. (2) The folk school—with a content predominantly of linguistic, religious, and national symbols. This is a part-time school.

The parochial school is generally associated with the Roman Catholic Church system and in Yankee City is confined to the Irish and French-Canadian communities. The emphasis placed by the Catholic Church upon the parochial school is to be seen in its doctrine, "The school alongside the church." An early New England bishop put it even more strongly: "The school before the church."

Fundamental in this philosophy is the defensive role of the church toward its family components. By the deprivation of the family's integrated and centripetal self-sufficiency and the division of its original functions among disparate structures in the American social system, parental control of the child is greatly weakened. The church must provide a secondary structure which will supplement the control functions of the family. Second, the functions of orientation of the family, assumed by the American public schools, threaten to separate the child from the sacred representations of the church. An F^2 father of the upper-middle class recognizes this fact: "I had a public-school education but I am sending my children to the parochial school, and other prominent business and professional men are doing similarly, for the reason that I want to give them some of the religion which I, as their father, haven't time to give them."

Therefore the Catholic parochial school is organized to perform a threefold service for the church. First, it tightens the behavioral controls over the child, as expressed by an early Irish writer[4] in the following:

The [Irish] youth of the country rapidly catch the prevailing spirit, and thus become impatient of restraint at a period of life when restraint is indispensable to their future well being. This is peculiarly observable in the youth who are educated in the Public Schools. The boy who is trained in these institutions is too apt to disregard, if not altogether despise, that authority which is held so sacred in Ireland; and once this first and holiest of all influences is lost, on goes the headlong youth, reckless of consequences, and the slave of every impulse. . . .

The Catholic Schools, on the contrary, inculcate obedience to parental authority—respect for the head of the family—reverence for holy things—for what is great and good and noble; while at the same time they carefully prepare their pupils for the ordinary pursuits of life, and fit them to make their way against difficulty and temptation, and they give him a resource on which he could fall back at every period of his future career. . . .

4. J. F. Maguire, *The Irish in America*, pp. 493, 494.

Second, the parochial school organizes the child's personality around the sacred symbols. Third, it defends the child against certain elements in the American social logics such as "materialistic ideals, independence of judgment and a certain basic scepticism (except where patriotism is involved) . . ." [5] A Yankee City Irish informant states explicitly: "They [the priests] urge the parents to send their children to parochial schools because the church wants its own people to be educated in its own schools and also to give the pupils religious instructions. It feels that a child who goes to the public school drifts away from church."

The interdependence of these functions is revealed in the church's insistence upon the synthesis of "church and school, religious education and secular instruction." The school, a prominent Catholic educator[6] declares, must be able to teach children "good citizenship in the Republic and to prepare them for eternal citizenship in the Kingdom of God." Because of this conception of the necessity of fusing the religious and the secular, the curriculum of the parochial school structure includes not only religious training but elements paralleling those of the public schools as well.

A church publication asserts of the parochial school of the Yankee City Irish community: "Such education as is absolutely necessary to fit them for the future is there provided them, while at the same time they are living in an atmosphere of faith and drinking in the knowledge of truth that will strengthen them in this world to win the crown of the world to come." In other words, the effort of the parochial school is to integrate American and Catholic and ethnic elements into a single representational whole, preparing and conditioning the child to maintain all three sets of elements in his own personality.

This philosophy is applied in the Irish and French-Canadian schools. Their settings are sacred in character. The schoolhouses of both immediately adjoin the church edifice. Sacred symbols of Jesus, the Cross, Mary the Mother, and the saints are on the walls of classrooms and halls. Prayers are said in unison several times during the day. The school as a collective unit observes most of the holidays in the Catholic ritual calendar. The children are articulated to the church through the school structure.

The seating arrangement at the children's Mass each Sunday prescribes: (1) Sharp differentiation of the sexes. (2) Differen-

5. W. F. Adams, *Ireland and Irish Emigration to the New World*, p. 361.
6. Rev. Dr. C. L. O'Donnell, "The Method of Catholic Education." Address on the National Radio Catholic Hour, September 14, 1930.

tiation of parochial-school children from public-school children. (This symbolizes a greater ritual importance for those more completely in the church fold because of attendance at its school.) (3) Differentiation of age. (The older the child, the farther forward he is, signifying greater ritual importance.) That this arrangement is not carried out for public-school children is curious but seems to suggest that age grading is the function of the school rather than of the church. In church, each school is treated as a group; and since the parochial school is an arm of the church its age grading is observed in the church seating. The public school is not related to the church and its age grading is not observed. It is also to be noted that, whereas the children originally attended Mass in the chapel, their important ritual status was raised with their attendance at Mass in the church proper.

The importance of the children is again brought out in a news article in the local paper which reports that a visiting bishop had addressed the "children of the parish" at a Sunday Mass.

The following newspaper excerpt records that the priest follows each Sunday morning Mass with a "talk." In speaking of the loss of a child it is significant that he lists those to whom he is lost in the following order: church, home, country.

In his Sunday morning talk yesterday to the children of this parish at their special 8:30 mass, at the Church of St. Mary which is also attended by parents and other adults, Rev. Leaf, while deeply sympathizing with the bereaved family of the little lad who lost his life by drowning the past week, took occasion to revert to his safety talk of a previous Sunday, reiterating his warning against the dangers of holiday time, stressing those of seashore and road motor traffic as well as the more approximate ones of our rivers and ponds.

He reminded his young listeners that, while the relaxation of vacation days brings freedom from the duties of school, the great responsibility still is theirs, of obeying the rules of safety laid down for them. He spoke feelingly of the loss of a little child to church, home and country, and of the sorrow such a loss brings to loved ones.

Rev. Fr. Leaf allowed his talk to turn toward a spiritual channel, making an earnest and most impressive plea to the little ones to follow the guidance of church and parental teachings as a safeguard against the moral and physical dangers of school holiday time.

These "talks," it is evident, are sermons simplified and shortened, which yet carry moral exhortations by the simple logic of concrete illustrations, such as that of a boy who had lost his life.

Admission to the church is marked by the ceremony of the first Communion for children at the age of about six.

A "course of instruction" is first necessary before participation in Communion. The rite itself was preceded by the elementary ceremonial practices of singing and praying.

Full ritual participation in the church is not achieved by the child until the ceremony of confirmation near the age of puberty. The ceremony is held every four years. The preparation for confirmation takes place in the school and is described by a Yankee City parish curate:

The children are trained in the school by the nuns and examined by the priests. This is in connection with religious education and not secular education. They are given training each day in the matters relating to the church and at the end of the time when the child is getting ready to be confirmed, then in the school the priest examines him in the Catechism and determines if he is sufficiently trained.

In the case of the public school children who are Catholics they meet twice a week during the school year in the afternoon and they are taught and examined by the priests. The purpose of this is to teach the fundamentals of the church.

Not only do the parochial-school children participate in the church as a unit, but the school also serves to train the children for entrance into the church. In addition to being in the sacred atmosphere of the schoolhouse and participating in the rite of admission into the church collectively, the children are in constant contact with sacerdotal personalities within the school structure. Their teachers are nuns of the Order of Sisters of Mercy, and their examiners are the priests themselves.

How effective is the authority of nuns and priests is described by a P[1] Irishman, janitor in a public school, who makes the following comparative observation: "If the kids over at the parochial school get a licking from the nuns or the priest, they don't go home and talk about it, because they know they'll probably get another one. They are all scared of the priest over there. He gives them a licking any time. He keeps them pretty well that way, and the family of course also. If a kid goes home and the mother comes up and a lot of the nuns tell her the story straight, she believes it and then the kid will get another one, so he doesn't say much if he gets a licking. In the public school the kid goes home and tells how he was doing nothing, how the principal and teacher thought he had, and gave him a licking and it was all so and so's fault. Then of course, the mother comes up and says, 'I never knew my boy to lie.' So they [public school officers] have a tough time. They don't do any of that licking of the kids now. They ought to, though. A lot of these kids ought to get a good whaling."

The curricula in the Irish and French-Canadian schools are alike in certain standard subjects taught in English: reading and literature, English, penmanship, arithmetic, music and drawing, American history and civics, and geography.

In both schools, from the first grade through the eighth, thirty minutes a day are spent on religion which, according to one Sister Superior, includes "the creed, some of the Bible, and church history." In addition, twelve minutes each day are devoted to "opening and closing exercises." In the Irish school the services and religious instruction are in English, but in the French-Canadian school they are in French. Another difference is that the French-Canadian school supplements American history and English by Canadian history and French.

The history of Ireland was once taught in the Irish school. An aged Irishman reported: "It used to be that Irish history was taught in the parochial school, but it has been discontinued. The Hibernians used to give a prize to the pupil writing the best essay each year on Irish history, but with the discontinuance of the teaching of Irish history this also has been discontinued." One F[2] Irish woman said: "When I was a child I and all my family knew all about the Irish heroes, but the children of today know nothing about them."

Formally, therefore, the Irish parochial school, like the Irish church, can no longer be said to be Irish in its content. The school, like the church, is no longer ethnic in both a national and religious sense, but in the religious sense alone. The ethnicity of school and church consists in their Catholicity, which continues to organize the group as a distinctive community. Not so the French-Canadian school, which maintains a curriculum of American, Catholic, and French-Canadian elements. In the Irish school, Irish symbols still appear in celebrations, but these are the last weak expressions of the school's original orientation to the society of Ireland. The Irish group is almost assimilated as an American-Catholic community.

While the French-Canadian school maintains its national elements there are indications that it too is dropping off its purely French-Canadian elements. As already noted in an earlier section the French language is losing ground rapidly among the native-born generations. At the present time the differences in the national elements of the two parochial schools are revealed in their nonsacred school rituals. The French-Canadian school is bi-national, i.e., both American and French Canadian. For example, its Memorial Day exercises consisted of these numbers: recitation, "Memorial Day"; song, "Sleep Soldiers"; dialogue, "Decoration Day"; song, "Old Glory"; recitation, "Dotty's Thought"; song, "America." Without exception, these are completely American in reference and parallel the programs in the Irish parochial as well as those in the public schools.

In 1932 graduation exercises of the French-Canadian school consisted of performances by pupils of various grades in the school: "Bienvenue" "Welcome"; recitation, "Grandma's Minuet"; chant, "Bébé Rose"; play, "Vacation Time"; *comédie,* "La Colère"; dialogue, "Tickets, Please"; recitation, "Model Letter to a Friend"; *saynète,* "La Greve"; dialogue, "The Lost Prize"; recitation, "The First Flag"; song, "Night Fancies"; and awarding of diplomas and prizes. Only four of the twelve numbers on this program were in the French language.

The graduating ceremony of the Irish school is of another type in which presentation of the diplomas is preceded only by the sermon of a visiting priest. A newspaper report describes one of these ceremonies:

In the presence of relatives, friends, and parishioners that filled the seating capacity of the St. Mary Church, 50 graduates of the parochial school received diplomas last evening at impressive commencement exercises. The address of the occasion was delivered by Rev. John E. Doyle of Boston, and the diplomas and awards were presented by the pastor, Rev. Leaf.

The program opened with the singing of a hymn by the graduates. Rev. Fr. Doyle then ascended the pulpit and made a short address. In part he said: "You graduates are about to open the door of the future, after completing eight years of schooling under the guidance of the Sisters. You are about to step across the wide corridor of life. For the past eight years, the Sisters have labored to train you according to the laws of God, and they hope you will be good citizens. If you fail, then the labors of the good Sisters will seem in vain, but if you are a success, then it is an incentive for them to labor more zealously.

"There are many mysterious doors along the corridor of life, and each must open a door which leads to a different calling. The next four years is the time of forming your character. You must decide what course you are to take in life's struggle, but whatever step you take, always remember the teachings of the school. To succeed in any vocation, you must give the best that is in you, regardless of what line of endeavor is selected.

"Living honorable and clean lives is the only key that will open the door to success, so that in the end, you enter through the door of eternity, to enjoy everlasting happiness with God in heaven."

At the close of the address, Rev. Fr. Leaf addressed the graduates before awarding the diplomas. He told them they had a debt to pay, not only to the parishioners who provided the school of education, but to the Sisters, who labored for their success. He urged them to frequently receive the sacraments of the church which will always keep them in the good graces of God. . . .

Success in one's "calling" is a concept that is Calvinist in source and associated with an industrial, capitalistic economy and "democratic" class strata such as characterize the American social system. To a large extent it is measured by the acquisition of value symbols, which the Roman Catholic Church would consider materialistic. Yet both the pastor of the Yankee City Catholic Church and the visiting priest emphasized the concept of success, although it was placed in a Catholic context by being made contingent upon "living honorably" and reaching "everlasting happiness with God in heaven." This is a further illustration of the changing content of the church. It is also to be noted that the principal speaker identified education in the parochial school with "training according to the laws of God." In this rite of passage of the graduates from the parochial school into "the wide corridor of life," the last word of the pastor was to urge them to participate frequently in the cult of the church. The representations in this ritual, like those of the curriculum, were made up of a fusion of American and Catholic elements.

At the golden anniversary of the founding of the Irish parochial school, a program was presented by the pupils of the school for the entire community. Among twenty numbers on the program only one had an Irish reference, a recitation entitled "That's How You Can Tell They Are Irish."

3. *The Hebrew School*

WHAT we have called the folk type of ethnic school is found in the Jewish, Greek, Armenian, Russian, and Polish communities. The first two will be used as examples.

The folk type of school represents a slightly different conception of ethnic education than was observed in the parochial type. The latter conceived education to be a process of integrating within a single school structure American religious and national representations. The folk school, on the other hand, allows the public school to orient the ethnic child to the American social system, reserving for itself the function of orienting the child to the ancestral social system of the community. It places primary emphasis upon the ethnic language, secondary emphasis on the folk society's national history, and third and minor emphasis on the ancestral religious system.

The curriculum of the Hebrew school is described by its teacher as follows:

Our first grade has children from six to nine years of age, and I start them with elementary Hebrew reading and writing and Biblical history in English. In the second grade we have children from nine to ten years of age, and here we teach Hebrew as a language, that is, conversational Hebrew; and with the beginning of a preparatory course in the Bible and in History we take up the period from the Conquest of Canaan to the destruction of the first Temple—this, of course, in English.

In the third grade the instruction is expanded into four divisions: (1) History, the period of the Commonwealth from 536 B.C. to 1 A.D.; (2) A reading of the text from the Hebrew Bible; (3) The third-grade books of Hebrew readings; and (4) We begin Hebrew grammar and all parts of speech except the verb.

The fourth grade: the instruction is divided into three sections. First of all, modern Jewish History; two, reading of the Talmudic literature from the Gaonic period of the ninth century through the Middle Ages; and three, a thorough study of the Hebrew verb and conjugations.

In the fifth year we study the period of the Spanish Inquisition, American-Jewish History, and the outstanding Jewish personalities.

The Hebrew language and history of the Jewish people are both begun in the first year. The former begins with the elements of the language and proceeds to a reading of the Talmud, the definitive codification of Jewish Law. The study of history begins with that provided in the Scriptures and proceeds through the history of the Jews in America.

In a discussion of this type of Hebrew school, one writer[7] states the purposes of the curriculum:

1. To give a knowledge of the Hebrew language.

   a. To open up for direct appreciation the storehouse of classic (Bible, etc.) and modern Hebrew literature.

   b. To teach its peculiarly significant concepts which deal with social and religious ideals.

   c. To form a bond of union with the Jewish past and the Jewish present in other lands, especially with the new life in Palestine.

2. To transmit the significant cultural, religious, and social heritage of the Jewish people through a knowledge of its history, literature, customs, and religious practices.

3. To bind the child in loyalty to the Jewish People so that he may strive for a continuous development of its ideal—cultural, social, religious—aspirations.

4. To give some notion of the general problems facing the Jewish People in its desire to perpetuate itself as a free society and the particular problems involved in the task of adjustment to life in America.

In short, the work of the Talmud Torah consists in converting the physical Jew, who is so by birth, into a spiritual Jew, who remains so by reason of the ideal significance of Jewish life. . . .

[The function of history is] to put in proper perspective, to clarify the significance of the events, products and customs of Jewish life . . . because the Jewish people is conceived of as still living, Jewish history is brought up to modern times, and equal emphasis is given to biblical and post-biblical periods. The course includes, for instance, a year's work in the history of the Jews in the United States. Too often the teaching of "history" in the Sunday schools has left the pupils with the notion that the Jewish people is a strange extinct people who lived in the dim past, governed by super-natural laws of development.

Therefore, the school seeks not only to appropriate the traditions of Jewish society but to bring them down to the present and

7. I. B. Berkson, *Theories of Americanization* (New York, Teachers College, Columbia University, 1920), pp. 200, 202.

to validate them in the modern American context. The Hebrew school attempts to relate the Jewish child to the history of Jewish society—a history concerned in large part with the religious representations of the society—and also attempts to organize the children into something of a junior synagogue. As the Yankee City teacher said: "You know, we conduct Saturday morning services for the school children after those of the older people. They are held by the children themselves. They sing the music of the chants—a dozen in all—and the responses which the older people read in Hebrew they read in English. That is, there are selections from the regular services. We have a small Holy Ark with a small Torah scroll. This is taken out and each Saturday a boy is prepared beforehand to read from it. Then one of the boys gives an explanation of the Law for the week, this in English, of course. And we end by singing of hymns in both English and Hebrew. Our services are frankly conservative."

By means of this junior synagogue, patterned after the conservative type, the children are prepared for entrance into the synagogue structure of adults. However, the Jewish children, like those of the other ethnic groups, exhibit a strong reaction against their folk school. Typical is the charge of one Jewish boy: "I don't like the Hebrew school. After all day in [public] school, you don't feel like going to school some more in the afternoon. Besides, what good is Hebrew? It's a dead language anyway." Expressions of similar attitudes among the Greek children reflect the fact that the ethnic child finds it difficult to reconcile two schools so remote in their content as the public and the folk. Since the former carries so much more value, reaction is directed against the latter.

The P generation Jews, however, both P^1 and P^2, vehemently attest the importance of the Hebrew school. One elder P^1 Jew was asked whether the Hebrew school was doing any good among the children. "Absolutely. Without it the children would become Goyim!" A P^1 Jewish woman, after complaining about the cost of the school, was asked if the Hebrew school would be given up. "No, no, no. The Hebrew school is the best thing in the city. We'll never give it up." As among the Catholics, the school is placed by this woman before the synagogue itself in importance to the community. A P^2 Jew said: "The Hebrew school is the foundation of the community just like the foundation to a house. We *must* keep it up. We must keep it going because without it the children won't know anything about Jewishness." Another P^2 Jew put it that "the Hebrew school is the heart of Jewish national life."

An annual entertainment by the Hebrew school children for the school funds was held in the vestry of an upper-class Episcopal church.[8] Apropos of the incongruity of the situation, a P² Jew remarked: "The interesting thing is this: This is the vestry of the Episcopal church, the richest and most orthodox church in Yankee City; the concert is being held on Christmas night by the Jewish Ladies' Aid Society for the benefit of the Hebrew school; and the concert is in celebration of the Chanukah Festival. Isn't that paradoxical? You know the money for the church was given mostly by two different people; one of them, a German Jew, who gave $50,000, and here we are, counting the pennies and raising money for our shul. Well, that's the Yankee City spirit for you."

4. *The Greek Schools*

THE folk school of the Greek community exhibits most of the elements of the Hebrew school. The most striking difference is that, whereas the Hebrew school combines national and religious symbols, among the Greeks these are in two separate school structures. One of these, which we call the Greek Afternoon School, is devoted to teaching the national-folk language and history; the other, the Greek Sunday School, is something of a junior church. It must be added that there is an age-grade differentiation between these two schools. The Afternoon School takes children from about the age of eight through a progression of five grades and keeps them until they are thirteen. The children in the Sunday School, however, are adolescent, ranging from fourteen to eighteen years of age. In other words, a child is normally expected to proceed from the Afternoon School into the Sunday School and finally to enter the church.

The parallelism between the curricula of the Hebrew and Greek Afternoon Schools may be noted in the Greek teacher's comment: "I teach the Greek language, Greek literature, Greek history, and some from the Greek philosophers." A Greek informant states the case similarly: "The school is for the purpose of giving the children an insight into Greek history, culture, thought, literature, and philosophy."

Of the Sunday School, an informant said: "It trains them in the Orthodox Church, in the Bible, Catechism, and things like that."

As already noted elsewhere, the two curricula are integrated in

8. This occurred while the new synagogue, described in the last chapter, was being acquired.

the homeland in one public-school system. A Yankee City Greek corroborated this: "There are no Sunday Schools in Greece. Here they try to imitate other churches and have Sunday Schools."

Why should this dichotomy of schools, on the basis of subject matter, appear in this little Greek community of Yankee City when there is no precedent for it in Greece itself? A suggestion is found in the informant's remark just quoted and in the fact that the two Greek schools are age graded.

The Greek community of P generation adults is defensive in keeping the American social system from carrying their children away from the Greek community and its traditional representations. Their associations are part of the defenses which would keep the child from drifting off into the open American associations. But there are two other important and threatening American currents.

The first is the public school, which takes the child at the age of six. The second is the American Protestant Church Sunday School, which might take the child around the age of thirteen. Since these threats come from two different directions, the Greek community organizes to meet each one of them separately and in turn.

The Greek Afternoon School takes in the children very soon after public schooling has commenced and matches the latter's curriculum with its own secular curriculum of Greek studies. Then at the age when the child might be drawn into the Sunday Schools of the American churches the Greek Sunday School absorbs him and provides him with the religious representations of the Greek Orthodox Church.

The unified school pattern of Greece is split up to meet two differently formulated threats and is divided between the age grades at which those threats are directed. The "imitation" of the other churches that have Sunday Schools must be interpreted as the matching of weapon for weapon.

Another highly important factor is the conflict between the "church and state" revealed in the controversy over the priest's teaching of the Afternoon School, described in the last chapter. Although the Afternoon School teacher is independent of the priest, the hierarchy of the Greek Church in America under its own bishop has recently succeeded in effecting a control over the Greek teachers. The Yankee City Greek teacher said of this: "The Greek teachers used to have an organization, but it wasn't very strong and they were fighting among themselves. Then about six months ago they made some changes. The priests decided that they should have a general committee which would oversee school affairs and the teachers. The bishop is not on the committee but it was formed at his say-so. Every teacher contributes a fixed monthly amount for the salaries of the committee, and also 1 per cent of his salary to pay the bishop's salary. The bishop is more or less over the teachers as well as the priests."

Although the teacher is formally subordinated to the American hierarchy of the Greek Church (which apparently has been moving to represent the larger Greek community in the United States), within the immediate community the priest has no direct control over the teacher or the Afternoon School. As we shall see later, however, the priest had a ritual function at the commencement exercises of the Afternoon School; but this was an expression not so much of his control as of his ritual leadership of the Yankee City Greek community.

How successful are the Greek schools in orienting the children to the ancestral Greek social system? There are only eleven Greek families in Yankee City whose children are not sent to the Greek schools. Nine of these families represent out-marriages of Greek men. Their children face two different social systems in the personalities of their parents and always follow the direction of the dominant one—the American. In such a divided house no compulsions are present to send the child to the Greek school, especially when the Greek father, who alone could insist upon it, has broken with Greek traditions in his out-marriage. In one of these nine cases, the mother is Irish Catholic, and the children are sent to the Irish parochial school, indicating the stronger pull of the Roman Catholic Church and its schools.

The remaining two of the eleven families are homogeneously Greek. The children of one go to the French parochial school, and the sons of the other attend the Baptist Sunday School. With the exception of these two variant families, all the homogeneous Greek families have consistently sent their children to the Greek schools.

As indications of the children's attitudes toward the Greek school, we have the Greek teacher's records of his pupils for one year and the grade he has assigned them for their work. These provide indirect but trustworthy evidence of attitude, since they can be compared with the report of the public-school authorities that the Greek children as a group are among the brightest elements in the schools. In the test year, there were 59 pupils in the Greek school, distributed as follows among three classes of grades:

unsatisfactory—21, or 36 per cent; fair—24, or 40 per cent; good—14, or 23 per cent. That is, less than one in four children did work worthy of the mark "good," and more than one in three did "unsatisfactory" work.

This is in such marked contrast to the type of work done by the Greek children in the public schools that the factor of ability can be canceled out, and the effective factor in the differential grades of work done for the two schools may be assumed to be difference in attitude. Ample corroboration is obtained from the Greek parents who reluctantly admit that in the conflict of the American and Greek schools for the attention and interest of the Greek children the latter comes off a poor second.

A P[1] Greek father reported: "The children all go to public school, and then practically all of them attend the Greek school where they learn to read and speak the language. The children are not all very enthusiastic about the school; they prefer the public school. The children seem to think that it's extra work that they don't want to do."

Another P[1] Greek was anxious to explain away the children's antipathies to the Greek school: "Well, some of them don't like it very much, but they go. Children don't like school anyway. Of course, as they get older they don't like to go much. For one thing, they get too old for it. They start them out too old. They don't put them in school until they are about eight and they are too big. They don't like to go to the Greek school. Then they only teach them up to the fifth grade, so they don't go very long anyway. Of course, some of the children like it, but a lot of them don't."

The difficulties of forcing the child's attendance at the Greek school are recognized. The president of the church committee said: "I don't know whether children get much out of Greek schools. When they are in the grammar school and study, they don't have much time to do other work and take on something else. I don't send my boys until they are older than they are now. They are now six years old. In a year or two I will send them." The conflict of the public and Greek schools among the children is put in terms of competition for limited time. But the informant immediately went on to talk about sending his boys to school—conflict and competition notwithstanding.

The Greek priest is of the following opinion: "You and I know about the melting pot of America. In another generation there won't be any Greeks or any other nationalities at all left. All will be American. Consequently, the Greek school really exists for the purpose of teaching the Greek children to think for themselves." Training in the Greek school will help them "think for themselves," i.e., be Americans though Greeks, and Greeks though Americans.

The president of the G.A.P.A. likewise foresees the assimilation of Greeks in the United States and in a much shorter period: "In fifteen years there'll be no nationalities here, all will be American. Since immigration has been stopped, soon there won't be any of the old-country people left and all those born in America will feel that they are Americans. They won't think that they are Greek or any other nationality. The Greek school won't do much good. Here it doesn't matter whether they know any languages except English; it doesn't do any good."

Here are the leaders of the Greek community who stand at the very center of the Yankee City Greek community system, yet in the face of the progressive defection of their children admit that they are fighting a losing battle and that ultimately that system will dissolve and crumble. But the community and the school embody the representations of the P generation Greeks at least, and the Greeks attempt to maintain both so far as they can. An instance of this is the graduation exercises of the Greek school which will be described in some detail because so much of it symbolizes and corroborates the discussion of the Greek language and school up to this point.

This ritual occurs in June, the end of the school year for both public and Greek schools. It begins with an "examination" of the school children by the church committee, a function performed in the schools of Greece by the school committee of the community. When asked the character of the examination a member of the church committee explained: "We just come down and listen to the children recite."

The ritualistic aspect of the examination is further suggested in this Greek's answer to the question whether all the children passed: "Oh, yes, everything was all right." That is, it was not so much an examination in the customary sense as it was a supervisory visit at which the children were expected to perform for the committee.

Several weeks later a similar ritual was performed, not in the regular school quarters but in a special hall with ritualistic accouterments and before the whole Greek community. This was not just a graduation of the top grade in the school but a celebration of the "passing" of all the children from one grade to the next higher. At the entrance to the hall were seated the members of the school committee. Opposite, on a dais, were seated the priest with the G.A.P.A. governor and the former president of the church committee at one side and the president and vice-president of the church committee on the other. Down the center of the hall were the children and at each side the spectators. The Greek flag was placed at one end, the American flag at the other.

The Greek priest, dressed in black vestments, with a red surplice, opened the ceremonies with a prayer, followed by the children singing. Only a few of the people took part in the singing. They first sang the Greek national hymn and then "America." During this the audience all stood. Following the opening, the priest removed his robe and sat in his regular street costume of black with a stiff collar.

The prayer, of course, is the traditional opening for every Christian nonsacred ceremony and serves to solemnize the occasion by binding together the group through communion and evoking the presence and blessing of God. This part of the rite was made even more sacred and impressive by the priest's wearing his sacred vestments, which he wore through the singing, it will be noted, of both the Greek and American anthems. The singing of the two anthems has the same significance as the use of both the Greek and American flags.

The program follows, with titles translated by the teacher. All the speeches and readings, with one exception, were in Greek. The priest's prayer, "To Progress of Countries," was followed by the singing of the Doxology and the Greek and American anthems. The ex-president of the church committee and the G.A.P.A. governor delivered speeches and the teacher gave an address, "The Promise and Knowledge of America and Knowledge of the Greeks." The remainder of this portion of the program was given over to recitations by students. During the intermission refreshments were offered. Then the priest and the president of the church committee gave speeches followed by pupils' recitations. The ceremony concluded with the presentation of certificates by the president of the church committee.

Analysis of the program, including the recitations, shows ten references to the family, seven to God, seven to Greece and America, six to Greek symbols, and seven to "neutral" subjects. Disregarding the neutral and heterogeneous group, there were thirty references, twenty-four of which dramatized the Greek family, the

Greek religion, and the Greek national tradition, the three dominant motifs in the ancestral Greek society.

In this rite of passage is also indicated the secondary and sup-
plementary function of the ethnic folk school—not only to present the values and symbols which underlie the framework of the
ethnic community system, but also to validate that framework
within the American social system. In other words, the school
recognizes formally that the American system has begun and will
continue to impress itself upon the ethnic child. There is no escape
from this fact. Therefore, the school, by the act of linking ethnic
and American values and symbols, to a degree identifies them so
that they may not be conceived as altogether discrete and mutu-
ally exclusive. Such a link insures that the child will not be thrown
into the dilemma of choosing one or the other and be tempted to
abandon the ethnic in the face of the commanding challenges of
the American.

IX

ASSOCIATIONS

PRECEDING chapters have shown that the ethnic community in Yankee City was originally directed to the preservation and stabilization of the ethnic personality and family structure. Under the P^1 generation, the church and school structures functioned to maintain the ethnic personality type by organizing the group around the religious and cultural symbols and behavioral modes of the fatherland. In so doing, the community attempted to sanction the family's exercise of its traditional controls and at the same time apply a brake to the personality change which was a challenge to those controls.

But in spite of the efforts of ethnic church and school, personality change proceeded at an accelerating pace, and the community was called upon to create secondary relational structures to keep its members within the controls of the community system. The unprotected aspect of the community system when it consists only of church and school structures is leisure-time behaviors. The father of the family, unless a storekeeper, works eight hours and has four or five hours each day which have no organized focus except the home. He may often spend these hours in informal clique relations with men of his age in the ethnic group chatting or playing cards. The mother, with the regimen of housekeeping lightened by the American technical accessories, will likewise have leisure hours during which she often seeks the company of other women of the ethnic groups. The child, finally, when not in either the public or ethnic schools, has his play relations with fellow ethnics and others. As the personalities of the various members of the family change, the clique relations tend to be less and less exclusively composed of members of the ethnic group—such development varying in degree, of course, for child, father, and mother. The ethnic family, once organized centripetally around the plot of land, its meager leisure centered chiefly in the family itself, is now centrifugally organized, its extended leisure directed in an important degree beyond the home. As each personality changes, the range of his relations external to the family widens progressively. The individual may enter relations with people outside of his group, including natives; and he may follow them into the American or "open" associations. Such developments tend to reduce his relations within the ethnic community and to hasten his personality change, weakening both the family and the community.

The P^1 generation counteracts this tendency by creating a secondary defensive ring about its community system through organizing leisure time within associational structures. These associations are in all cases explicitly "closed" associations, in contrast to the "open" associations of the Yankee City system, and tend to keep the individual associated within the community system.

The Jewish group, totaling about four hundred individuals, has eight associational structures, bisected according to sex and divided into four distinct age levels. It is a system of age-graded associational structures which a Jewish child enters at the age of thirteen when he has just been graduated from Hebrew school, and through which he can progress grade by grade until he reaches the topmost. Complete associational subsystems are also found in the Armenian, French-Canadian, and Irish communities. In such a system the superordination of husband over wife and of father over child may be effected by the higher position of the father's association in the system. In so far as these associational structures serve to organize and control their members they supplement the church and school in functioning in an area in which the family has been deprived of effective controls.

These closed associations have more than the function of integrating the individual, the family structure, and the community system, for they discharge certain functions which in the ancestral folk society were performed by the local village community. Varyingly among the ethnic groups, these include caring for the needy, sustaining the family in the crises of sickness and death, supporting the school and the church, and organizing nonsacred festivals.

The village community in the "old country" was a relatively autonomous, inclusive social system with responsibilities of integrating its various component structures and discharging the specialized obligations of the whole system. The ethnic community system in Yankee City has no such definitive autonomy or set of responsibilities, since these are assumed by Yankee City itself. The ethnic community is a system of structural parts, with no superstructural system to integrate the parts except the church, which assumes relatively few secular functions. Some of the larger responsibilities, such as dispensing charity, are met by church and school committees, and the rest by the associations.

As the associational subsystem of the community grows, moreover, there appears a progressive division of functions among the separate associational structures. In other words, where the controls of the village community in the ethnic folk society were essentially with the fathers, who collectively discharged the common functions of the village, in the Yankee City groups which have a complete age-graded system of associations, the controls are with all members of the family above a certain age. Each age level is organized into associations, each of which has certain distinct community functions. There are variations, of course, in the degree to which this development is found in the associations of the various ethnic groups, but it is lacking in none of them.

The development of ethnic associations is correlated with residential phases of the group, class strata, national and church representations, interaction-time and generations, and numbers in the group. In the following descriptive section these factors in each ethnic group will be evaluated, with special emphasis upon the last two.

1. *The Informal Association*

INFORMAL associations are groupings larger than cliques having a regular meeting place and organized around recreational activities. These informal groupings have no administrative officers, no defined membership criteria, techniques for perpetuating membership, definite functions, or explicit representations. At a specific point this type of association will be seen to crystallize into a formal association with the essential attributes of the type. Informal associations have been observed among five of the newest ethnic groups—the Poles, Russians, Greeks, Armenians, and Jews. Each will be discussed in turn.

There are four provision stores along River Street, three owned by Poles and one by a Russian. They are the general meeting places for the men, who pass most of the day there when not at work. They are filled with chatting visitors, sitting and standing around, engaged in animated talk that sometimes reaches a shouting stage. Conversations of great length are carried on, the storekeeper participating except when he is waiting on a customer. Yornick's (the Russian's) store has a bulletin board with notices of Polish and Russian activities.

The officer of one of the two formal, recently organized, Polish associations uses these stores as an organizing base and as a place to meet fellow members on association business. At a time when this man was unemployed his daughter said of him: "He usually spends the afternoon in one store after another. He runs all around with checks and letters for the club members, and goes from store to store, getting people interested in the club and talking it up." Another Pole, who had been ill for some time, was asked a question relating to the Polish group: "I don't know. I haven't been down to the store lately."

These stores serve the men somewhat as clubhouses and are the basis for the intimate relations existing among the Polish and Russian groups. The most important of the stores, that run by the Russian, is also something of a community center, where, through its bulletin board, the two groups are kept in touch with community affairs. Through the bulletin board and more generally through conversation, the men, who are still strongly in control of their families, keep in close touch with each other. These stores serve as foci of informal associations of adult males, and these associations in turn serve to integrate the family units of the Polish and Russian communities, and to link the two communities to each other.

The proprietors of the stores, moreover, are usually sought by mail carriers and other "outsiders" trying to locate some Pole or Russian, and in this way the stores furnish a point of contact between the external society and the internal community.

The first of the stores appeared in the decade census of 1913 when there were only about fifteen Polish and Russian families recorded in the City Directory. In all probability, then, the informal association as centered in the store emerged very early in the development of these groups. But there is no critical necessity for an informal association to center on a store. If a Polish-owned store had not appeared, it is likely that such an informal association would still have emerged and sought some other available focus, as happened among the Jews and Greeks.

One of the foci of the Jewish men was a Jewish-owned grocery store in the center of the Jewish residential nucleus off Wharf Square. A P[2] Jewish informant said: "In the old days the Jewish grocery store was the clubhouse. All the news of the world was there, and they even got their mail there. This right up to the war was the center of things. On a hot summer night there may have been as many as twenty-five or thirty men sitting around on boxes reading papers and discussing. The older men also came there. Everybody used to live on Wharf Square. It was very tawdry but still it was beautiful. It was clean inside and had that Russian quiet, peaceful life." The store referred to is recorded first in the City Directory of 1903, when the Jewish community, like that of the Poles and Russians, numbered fifteen families.

But according to the same informant, there was another and earlier associational focus for the Jewish men: "In those days the older men used to almost live at the shul. It was their club and home." The informant identifies the synagogue itself (located before 1907 in a store loft) as the focus of the older men, whereas in his first remarks he commented that "the older men also came there." It may be inferred that the synagogue was the exclusive focus of the older men, whereas the store was primarily the focus of the younger men and only secondarily a center for the older men.

Of course, the congregation, that is, the church organization of the Jews, is itself a religious association. Unlike the Roman Catholic Church, which transcends the individual and explicitly conceives of itself as "absorbing" the individual, the congregation exists the moment ten adult Jewish males come together for worship. By their association these ten men literally create a congregation. A simple congregation of this number may be organized, have officers and a specially defined membership, and hence be a formal association; or it may be a temporary, unorganized congregation and fall into the classification of an informal association. In the late 'eighties, according to the oldest living Yankee City Jew, there were about eleven Jewish men who came together regularly in private homes for purposes of worship, and it was not until 1896 that this group was formally organized as a congregation. It is likely that these Jews who early joined in religious services were also an informal recreational association. Certainly, according to our P^2 informant quoted above, this was the case for older men when the congregation was organized and had its synagogue in a store loft on Wharf Square. "The shul was their club and home."

Today the older P^1 Jews and the younger P^2 Jews are organized into two separate formal recreational associations. It is significant that the informal recreational association of the P^2 men no longer exists, whereas that of the P^1 men, with its center in the synagogue, still continues. These older men go to the synagogue each day at half-past six for morning prayers, which are generally completed by seven. These men were encountered on several occasions near the synagogue at a quarter-past or half-past eight on their way back to their homes for breakfast. When asked why they were so late, one replied, "Oh, we finished praying and sat around gabbing all this time."

Among the Poles, Russians, Greeks, and Armenians, as well as among the Jews, the P^1 generation has been organized into a formal association which does not interfere with the preëxisting informal association. The two exist side by side, and from the facts to be reviewed later, the informal appears to be the more important of the two associations for the men of this generation. On the other hand, the P^2 and F generations tend to shift from the informal to the formal type of association, leaving little trace of the former.

The essential factor contributing to this differentiation between the P^1 and subsequent generations is this: The P^2 and, especially, the F generation already have their clique relations in large part within the external Yankee City social system. The P^1 generation, however, has these relations centered predominantly in the ethnic community. Therefore, while this adult immigrant generation may organize itself into a formal organization, such organization in no way affects its recreational clique and informal associational relations. The informal association of the younger generations in time becomes the only extended recreational relation which it has with the ethnic community, and when this generation is organized into a formal association, this association absorbs the hitherto informal association, leaving no trace of the latter.

The informal association is seen in its highest development in the coffee house of the Yankee City Greek community. In Greece the coffee house was the most important single focus of the leisure behavior of the male adult population. A Greek informant, for example, in speaking of the coffee houses in Greece, commented: "They have them everywhere. Yes, even every small town has a coffee house. Of course, the best ones are in the big cities." Xenides[1] corroborates the statement: "The most prevalent mode of recreation in Greece and Turkey is sitting in groups in houses or at the coffee houses talking, discussing politics and sipping Turkish coffee."

The coffee house in Greece was really the informally organized men's club, where the leaders of the society, the adult males,

1. J. P. Xenides, *The Greeks in America,* p. 46.

through gossip and discussion, thrashed out the events of the group. It served as an instrument for the expression and renewal of the society's representations and also for the exercise of social controls. Every deviant act of an individual was the object of comment, and thereby emphasis was given to the approved modes of behavior.

Mention is made by several Greeks of the "joking" carried on in the coffee house. For example, there is the following remark of a Yankee City Greek: "The Greeks have these coffee houses. They sit around, joke with each other, call each other names, all in good fun. It is all understood. But when one goes into a Greek's home, he won't joke with the husband or anything like that. He keeps the jokes for the joking places. In the home they are dignified." The coffee house is the place par excellence to relax from the formalities of the home.

It was inevitable that so conspicuously central a focus of the Greek social system as the coffee house should be reproduced by the Yankee City Greeks. What has been said of the synagogue— that where ten Jews meet there springs up a synagogue—may with equal force be applied to the coffee houses of the Greeks. Both are primary foundations upon which the community system is later constructed.

The first Greek coffee house in Yankee City is recorded in the decade census of 1913. In that year there were only five Greek families listed for the city, but these were supplemented by twenty-two single males, making twenty-seven adult males in all. A coffee shop generally serves nothing more than Turkish coffee and *Baclava*, a Greek pastry. Yet a Greek coffee-house keeper could maintain himself at that early date with a small group of customers. The coffee house must have served its function as a center for the men or it could not have survived.

The coffee house remained the sole community structure of the Yankee City Greeks for at least eleven years. It was not until 1924 that the community established its own church and school structures. At about that time, with a large influx of Greeks, a second coffee house made its appearance, although it was only an adjunct of a general store. Not until 1929 was the group's first formal association, the Greek-American Progressive Association, organized.

The coffee houses will be described in their present aspect and interpreted in terms of the community system. Behind the cases and filling the back part of Taksas' store are white-topped tables where coffee is served and where the Greeks gather to read the Greek language papers, to joke, gossip and play cards. Church notices, Greek school notices, and occasionally political handbills are posted on the walls. In a wire rack are sometimes a few undelivered letters to members of the Greek group. On the wall is also a framed sign stating that Bank of Athens drafts may be bought here, but Taksas said that "since foreign exchange is so uncertain that business has stopped." The discussions in the coffee house take many directions and are usually all in Greek.

Miksos' Coffee House differs from Taksas' in that he has no store connected with it but depends entirely on the sale of coffee. The large room is filled with white-topped tables. Two pool tables in the rear are seldom used. In a small partitioned area in the rear the proprietor prepares the coffee, the entire equipment being a sink for washing the cups and a small gas burner for heating the Turkish coffee which must be prepared fresh for each order.

This is the most popular coffee house, always having more people in it than Taksas' place. At all hours of the day idle Greek men are found here talking, reading Greek language papers, playing cards or backgammon. It is also frequented by a few Armenians who come to drink coffee and play cards.

Both these coffee houses are very informal; anyone is admitted and there is no urging to buy coffee. Only coffee and baclava are served. Cards, dice, or backgammon boards are furnished free. All the men read the Greek language newspapers (printed in America). In the evenings or on days when the factories are closed, the places are crowded, and in cold and rainy weather the idle men will frequently spend the whole day there, leaving only for meals. Not all the Greeks frequent the places; it is very unusual to see any of the Greek shopkeepers there. Practically all the factory workers and barbers are habitués.

The conspicuous absence of the shopkeepers, who are for the most part restaurant and confectionery store owners, is probably due to the fact that their businesses do not have the limited hours of the factories and allow them little leisure.

Both coffee houses have from the first been located on River Street, directly adjoining the area of Greek residential concentration. This relation likewise existed among the Polish, Russian, and Jewish stores.

The associational aspects of the coffee house are established in the interview data. For example, the Greek priest, himself an habitué, says of the coffee house: "It is almost a club, but the manager runs it on a business basis. The Greeks visit the coffee house when they have nothing to do."

Another Greek informant says: "The Greek coffee shop across the street is just a sort of club like Americans have. People go in there and play cards and dominoes and drink coffee and talk. Foreigners [*sic*] can go in, but only Greeks go there usually. They all talk Greek and play Greek games and nobody else goes around there much. It is a nice place to spend the time. I spend all my spare time there."

One Greek, when asked whether he had heard one of the local Greek women sing on the radio the day before, answered: "No, I hadn't heard about it. Well, I'll be down at the coffee shop tonight and I'll hear all about it. I always go down to the coffee shop in the evening. It's a good place to talk. Everybody is there. We play games, gossip, and talk, especially on Saturday evenings."

The proprietor of one of the coffee houses invited the investigator to join him in a cup of Turkish coffee "on the house": "I always want my coffee, but I don't like to drink it alone. I have to get somebody to drink with me." Especially significant is the following report of a young Greek: "About a month ago a traveling puppet show came to town and they held it at Miksos' coffee shop. The whole thing was in Greek. But it only stayed a couple of days. When times were good they were here two or three weeks."

The behaviors of the Yankee City Greeks in their coffee houses represent essentially the same pattern which existed in Greece. The importance of the coffee houses in the Yankee City Greek community may be measured by the fact that, whereas the G.A.P.A. meets once monthly and the church once weekly, the coffee houses are filled day in and day out. The coffee shop's function as a community center is revealed in the church and school notices which are tacked on the walls and in the undelivered mail for local Greeks in a special rack. The traveling puppet show used the coffee house as a community theater, in spite of the fact that church, school, and G.A.P.A. all have separate and adequate meeting places. The coffee houses not only bind the adult males into an informal association but have wider community functions.

The Greek coffee shops serve in greater degree than do the stores among the Poles, Russians, and Jews, to tie the ethnic community to the homeland—not only through such traditional symbols as coffee, backgammon, and the Greek language, but through more recently acquired symbols, such as Greek newspapers and the Bank of Athens notices. The coffee house represents to the P[1]

Greek an aspect of his ancestral society which is less changed from the original than any structure of the community, the family not excluded and the Greek church alone excepted. In the coffee house he can be more completely the Greek personality he knew himself to be than anywhere else in his new environment. This illuminates the behavior of the men who spend almost all their leisure time in the coffee shops and remain sometimes through a whole day.

Symbolically, American society has crept into the coffee houses in the guise of an American play form. The Greek priest, speaking of the games played, says: "They play a kind of whist, something they picked up in America. Occasionally they have whist parties." Incursion of non-Greeks into the coffee houses occurs, although to a limited degree, as suggested in the following report of the investigator: "One coffee house, that of Miksos, is frequented by Armenians, and they frequently mix with the Greeks, especially in the card games. In Taksas' place, the variety store, there is a continual influx of salesmen calling on him, and they stop and chat with the Greeks who are present. Aside from the salesmen at Taksas' and the Armenians at Miksos', it is very seldom that any non-Greeks are found in the places, and if one who was a stranger should come in he would be served by the proprietor and ignored by the others."

Since most of the Armenian stores are on the principal business streets of the city and all serve the society at large, the Armenian men have had no available focus for their informal association except the Greek coffee house. The coffee house existed in Turkish Armenia; hence as a center of recreation for the Armenian informal association it has been especially congenial. Moreover, the Greeks and Armenians are in some senses cultural kin. Certain of the Greeks came from Greek colonies in Turkish Asia and possess, in common with the Armenians, the Eastern Orthodox Church system and recreational and dietary forms. Just as the Poles and Russians "mixed" naturally in their stores, so have the Yankee City Armenians and Greeks mixed in the coffee house.

The Greek coffee houses, to a greater degree than the Polish and Russian stores, are points of articulation between the ethnic community and the Yankee City social system. This is indicated in the following observation of the investigator: "During the elections there are vigorous discussions regarding the political parties and candidates, with most of the Greeks favoring the Democratic party. And before city or state elections, the candidates often come to the coffee houses to talk to the Greeks. For example, at the last election George Nidos, president of the G.A.P.A. Juniors, escorted a Democratic candidate around to both the coffee houses in Yankee City." The coffee shop is recognized by the candidates as a place where they can conveniently reach the men of the Greek community in a group.

The persistence of the coffee shop as a focus is suggested in the following statements of the investigator: "Since Miksos' place has been closed [as a result of a mortgage foreclosure] and converted into a diner, another coffee house has been opened by another Greek. This is just across the street from Taksas and is a duplicate of Miksos' place except for size. It also has about the same crowd as Miksos had. It has the usual church and school notices posted on the walls.

"The change in coffee houses seems to have made no difference to the group. Taksas has no more customers than before and his coffee shop remains a subsidiary to his store. The individuals go from one shop to the other and sit and chat just as they did before. Apparently the important thing is the coffee house, not the individual who runs it."

There is no record of informal recreational associations among the Italians, who are few in number and sharply split on sectional lines, nor among the two largest and oldest groups, the French Canadians and the Irish. Such associations must have been characteristic of the village communities from which these groups emigrated, as of those from which the Poles, Russians, Greeks, and Armenians came. And it is likely that the Italians, French Canadians, and Irish had informal associations at an earlier stage of their Yankee City development than that observed in this investigation. This applies especially to the Irish, who established no P generation formal association until as late as 1888, and to the Italians, who have no formal association to this day.

2. *Elements in the Ethnic Formal Association*[2]

UNLIKE the informal association, the formal association is complex in both form and content. The following criteria have been worked out to aid in classifying these associations: membership composition (generation, age grade, sex, class, and number); representational content; explicit function; recreation at meetings or at periodic festivals; and formal affiliations.

2. Hereafter, unless otherwise qualified, the term "association" will be used to refer only to formally organized associations.

Russian and Polish Associations

In 1924 the Russian adult males created a formal association called the Russian Benefit Society. At that time there were twenty-two families in the Russian group, and the society had a charter membership of eighteen. The membership was composed of P[1] adult males, numbering twenty-five in 1929 and twelve in 1933. Its representational content is organized around the ethnic community. This association functioned as a benefit society, paying its members $3 weekly for the first six months of illness, $5 a week for the following six months, $100 at death, and $50 at death of wife "if the man needs it badly." The association is represented at funerals of members, furnishes pallbearers, and sends flowers. There are no recreational interests except an annual summer picnic. Meetings are held monthly at the homes of various members.

The Poles have an association called the Polish Benefit Society, whose elements repeat those of the Russian society in almost every detail. Like the latter, it was organized in 1924. At that time there were about fifty families in the group and all their P[1] male adults joined. With the rapid expansion of the group, the membership of the association grew to about one hundred in 1929, but unemployment by 1933 reduced its numbers one half, just as in the case of the Russian Benefit Society.

Both of these societies are formal associations of the adult P[1] males of the group. Their representations are implicitly communal in contrast with other associations to be examined which have national representations. That is, they are identified solely with the local community. Their principal function, as suggested by their title of "benefit," is crisis stabilization. The two most serious family crises are illness of the head of the family (and consequent unemployment) and death of the husband or wife. By assigning a committee to attend the bedside of a member who is seriously ill, by sick benefits, by attendance at the funeral in a body, and by death benefits, this type of association serves to strengthen the family and tide it over a period which threatens its stability and existence. Since the association in normal times consists of most of the men in the group who are heads of families, it represents the community itself, organized collectively to protect the endangered familial component.

It has been mentioned elsewhere that the attitudes of the P[1] generation to the function of money have a certain crisis aspect. Money to them must be used only productively, must be set to reproduce itself, and is not to be "frozen" in the form of consumers' goods, for the reason that money assures economic stability to a family that does not feel itself stable within the context of the Yankee City social system. The most serious crisis which such a family can encounter is loss of its income and, even more serious, of its source of income, namely, the money producer of the family. The benefit or mutual-aid type of association reflects this crisis attitude and converts such a crisis from a purely family affair to an affair of the whole community. The benefit aspect will be found in varying degrees of development in most of the ethnic associations to be examined, but it will be established later that the older the ethnic group, the less emphasis is placed upon sick and death benefits. This aspect will also be seen to recede in importance progressively with the associations of successive generations.

Furthermore, there is a correlation between the relative development of the benefit and of the recreational element in each association. Among the P^1 generation associations in which the benefit element is prominent, the recreational element is negligible; whereas among associations of the P^2 and F generations the recreational element is generally primary and the benefit element either minor or absent altogether. For example, the monthly meetings of the Russian Benefit Society (P^1 men) provide no recreational forms whatsoever. As the president told us: "We don't have a regular meeting place. We take turns about meeting at the houses of the members once a month. At the meetings we collect the dues, give a statement as to how much money we have, how much is spent for people that are sick, etc.—just business."

The only recreation which the society organizes, in fact, is the annual summer picnic which the entire group attends together with kin and friends from near-by cities. The association, then, acts to provide the group with its only community festival, at which recreational forms of the folk society are organized, such as folk music and dancing, and at which, incidentally, money is raised by selling food and auctioning objects of value.

Lack of recreational activity at the monthly meetings can be explained in part by the existence of the informal association which absorbs the leisure of the men. An added factor is that the P^1 generation, especially in groups as recently arrived as the Russians and Poles, is as yet unfamiliar with the associational structure and its recreational potentialities. The association structure in their folk societies had political and economic functions almost exclusively. Leisure had not been formally organized for purposes of recreation. In fact, the recreation type of association is peculiarly an urban relational structure which has reached its highest form in American society. It will later be observed that the more "Americanized" generations and groups strongly emphasize the recreational aspect in their associations.

The Polish Benefit Society has greater opportunity for adding recreational forms to its meetings than has the Russian Benefit Society in that it owns a building, called Polish Hall, which serves as a clubhouse. Yet of the society's meetings an officer says pointedly: "We don't go in for cards or pool or anything like that." Its meetings are also "just business."

However, the clubhouse does supplement the stores in providing a center for the informal associations of Polish men. In somewhat the same fashion as do the Greeks in the coffee houses, the Polish men gather in one of the rooms of the hall to drink beer and play cards. However, use of the clubroom is not restricted solely to members; Polish nonmembers are also welcome. Hence the distinction must be made that the P.B.S. offers in its hall a focus for informal recreation for the men of the entire community, without formalizing recreation as an aspect of its own program of activities. The P.B.S. arranges an elaborate program of entertainment for the entire community, including dances and picnics, by which it adds to its depleted treasury. By the profits from these community affairs the society has been able to carry on its benefit functions throughout the economic depression, which affected the Polish group severely.

The final datum indicating the position of the P.B.S. Hall as a community center is that when the Polish school was established its meeting place was one of the rooms in the hall. And when a second Polish association was organized in 1930, it likewise used the hall for its meetings and affairs. But whereas the P.B.S. furnished the hall free of charge to the school, the new association paid rental for its use. The P.B.S., therefore, was in an important sense contributing to the support of the Polish school.

The more recently formed Polish association, called the Polish-American Club, represents a combination of elements differing markedly from that of the Polish Benefit Society. The membership includes P^2 as well as P^1 males, averaging thirty-five years of age, and numbering fifty in 1930 and twenty-three in 1933. In representational content this association is bi-national, Polish-American, rather than simply ethnic-communal. Its explicit function is concerned with naturalization. It provides recreational activities such as card games and political speakers. It is affiliated with the national organization of Polish-American Clubs.

The membership of the Polish-American Club overlaps in part that of the P.B.S., but the former has an important proportion of members of the P^2 generation younger adult age grade (twenty to thirty years) who are not found in the P.B.S. In another connection it will be seen that the Polish-American Club is, in fact, an organization formed by the older men to attract the younger men.

To analyze the Polish-American Club's representational content we must first examine its functions as defined by officers of the club. One states: "The club is mostly for the benefit of the people wishing to get their citizenship papers. We charge ten cents a month, and any member that is getting papers, we pay for the witnesses that have to go up with them. Sometimes they have to go to Boston or other towns to get the papers. Members of the club go with them as witnesses and the club pays the expenses. This makes it much easier for a person to take out their papers. There are a lot of other expenses also connected with it, and they might have trouble getting witnesses, etc."

Another officer elaborates: "The club purpose is to help the men with their citizenship papers, to provide witnesses, and swear to their character. By law the witnesses have to know the fellow for five years when he comes up for examination at the naturalization court. We give him the answers to the examination questions, tell him the governor, the senators, and the congressmen, and all the rest. The witnesses have got to tell the truth and tell whether or not he's been in jail and what for, if they know. You can't tell lies, because if they find out, they take your own papers away from you."

Therefore, this association converts the rite of passage of naturalization from an individual matter into a community concern. It is a collective effort to articulate the community with the legal status of citizenship in the American social system. Hence the club is representationally bi-national, as its name "Polish-American Club" suggests. This contrasts with the Polish Benefit Society whose function is directed to the inner stabilization of the immediate group. The Polish-American Club, as one unit in the national order of Polish-American Clubs, performs the service of linking the community externally, first, to the entire society of Poles in America, and second, to the American society itself.

The latter aspect is shown in the political activities of the club. Candidates for local, state, and national offices are invited to speak and political forums are held. This is the American side of the bi-national, dual character of the club. The Polish side is revealed in the Kosciusko celebration organized by the club for the community. Kosciusko is the hero through whom American Poles can identify themselves with the most important phase of American history. Thus the celebration has its bi-national aspects. This is especially apparent in the following remarks of a young P^2 Pole, who is the only professional man in the Polish group: "When the Poles had a Kosciusko celebration here a couple of months ago, Mayor Ronnell spoke and they asked me to speak. I told them that if ever a Yankee stopped them on the street and said, 'You are not an American,' you tell them that Kosciusko and Pulaski gave their money and their efforts to the Revolutionary War at a time when the Yankees themselves were deserting Washington and the cause. These Polish heroes fought for American liberty, and all Poles should be proud of them. No Pole need walk down the street feeling ashamed but should hold his head high as a Pole and as an American, and they should act in a way that would make others proud of them."

When unemployment brought the Poles to severely reduced circumstances, the Polish-American Club was more seriously affected than the Polish Benefit Society. The latter society had a larger membership and was able to bolster its finances by an extensive entertainment program, whereas the Polish-American Club, officered by the older men who were also members and officers of the P.B.S., had no recreational program for the community. Also, the benefit function of the P.B.S. was far more important to the community than was the naturalization function of the P.A.C. Hence, while the memberships of both were cut in half by 1933, the P.A.C. was less able to withstand the shock and its continued existence was seriously threatened.

At that juncture a P^1 Pole who was an officer in both associations produced the following plan for strengthening the P.A.C.: "We are planning, in a few weeks, a big drive for the club. We have written to the central offices for Polish speakers to come some Sunday soon and address the people. We want to enlarge the club and bring in other people of other religious affiliations [Russian Orthodox] and Roman Catholics. Now the club is reduced to about twenty-five members, all Polish and Roman Catholic. Most of them are oldish, the ages admitted being from eighteen to forty-five. We want to bring in particularly the other younger Poles and the Russians. The constitution has been remodeled to admit other religions. This is a tribute to American democracy. Especially, we want to interest the young fellows who are just growing up now—those of about eighteen and twenty. They haven't any place to go now at all, and we would provide them with something to do. I am sure that we can get them and also get the Russians."

Another officer had more restricted plans: "There is a new batch of fellows going up this spring for their papers. We want them in the club now." That is, the officers were concerned about the "younger fellows who are just growing up now" and proposed a "drive" to bring them into the club. They were also concerned about the falling membership of the Benefit Society, yet they proposed no such "drive" to add young men to its membership, primarily because the death benefits are conceived in terms of their function for the family, and these younger men were almost without exception unmarried. The P.A.C. was definitely the place for the younger men. Since the club was directed by older men who were also the officers of the P.B.S., it is evident that the club was an adjunct of the P.B.S. designed to absorb the younger men who were not interested in death benefits. As an attraction, however, they established in the club what was known as a "sickness fund," from which members could make limited loans to tide them over periods of unemployment enforced by illness. That is, they added to the club one of the benefit elements which was important in the P.B.S. and which would have meaning to the younger unmarried men for whom the P.A.C. was designed.

A second meliorative plan was to include the Russians in the club but not in the Benefit Society. By its important internal functions for the Polish community the Benefit Society was implicitly identified with the community and hence was exclusive in its membership. The existence of the Russian Benefit Society had a corresponding relation to the Russian community. The P.A.C., however, had externally articulating functions which, apparently because of the close relations between the Poles and Russians in the informal associations of the stores, could be extended to include the Russians. The distinction is, then, that the Russians could not be organized formally with the Poles in an association having internal functions for the Polish community, but could be included in an association with external functions. The club, it was planned, should articulate both the Poles and the Russian groups to the American social system.

The young adult grades in both the Polish and Russian groups were moving into American open associations, especially into the

Moose. Twenty-two young male adults among the Poles and ten
among the Russians were in this movement. One of these Poles, a
married man, asked why he joined the Moose, answered: "Well,
I suppose protection is one thing. They give good protection.
Then it is a place [the Moose clubhouse] to go play pool, shower-
bath and the library. They like to use the library. They sit there
and read, and it is a good place to go in the evening and talk.
Even the married men want to go out in the evening and that's a
fine place." By protection he means the insurance aspects of the
Moose, but his principal emphasis is on the recreational facilities
provided.

With this development the Polish club was indeed at a critical
stage, and the final move, on admitting failure, was to merge the
two associations. Actually the P.B.S. absorbed the P.A.C. A Pole,
questioned about the P.A.C., replied: "Oh, that is the same thing
as the Benefit Society now. They have moved in together. The
members of the Benefit Society pay five cents extra dues a month
to help keep up the Polish-American Club. It is all one thing now."

As the informant intimates, the Polish-American Club nominally did not go out of existence. The memberships were merged
but the functions were kept distinct. The benefit and recreational
functions continue to be administered under the name of the
Benefit Society. The naturalization and political functions, however, are performed under the name of the Polish-American Club.
By distinguishing the two sets of functions in spite of the union
of the two associations, the Poles are emphasizing the important
distinction between internal and external functions.

The F^1 male adolescent age grade among the Poles, joining
with the Russian boys, formed an informal athletic association in
1931. Then a prominent P^2 Pole, who is now in a professional occupation and who was a "star athlete" in the local high school and
in college, returned to the city and joined the coaching staff of
the Y.M.C.A. He described the subsequent developments:

"I want to tell you about my club work here. Through the Hi-Y
Club [when he was in high school], I became associated with the
Y.M.C.A., its teams and its activities under the three different
secretaries. When Mr. Clarence, the present secretary, came, he
organized all the boys into clubs and he made me the leader of six
of them. I realized that, to make the clubs successful, they would
have to be cohesive around common activities, so I drew up constitutions for them, organized teams, gave them names, had a little
ritual, and they all worked very well. Then the Polish boys came to

me and said, 'If you can do this for them, why can't you do it for us?' So I organized them, brought them into the Y.M.C.A. club system, but in the constitution I provided that each member should go to Communion once a month; this of course because the Poles are Catholic. But at the end of the first year the Polish people began to kick. In the first place, the Irish Catholic priest wanted the boys in the Catholic Club. And the boys had been in the Catholic Club, but they said that the priest was Irish and favored the Irish boys. Secondly, the young Polish Catholic priest from Essex came to Yankee City to hold services at stations, and he was against the boys' being in the Y.M.C.A. because it was Protestant and anti-Catholic. I told them that I don't know about the Y.M.C.A. elsewhere, but I do know that here it is nothing of the sort. At any rate, at the end of the year the Polish boys withdrew and formed their own club, called the Polish Club, and I was asked to be their leader. I drew up a new constitution for them and coached their teams. They needed some money to fix up a clubroom in Polish Hall, so they put on little vaudeville skits, ideas they got from the movies, etc., and they charged ten cents a head. Pretty soon they had collected $75. Then by getting a seven-tube radio speaker to which was attached a phonograph device, they could get the best dance music—Paul Whiteman, etc., and hold dances without paying for an orchestra."

The informant's last comment, on the dancing facilities acquired for the club, introduces the next associational development in the Polish community system, organization of the girls of adolescent age. Female dancing partners could be invited to the club informally, but only recently the leader "decided that it would be better to have the girls come as a group, so I organized them into a Polish Girls Club."

This Pole, only in his late twenties, assumed leadership through the boys' and girls' clubs of the Polish community. By influencing the clubs to orient their organized behaviors to the standards of the "elite of Hill Street" he meant to lead the adult P generation and the community to "better things—higher things." Through his prestige as an athlete and college and professional man, he has been the factor in organizing the Polish F[1] adolescent age grade into associations at a much earlier stage in the development of the Polish community system than will be observed for most other ethnic communities in Yankee City.

His prestige may be defined in terms of the value symbols which he incorporates in his social personality. He represents a personality whom those younger than himself in his own ethnic group would seek and accept as leader and guide. To both the Polish Boys Club and the Polish Girls Club he has served as an organizing focus, without which, to judge from the evidence of other ethnic groups, their respective associations would not have emerged at so early a stage in the evolution of the community. Adolescent associations of other ethnic groups have in most cases been formed by the P[1] parents, removed in age generation and system orientation from the F generation. In all groups except the Irish these associations have proved relatively weak in either attracting or holding the adolescents for whom they were designed.

Greek Associations

The extent to which the coffee shops absorb the leisure time of the Greeks is seen in the fact that no formal Greek association was organized until 1929. The Poles, who arrived in Yankee City during a period five years later than the Greeks, had a formal association in 1924. The Greek-American Progressive Association parallels the Polish-American Club in almost every detail. Its fifty members[3] are P[1] and P[2] adult males. In representational content it is bi-national, and it functions for purposes of naturalization. There are no regular meetings. Annually a ball and a concert are given. This association has national affiliations.

Although the membership is fairly evenly divided between young adults (thirty to thirty-nine) and adults (forty plus), the G.A.P.A. holds 75 per cent of all the young Greek male adults and only about 33 per cent of the older adults. These older adult males are the Greek men who have been longest in this country and in Yankee City, some of them having arrived as early as 1900. Therefore, the young-adult grade and those of the adult grade longest here comprise the membership of the G.A.P.A. Testing this conclusion by the factor of ethnic generation it is found that the G.A.P.A. holds thirty (32 per cent) of the ninety-three P[1] male Greeks in Yankee City and twenty (71 per cent) of the twenty-eight P[2] male Greeks. Of the P[1] members, many arrived as young men and fall close to the P[2] category.

3	Age Grade	Greek Males in Yankee City	Members of G.A.P.A.
	02–29	9	0
	30–39	28	21
	40–49	66	23
	50–59	19	6
	60+	4	0

Control of the G.A.P.A. is almost evenly balanced between the two age grades. Its board of directors includes the four officers, together with a chaplain and five councilors. Over a period of three years these offices were filled by thirty men divided on the basis of age and generation as follows: sixteen of the P^2 generation (age thirty to thirty-nine) and fourteen of the P^1 (age forty and over).

The class composition of the G.A.P.A. is 50 per cent lower-lower, 46 per cent upper-lower, and 4 per cent lower-middle.

In its representational content the G.A.P.A. is bi-national, as is indicated in the following statement of the "Objects and Principles of the Association" which appears in the Souvenir Program of the Annual G.A.P.A. Ball:

Sec. 1. To promote and encourage loyalty and allegiance to the United States, its constitution and laws, including the Constitutions of the several States and their subdivisions. To teach and educate persons of Greek nationality residing in the United States of America the principles, ideals and doctrines of American citizenship; to educate its members in the fundamental principles of constitutional government; to teach the science of political economy and to afford its members social culture and enjoyment.

Sec. 2. To urge its members to become citizens of the United States in order that they may fully appreciate the privilege of citizenship and participate in the political, civic, social and commercial life in the United States.

Sec. 3. To promote a better understanding between the American and Greek peoples, and of the ideals of Hellenism, and its influence on the United States.

Sec. 4. To cultivate the Greek language, and the religious sentiment of members according to the dogmas and Holy Canons of the Greek Orthodox Church, and to assist it in order to fulfill its spiritual mission in America through an educated, disciplined and learned English-speaking clergy and by means of Sunday Schools, Bible Classes and Social Work.

Sec. 5. To coöperate in benevolent and charitable matters, and in the maintenance of high moral standards; to promote good fellowship and a spirit of altruism among its members; to impress the duty of its members to help, encourage and comfort each other, in every possible manner.

In the application for membership is this pledge:

Relying upon the assurance that the G.A.P.A. is an organization consecrated to the ideals and traditions of America; that it pledges its membership in obedience to the duly constituted Federal, State and Municipal authorities of the United States; that it obligates its membership to the practice of the fraternal principles of brotherly love, benevolence and self sacrifice, I do hereby respectfully request admission. . . .

These are especially clear statements of the representational content of the bi-national type of formal ethnic association. Such an association is almost inevitably a structural component within a system of associational structures embracing most of the communities of a particular ethnic derivation found in the United States. The extended system attempts to articulate the community components of the total ethnic group in the American society, and hence the individual communities to (1) the American representational system, e.g., the "principles, ideals and doctrines of American citizenship"; (2) legal status in the American social system, by urging "its members to become citizens of the United States"; and (3) the "political, civic, social, and commercial" subsystems of American society.

On the other hand, this associational system seeks to preserve and strengthen the community's ethnic representational system by emphasizing, as in the case of the G.A.P.A., the "cultivation of the Greek language . . . the Greek Orthodox Church," and Greek schools. That is, while giving each community system status in the American social system, the national G.A.P.A. would nevertheless have that community system maintain its essential Greekness.

The community, as the name of the association suggests, must be both Greek and American at one and the same time, to sanction, while still articulated to the American social system, the preservation of its Greek elements. The association seeks "to promote a better understanding between the American and Greek peoples, and of the ideals of Hellenism, and its influence on the United States"; that is, it would have the American society understand why the Greek community should preserve its Greekness in America.

The bi-national representational content of the G.A.P.A. is also manifest in the fact that the Yankee City G.A.P.A. has taken as its chapter designation the name of a Greek-American boy from New England who was killed in the service of the American

Army during World War I. The parallelism with Kosciusko in the bi-national Polish association, the Polish-American Club, is obvious.

Regarding explicit function, most of the informants contrast the G.A.P.A. with the other great Greek-American order, the American-Hellenic Progressive Association, otherwise known as the Ahepa.[4] A P[1] middle-aged Yankee City Greek who has been in this country about twenty-five years and who is not a member of the G.A.P.A. said, "The G.A.P.A. has no political importance. It is just an organization sponsored to teach the Greeks to be good Americans as well as good Greeks. It encourages the truth and wants them to learn Greek and know all about Greece. There is another organization, the Ahepa. It is not quite like the G.A.P.A. The difference is that at all meetings the Ahepa requires English to be spoken. It only takes in citizens, and if a person wants to join they have to become a citizen first. But the G.A.P.A. takes in anyone and their meetings are in Greek. The G.A.P.A. wants them to be good Greeks and good Americans, but the Ahepa wants to teach them to be Americans first. All the best people— doctors and lawyers—among the Greeks belong to the Ahepa. It is a much better society than the G.A.P.A. If I wanted to join anything, I'd join the Ahepa."

The president of the G.A.P.A. said: "The G.A.P.A. is smaller than the Ahepa and is known primarily for developing citizenship among the Greeks. It does not take part in politics [but see below]. It is rather new. The Ahepa takes a great deal of interest in politics. Only members of the Greek Orthodox Church can join the G.A.P.A., while any Greek may join the Ahepa."

The remarks of one Greek were more direct: "The G.A.P.A. has a social side, but its primary purpose is educational [his implication seems to be, education into Greek representations]. It works also for Americanization in helping people to take out their first and second citizenship papers."

And finally, there is the comment of a G.A.P.A. member: "The G.A.P.A. encourages Greek things in every way they can. It [the national order] used to send a group of selected young people on trips to Greece, in order to imbue them with Greek ideals and Greek traditions. That is in contrast with the Ahepa. The G.A.P.A. and Ahepa are in strong competition with each other.

4. There is no chapter of this lodge in Yankee City, although three Yankee City Greeks belong to chapters in other near-by cities.

G.A.P.A. looks back to the old Greek life, and Ahepa looks forward, encourages American things and American ideas."

The linkage, through contrast of the G.A.P.A. and Ahepa, in the mind of Greek informants gives the key to the whole function of the G.A.P.A. The G.A.P.A. and the Ahepa are both bi-national. Both have the explicit function of encouraging "the Greeks to be good Americans as well as good Greeks." But as between the dual national representations, the Ahepa emphasizes the American representations, e.g., in its formal use of the English language, its requisite of American citizenship for membership, and its indifference to the affiliation with the Greek church that is required by the G.A.P.A.

Two of the three Yankee City Greeks who are members of the Ahepa chapters in other cities are of the lower-middle and one is of the upper-middle class; all three are of the P^2 generation; none is a member of the G.A.P.A.

The G.A.P.A., as a bi-national associational structure containing both the P^1 and P^2 generations, is homologous to the Polish-American Club, the Armenian Progressive Club, the Lafayette Club of the French Canadians, and the Hibernians of the Irish in Yankee City. Especially among the Irish, the difference in emphasis of the two bi-national associations within a single ethnic community will be reproduced with identical correlations of generation and class composition.

The bi-national nature of the Yankee City G.A.P.A. is illustrated by the remarks of those Greeks who are antagonistic to the organization. The Greek priests in Yankee City represent the Greek community and the Greek church at the annual installation of G.A.P.A. officers; yet all claim that they "have nothing to do with the G.A.P.A." One of them, when asked about the G.A.P.A., replied sharply: "I don't know much about it; I don't belong to secret societies."

One middle-class Greek of the P^2 generation said: "I don't like the G.A.P.A. or the other Greek organizations. They will break up. I belong to the Veterans of Foreign Wars." Another, when asked whether he was a member of the G.A.P.A., replied, "No, I don't belong. I am a member of the Moose. I don't know much about the G.A.P.A. They are supposed to help people out. They don't seem much to me."

Those among the Greeks, then, who are still strongly oriented to the social system of Greece—the priests, for instance, and more recent P¹ immigrants—have refrained from joining the G.A.P.A. and are often antagonistic to it because of its American content. Those who have shifted their orientation to the American system have not accepted membership in, and are antipathetic to, the G.A.P.A. because of the Greek content.

Like the monthly meetings of the two Polish associations, those of the G.A.P.A. are devoted largely to business, although ritual elements may be inferred from the existence of a "chaplain"; and like the Polish Benefit Society, although to a far less degree, the G.A.P.A. serves to organize, for the entire Greek community, recreational affairs such as the annual ball, the annual celebration of Greek Independence Day, and periodic dances and concerts.

That the G.A.P.A. has begun to acquire recreational functions for its membership is suggested, however, in the plans of its president for acquiring a hall to be used as clubrooms as well as a meeting place. "An organization without a place of its own won't last long. When we go to the Knights of Malta Hall for meetings, it is not a home place; we feel that when we go out we can't come back. We can't go there any evening we want, we can't go there to discuss business; no place where we can always go and talk over the business of the club. If we had a hall we could make it a sort of club place, meeting place. Now if we want to discuss business we have to go to the coffee shop, but that's too public—no good. We need a place of our own. If we had one we could put in things to exercise with and have lots of entertainments and play games. I never go to a coffee house like some do; I've only been there twice."

This and other evidence indicate that the G.A.P.A. is moving toward usurpation of the clubhouse functions of the coffee shops by providing recreational facilities of its own. It has also begun to displace the coffee houses as the point of articulation between the Yankee City political candidates and the Greek community. Recently the G.A.P.A. has organized open meetings for the entire group at which contending candidates for political office have made campaign speeches. This, of course, parallels an aspect of the Polish-American Club. The liaison function which the coffee houses have been performing informally the G.A.P.A. is now carrying out formally. That there is antagonism between the two is seen in the concluding remarks of the G.A.P.A. president and in the fact that, while notices of the Greek school and Greek churches are posted on the coffee house bulletin boards, no G.A.P.A. notices have been observed there.

A formal male association covering the adolescent age grade

was organized in 1930 by the G.A.P.A. members as an auxiliary called the G.A.P.A. Juniors. This adolescent association was organized around a personality of a type similar to that of the Polish leader described above. Both leaders were of the P^2 generation, both had been brought to this country when they were four years old, both were star athletes in high school, and both went into professional occupations. The important difference between them was one of age. The Pole was twenty-five in 1934 when the Polish Club was established, whereas the Greek was nineteen in 1930 when the G.A.P.A. Juniors were organized. Because of this difference in age, apparently, the Greek "leader" preferred to become the first president of the Juniors, whereas the Polish leader accepted no office in the Polish club and preferred to wield his influence from "behind the throne."

In type, the G.A.P.A. Juniors is similar to the Polish club in that recreational aspects predominate. In all the major sports it has teams which compete in the Y.M.C.A. league as well as in a league of the New England G.A.P.A. Juniors. The senior G.A.P.A. provides these teams with uniforms bearing the names of both the national association and the Yankee City unit.

In addition to organizing athletics, the Juniors have a program of "social affairs," as they are called, e.g., an annual New Year's Day party for the children of the Greek Afternoon School and an annual musical entertainment for the community which features the Juniors' string orchestra. The orchestra also takes part in the musical program of all community affairs and appears on the entertainment programs of the Yankee City society itself.

The Juniors have thirty-two members, aged twelve to twenty-one, representing about 60 per cent of this age group. Eighty per cent of the members have fathers in the G.A.P.A. The G.A.P.A. and its junior auxiliary, therefore, represent corresponding age-grade associations which formally organize and relate fathers and sons. A member of the senior G.A.P.A. is the adviser of the Juniors, and the two associations have their annual public installation of officers jointly. A Junior officer states: "We have brought a lot of favorable attention to the Seniors because we were one of the first G.A.P.A. Junior chapters to be organized. We always work together with the G.A.P.A. seniors in anything that they are doing [in communal recreational affairs]."

Because of its wide age range, there appears a differentiation of function between the older boys and the younger boys among the Juniors. There are two sets of teams, the older being called by the association name, and the younger after a Greek mythological animal. An officer said: "The older fellows run the organization. There are a lot of kids about twelve years of age. That's when we first take them in. They don't amount to much. We sort of keep them in, giving them a little training, and teach them how to run the thing. But they are not very active anyhow until they get older." From 1930 to 1933 all officers were between the ages of sixteen and nineteen.

The Juniors, following the pattern of the parent association, "have a meeting every month except in the summer. We charge dues of five cents a week and collect it at the meetings. Otherwise we don't do much at meetings."

Analysis of the statements of informants shows that the G.A.P.A. established the Junior auxiliary for these purposes: (1) to organize formally the boys' recreation; (2) to articulate the boys into the Greek community system and, conversely, to keep them from dissociating themselves from the community; (3) to subordinate the boys formally to the controls of their fathers who are organized in the senior G.A.P.A., e.g., by means of the "adviser" to the Juniors; and (4) to use the Junior association as a "stepping stone" by which the F^1 generation will be led up into the P generation senior association.

Jewish and Armenian Associations

The ethnic-national association is found only among the Jewish and Armenian communities. In both communities, this type until recently organized adolescents as well as adult males and females, although in separate structures. In other words, almost the entire associational subsystem of each, sexually bifurcated and age graded, is oriented to the national representations of their respective ancestral social systems. Furthermore, this type emerged early in the development of each community system: among the Jews in 1906 and among the Armenians in 1908. The nationalist aspiration of the community for the ancestral society is the primary reason for these associations. Up to the post-World-War-I treaties, the function of the Armenian associations, linked in an international system, was to render moral and financial assistance to the Armenian movement for national autonomy and independence from the Turkish Empire. In 1933 there were six structures in the associational subsystem of the Yankee City Armenian community, and, without exception, all were explicitly organized around nationalistic representations.

The Jewish aspirations to the restoration of Palestine as a Jewish homeland are organized internationally in what is known as the Zionist movement. Between 1906 and 1918, almost the entire Yankee City Jewish community was distributed among three age-graded Zionist associations. Since that time, however, there has been an internal proliferation of associations, with a differentiation of functions and representations. In 1933 the Jewish associational subsystem consisted of eight structures— four female, three male, and one mixed. These are split into four age grades, and include the P^1, P^2, the young adult F^1, and the adolescent F^1 generations. Three of these are Zionist in their representations, affiliations, and functions, i.e., are of the national type. The rest are all of the community type, divided into subtypes: two for charity and benefit; two for recreation (adolescents) ; and one fraternal.

Irish and French-Canadian Associations

The Irish and French Canadians each present two complete overlapping age-graded associational subsystems. Because of the similarities between the two ethnic groups in this respect, only the Irish associations will be given since they appear in a more developed stage.

One of the associational subsystems among the Irish consists of six associations which are direct extensions of the church. Their recreational aspects are negligible except in the adolescent grade. The members meet in the parish hall adjoining the church and devote their time almost exclusively to religious instruction under the direction of either a priest or a nun. They attend Mass in a group monthly. Their most important function appears to be ritualization of their dead. These six associations are rigidly split into sex and age groups. All are developments of the last twenty-five years.

The second associational subsystem, dating from 1871, consists of six adult associations which maintain direct relations to the Irish church as reflected in their annual contributions to the church fund and ritualization of their dead within the church. Three of these associations are fraternal, five have insurance features, and one is the charity-dispensing organization for the community. All but one are sexually differentiated. All but one have secret rituals and developed recreational forms centered in their own clubhouses.

The associations with P and F^1 generation members are lower class and those with F^2 members are middle class. The P generation associations are bi-national, i.e., Irish-American; and the F^1 and F^2 generation associations are American-national.

3. *Summary*

FROM the evidence presented it is possible to establish a sequence of associational developments in the ethnic community of Yankee City and probably of most other American cities:

1. An informal association of males emerges when there are from ten to fifteen men in the group.

2. From ten to twenty years after this stage a formal P^1 association crystallizes, which supplements rather than displaces the P^1 informal association.

3. From five to ten years later a P^2 formal association appears which displaces the antecedent P^2 informal association. In most cases the P^2 are joined in the structure with the P^1 men longest in the city and most "Americanized."

4. There are no female informal associations since this sex never congregates around a "hangout" which defines the focus of such an association, and confines its informal recreation to clique relations.

5. There appear to be no formal P^1 female associations except among the Jews and Armenians. All groups except the newest, i.e., Russian, Polish, and Greek, have formal P^2 female associations.

6. Except among the three newest groups just named, both the P^1 female associations (Jewish and Armenian) and the P^2 are organized within five years of the P^2 men's association.

7. The crystallization of adolescent formal associations out of the informal type varies widely. Among the Jews one was organized in 1908, early in the community's development, but among the Irish not until 1921.

8. The minimum necessary to the crystallization of a formal association structure is in all cases about twenty. Increase of numbers in the ethnic group is followed by increasing numbers in the association's membership, rather than by the creation of a new formal association.

9. The primary differentiating factors of associational structures in a community system are sex, age, generation, and class. The numbers in the group are correlated with the class factor, for only when a group has expanded in population to the point where it is internally differentiated on class lines does class differentiation enter into its associational subsystem. Only among the Irish in Yankee City has this occurred.

X

THE AMERICAN ETHNIC GROUP

1. *Ethnic Groups in America*

THE ethnic groups of Yankee City are important in their own right, but their significance to us as Americans is greatly increased when we recognize them as representatives of other such groups which are an important part of our total population and vitally influence every aspect of American life. American ethnic groups are sometimes classed with the minority groups of Europe, but while they show certain general characteristics in common the groups in America are quite different from those in Europe and more like the minority groups of Australia and South America. The roots of the minorities of Europe are buried deeply in the soil of the dominant country. Often the history of the subordinate group in a region is more ancient than that of the dominant one. In the United States the ethnic group's origins are known and felt to be "foreign." Yet these minorities arrived only a short time after the dominant culture had established itself.[1] Both the immigrant and host societies know that the so-called "old-American" culture is itself new and ultimately "immigrant." This feeling creates a certain toleration in the attitude of the host society.

The forces which are most potent both in forming and changing the ethnic groups emanate from the institutions of the dominant American social system. Our political organization permits all adults to be equal within its structure. Although at first this equality is largely theoretical, it gives the ethnic members an attainable goal as the political success of the Irish, Germans, Scandinavians, and Italians demonstrates. Our developing industrial and factory economy with its own hierarchy permits and demands that ethnic members move up and out of their ethnic subsystems into the common life of America. The public school teaches the people to adjust to the central core of our life, provides them with technical skills for their own advancement, and gives them some of the power necessary to become upward mobile in our class order. The

---

1. The only exceptions are the American Indians and some of the Spanish-speaking minorities.

school, in belief and partly in practice, expresses the basic principles of American democracy where all men are equal; when the school cannot make them equal it struggles to make them culturally alike.

The American family system breaks down and builds up ethnic subsystems. The ethnic parent tries to orient the child to an ethnic past, but the child often insists on being more American than Americans. Marriage also may maintain or disrupt the ethnic way of life. At marriage an individual may move out of his ethnic group into that of his spouse; or an individual who has become partly American may re-identify with his ethnic group and become more ethnic than in the past.

Cliques and associations also operate to increase or decrease ethnic identification. If the child in school becomes a part of an American clique he is likely to move rather rapidly into the American way of life. On the other hand, if he is rejected and forced to participate in ethnic cliques he may become closely identified with the cultural group of his parent. This is also true for adult cliques and for adult associations. On the whole, however, the evidence from Yankee City shows that cliques and associations increase the participation of ethnic people in the life of the larger community and accelerate assimilation.

Our class system functions for a large proportion of ethnics to destroy the ethnic subsystems and to increase assimilation. The mobile ethnic is much more likely to be assimilated than the non-mobile one. The latter retains many of the social characteristics of his homeland. Most ethnics are in lower social levels. Some of them become self-sufficient, interact among themselves, and thereby reinforce their old ways of life. Some of the unsuccessfully mobile turn hostile to the host culture, develop increased feelings of loyalty to their ethnic traditions, become active in maintaining their ethnic subsystems, and prevent others from becoming assimilated. But, generally speaking, our class order disunites ethnic groups and accelerates their assimilation.

2. *Race, Culture, and American Subordinate Groups*

To understand the place of the ethnic group in the American social system it is necessary to see it in the larger framework of all the subordinate groups. A survey of the several types of subordinated groups in this country reveals that, excluding the subordination of lower-class old Americans, there are three basic types which are ranked as inferior. They are (1) the ethnic group, (2) the racial group, and (3) the ethno-racial group. The ethnic group carries a divergent set of cultural traits which are evaluated by the host society as inferior. We have seen in the Yankee City study how these cultural groups are identified with being different and given an inferior rating and how they form their own social world to nurse their members through a period of transition until these members "unlearn" what they have been taught and successfully learn the new way of life necessary for full acceptance in the host society.

The racial groups are divergent biologically rather than culturally. They possess physical traits inherited from their fathers and mothers which are divergent from those of the old-American white population. These traits have been evaluated as inferior. Such physical attributes as dark skin, the epicanthic fold, or kinky hair become symbols of status and automatically consign their possessors to inferior status. The Chinese, Japanese, and Filipinos of California, the Spanish Americans and Mexicans of the American Southwest, and American Negroes suffer from such evaluations of their racial differences. The cultural traits of the ethnic group, which have become symbols of inferior status, can be and are changed in time; but the physical traits which have become symbols of inferior status are permanent. Unless the host society changes its methods of evaluation these racial groups are doomed to a permanent inferior ranking.

From the researches done in Yankee City and on the Negro groups of the South and the North, and from the recent investigations made on the Spanish Americans and the Orientals of California, all of which are based on the body of knowledge that social scientists have collected on ethnic and racial groups, it now seems possible to present a conceptual scheme which places a subordinate group in its relative rank within our social hierarchy. It permits us to predict with some degree of success the probable degree of subordination each group will suffer, the strength of the subsystem likely to be developed by it, the kind of rank order it will be assigned, and the approximate period necessary for its assimilation into American life.

The conceptual scheme about to be described is based on the following propositions: First, the greater the difference between the host and the immigrant cultures, the greater will be the subordination, the greater the strength of the ethnic social systems, and the longer the period necessary for the assimilation of the ethnic group. On the other hand, those ethnic groups with small differences are quickly assimilated. Second, the greater the racial difference between the populations of the immigrant and the host societies the greater the subordination of the immigrant group, the greater the strength of the social subsystem, and the longer the period necessary for assimilation. Finally, when the combined cultural and biological traits are highly divergent from those of the host society the subordination of the group will be very great, their subsystem strong, the period of assimilation long, and the processes slow and usually painful. With these propositions in mind it is possible to construct a rough scale by which hypotheses may be developed about the relative ranking of each racial and cultural group in American life, the strength of its subsystem, and the period necessary for ultimate assimilation.

The people racially most like white "old Americans," the dominant people in America, are other Caucasians. Those least like them are the Mongoloid peoples, Negroes, and racially mixed, dark-skinned groups such as the peoples of India. The Caucasoid group lies at one extreme, and the Mongoloid and Negroid peoples at the other extreme of the range. To bring out the significant points about assimilation and to point up further questions on the subordination of subgroups, the Caucasoid immigrant population has been divided into those who are largely like the present old-American stock and those who are least like them. For convenience we can refer to the first as light Caucasoids and to the latter as dark Caucasoids. Those people with a mixture of Caucasoid and Mongoloid blood, in particular mixtures from Latin America, occupy the next place in the range. The mixed bloods of Mongoloid and Caucasoid stock who resemble Mediterranean Caucasoids are followed by Mongoloids and Negroes. These considerations provide us with five categories: race type I, the light Caucasoids; race type II, the dark Caucasoids; race type III, Mongoloid and Caucasoid mixtures with a Mediterranean appearance; race type IV, Mongoloids and mixed peoples with a predominantly Mongoloid appearance; and finally race type V, Negroes and all Negroid mixtures.

A similar scale can be constructed for deviation from the dominant American culture. For purposes of the present analysis, the immigrant cultures may be divided into differences of language and religion. (Other customary behavior is associated with language and religion.[2]) In the light of this study, and from the

---

2. A finer cultural screening necessary for making sharper discriminations would divide the culture into more categories, but for general placement of the

results of others, it is clear that emphasis must be placed on religious differences. The dominant old-American religion is Protestant, and much of our customary behavior is closely integrated with a Protestant outlook on life. Our customary way of life is most like the English, and our language is but one of the several English dialects. The ethnic people most like us are English-speaking Protestants with a body of customary behavior no more deviant from our way of life than their language and religion. This cultural type is followed by Protestants who do not speak English and whose way of life is slightly more divergent from ours. The third type includes English-speaking Catholics and other non-Protestant groups. The fourth cultural type includes Catholics and other non-Protestants who do not speak English. The types least like us are the non-Christians, some of whom speak English and others who do not.

When these two scales, the cultural and the racial, are combined into a table, thirty possible categories logically result since there are six cultural types for each of five racial types. However, several of these categories do not exist in actual fact. For example, there are no English-speaking, Protestant, dark Caucasoids.

Table 6 succinctly presents the ethno-racial scale of differences between the dominant white American host society and the present ethnic and racial groups as well as the entering immigrant groups. In the left-hand column are the five racial types in the order of their similarity to the old-American white stock. Next to this column are the six cultural types serially arranged according to their similarity with old-American culture. The repetition of the six cultural categories for each racial type reveals that the racial evaluations made by the American host society are far more potent and lasting in the ranking of divergent peoples than those applied to cultural groups. For example, English-speaking Protestant Negroes possessing the same culture as the rest of the American group cannot be ranked as a subvariety of other English-speaking peoples; and it is obvious that they must be placed in a position inferior to all Caucasoid peoples, regardless of the cultural deviation of all the white-skinned peoples. The peoples most like white Americans, and therefore ranked highest, are the

several groups, language and religion are significant; this is in part true because large bodies of customary behavior are associated with these two basic cultural phenomena.

The racial scale must follow the classifications of contemporary texts of physical anthropology, but these classifications may be simplified to fit the needs of the above racial categories.

TABLE 6

Scale of Subordination and Assimilation

Racial Type	*Cultural Type*
Racial Type I Light Caucasoids	Cultural Type 1 English-speaking Protestants
	Cultural Type 2 Protestants who do not speak English
	Cultural Type 3 English-speaking Catholics and other non-Protestants
	Cultural Type 4 Catholics and other non-Protestants, most of whom speak allied Indo-European languages
	Cultural Type 5 English-speaking non-Christians
	Cultural Type 6 Non-Christians who do not speak English
Racial Type II Dark Caucasoids	Cultural typing the same as for Racial Type I
Racial Type III Mongoloid and Caucasoid mixtures with Caucasoid appearance dominant (appearance of "dark" Mediterranean)	Cultural typing the same as for Racial Type I
Racial Type IV Mongoloid and Caucasoid mixtures that appear Mongoloid	Cultural typing the same as for Racial Type I
Racial Type V Negroes and all Negroid mixtures	Cultural typing the same as for Racial Type I

light Caucasoids who are Protestant and speak English. Those least like us are the non-Christian Negroes.

We will now turn to the second part of our analysis, presenting a way of ranking (1) the degree of subordination and social distance, (2) the strength of the racial and ethnic subsystems, and (3) the forms of American rank. A timetable predicts the approximate period necessary for the assimilation of each racial and ethnic group. For convenience a five-point scale has been set up for each. The degrees of subordination run from "very slight" through "slight," "moderate," "great," to "very great." The criteria for rating a particular group's degree of subordination are (1) freedom of residential choice, (2) freedom to marry out of one's own group, (3) amount of occupational restriction, (4) strength of attitudes in the host society which prevent social participation in such institutions as associations and cliques, and (5) the amount of vertical mobility permitted in the host society for members of the ethnic or racial group.[3]

The presentation here is designed to give no more than a résumé of the operations and present only those necessary to understand the whole schema of ethnic and social subordination and assimilation. Any one group may be slightly out of place as, for example, the Catholic French or the Hungarians, but the relative place of most of the groups is accurate. The importance of this system of analysis is that each group's place is established in a total configuration of American society as the result of applying scientific propositions about subordination and assimilation which appear to be laws governing the relations of ethno-racial groups in the larger American society.

The criteria for the strength of the cultural or racial subsystem are (1) the power of the "church" over its members and degree of divergence of the "church" from the Protestant norms; (2) the presence of separate schools and the amount of control they exercise; (3) and (4) the political as well as the economic unity of the group; and (5) the number and power of ethnic or racial associations.[4] Our hypothesis is that the light Caucasoids who are English-speaking and Protestant develop the least powerful systems while the Negroes have the strongest.

Criteria for a timetable of assimilation are (1) the time taken for an entire group to disappear, (2) the proportionate number of people who drop out of a group in each generation, and (3) the amount and kind of participation permitted members of the group by the host society. The same procedure as described for the other categories produces a rough index for a group's assimilation: "very short" (see Table 7) means that the group is assimilated in a period of not more than one generation; "short"

3. If each of these criteria is re-scaled from one to five and the results added and the sum divided by five, the quotient given provides a rough but fairly satisfactory index of the degree of subordination of each group. The light Caucasoids who are Protestant and speak English get an index of one, and the non-Christian Negroes an index of five, giving the first a rating of "very slight" and the latter "very great" subordination.

4. Each of the five characteristics of the strength of a subsystem can be re-divided into a five-point scale and the same procedure can be used for determining the strength of the subsystem as that described for the degree of subordination.

TABLE 7

Ethnic and Racial Assimilation

Cultural and Racial Type	Degree of Subordination	Strength of Ethnic and Racial Subsystems	Time for Assimilation	Form of American Rank

Racial Type I—Light Caucasoid

Cultural and Racial Type	Degree of Subordination	Strength of Ethnic and Racial Subsystems	Time for Assimilation	Form of American Rank
Cultural Type 1 English-speaking Protestants. Tests: English, Scotch, North Irish, Australians, Canadians	very slight	very weak	very short	ethnic group to class
Cultural Type 2 Protestants not speaking English. Tests: Scandinavians, Germans, Dutch, French	slight	weak	short	ethnic group to class
Cultural Type 3 English-speaking Catholics and other non-Protestants. Test: South Irish	slight	moderate	short to moderate	ethnic group to class
Cultural Type 4 Catholics and other non-Protestants who do not speak English Tests: ("fair-skinned") French Canadians, French, Germans, Belgians	slight	moderate	short to moderate	ethnic group to class
Cultural Type 5 English-speaking non-Christians Test: English Jews	moderate	moderate	short to moderate	ethnic group to class
Cultural Type 6 Non-Christians who do not speak English Tests: ("fair-skinned") European Jews and Mohammedans from Middle East	moderate	moderate	short to moderate	ethnic group to class

Racial Type II—Dark Caucasoids

Cultural and Racial Type	Degree of Subordination	Strength of Ethnic and Racial Subsystems	Time for Assimilation	Form of American Rank
Cultural Type 1	—	—	—	—
Cultural Type 2 Test: Protestant Armenians (other "dark-skinned" Protestants)	slight to moderate	weak	moderate	ethnic group to class

TABLE 7 (Continued)

Cultural and Racial Type	Degree of Subordi-nation	Strength of Ethnic and Racial Subsystems	Time for Assimi-lation	Form of American Rank
Racial Type II—Dark Caucasoids				
Cultural Type 3	—	—	—	—
Cultural Type 4 Tests: "dark skins" of Racial Type I, Cultural Type 4; also Sicilians, Portuguese, Near Eastern Christians	moderate	moderate to strong	moderate	ethnic group to class
Cultural Type 5	—	—	—	—
Cultural Type 6 Tests: ("dark-skinned") Jews and Mohammedans of Europe and the Near East	moderate to great	strong	slow	ethnic group to class
Racial Type III—Caucasoid Mixtures				
Cultural Type 1	—	—	—	—
Cultural Type 2 Tests: Small groups of Spanish Americans in the Southwest	great	strong	slow	ethno-racial to class or color caste
Cultural Type 3	—	—	—	—
Cultural Type 4 Test: Most of the mixed bloods of Latin America	great	strong	slow	ethno-racial to class or color caste
Cultural Type 5	—	—	—	—
Cultural Type 6	—	—	—	—
Racial Type IV—Mongoloids				
Cultural Type 1 Tests: Most American Chinese and Japanese	great to very great	very strong	slow	racial to semi-caste

TABLE 7 (Continued)

Cultural and Racial Type	Degree of Subordination	Strength of Ethnic and Racial Subsystems	Time for Assimilation	Form of American Rank
Racial Type IV—Mongoloids				
Cultural Type 2	—	—	—	—
Cultural Type 3	—	—	—	—
Cultural Type 4 Test: Filipinos	great to very great	very strong	very slow	racial to semi-caste
Cultural Type 5	—	—	—	—
Cultural Type 6 Tests: East Indians, Chinese, Japanese	great to very great	very strong	very slow	racial to semi-caste
Racial Type V—Negroids				
Cultural Type 1 Test: Most American Negroes	very great	very strong	very slow	racial to color caste
Cultural Type 2	—	—	—	—
Cultural Type 3 Test: Some American Negroes	very great	very strong	very slow	racial to color caste
Cultural Type 4 Tests: Negroid Puerto Ricans, etc.	very great	very strong	very slow	racial to color caste
Cultural Type 5	—	—	—	—
Cultural Type 6 Tests: Bantu Negroes and West African Negroes	very great	very strong	very slow	racial to color caste

means more than one but less than six generations; "moderate," more than six; "slow," a very long time in the future which is not yet discernible; and "very slow" means that the group will not be totally assimilated until the present American social order changes gradually or by revolution.

To test these hypotheses about subordination and predicted assimilation, let us examine Table 7 in which many of the ethnic and social groups now in America are placed appropriately in

the ethno-social scale. The people listed may also be regarded
as referring to populations now outside America who in the future
might be migrants should our present immigration laws be modified.

Most of the peoples of the British Isles, including the North
Irish but not the Catholic Irish, as well as the English-speaking
Canadians and the other English-speaking peoples of the Domin-
ions, belong to Cultural Type 1 of Racial Type I. According to
our hypotheses, their subordination should be very slight, the subsystems they build very weak, and their period of assimilation
usually less than a generation. Anyone familiar with the facts of
such people's position in America knows that their actual place
fits the one we propose for them. In Yankee City there were numerous Canadians, and a fair representation of Scotch, English,
and North Irish, but they had not formed ethnic groups and were
considered as members of the total population.

The Protestant Germans, Dutch, and Scandinavians of Cultural Type 2 and Racial Type I, according to our hypothesis,
are quickly assimilated into American life. The facts in general
support this theory. Some of the Scandinavians and Germans,
however, have formed sects that do not conform to the general
rule we have laid down and present special problems which demand
added dimensions to place them accurately in a timetable of
assimilation.

The non-Protestant Christian groups who do not speak English
are in Cultural Type 4. The great strength of the Catholic
Church in organizing and maintaining separate ethnic groups is
clearly illustrated here. The French, German, Belgian, and Dutch
Protestants, it seems likely, assimilate very rapidly, develop
less powerful subsystems, and are less subordinated than those
of the same nationality and language who are Catholic. The
Catholic Irish of Cultural Type 3 assimilate more slowly than the
Protestant Irish despite the fact that in all other respects the two
cannot be distinguished by most Americans. Whereas the Catholic
Irish develop moderately strong subsystems and take many generations to assimilate, the Protestant Irish form very weak ones
and almost immediately become assimilated.

Cultural Types 5 and 6 of Racial Type I include the light Caucasoid Jews, particularly those of Western Europe. We can best
understand the place of the Jew and of the other peoples in this
category if we glance down Table 7 to the same cultural types of
Racial Type II (see "dark-skinned" Jews). A comparison of

these categories of Jews tells us much about the place and problems of the Jew in American life. Jews and other non-Christians are likely to assimilate less easily than Christians, but the light-skinned Jew who is not physically different and thereby not burdened with negatively evaluated racial traits like his dark-skinned co-religionist assimilates more rapidly than those who belong to Racial Type II. In the first case five or six generations may see most of the group disappearing; in the latter the members of the group assimilate very slowly.

This general hypothesis on assimilation was developed after the field work had been completed in Yankee City, but the evidence points to the fact that the German, English, and other less racially visible Jews disappeared into the total population more rapidly than those who were racially variant.

The Catholics and non-Protestants of Cultural Type 4 and Racial Type II include a large number of nationalities such as Italians, Greeks, and French who are also found in Cultural Type 4 of Racial Type I. The subordination of the former group is likely to be greater and their period of assimilation much longer than those of the latter despite the fact that they are often co-religionists, speak the same language, and have the same body of customary behavior. The factor of race, or rather the strong negative evaluation of it by American society, is sufficient to explain most if not all the differences in ranking of the two groups.

The power of the evaluation of the racial factor becomes even clearer when Cultural Type 4, the Catholics and other non-Protestan Christians of Racial Type III (the Mongoloid and Caucasoid mixture), are compared with those of the dark Caucasoids. These Catholics, most of them dark-skinned Latin Americans, are heavily subordinated as compared with moderate and light subordination for the same type in the other two racial categories. The prediction for their assimilation is slow, which is to say there is no predictable time when they will disappear into the total population, whereas that of their co-religionists of lighter skin is predicted to be short and moderate. We see plainly that while the Catholic Church is a powerful instrument for the conservation of the ethnic tradition, it is much less powerful than the force of American organized "prejudice" against the dark-skinned people. The Negroid Puerto Ricans, Cubans, and West Indians who are of the same cultural type as the lighter-skinned peoples of these islands provide final and conclusive evidence that it is the degree of racial difference from the white American norms which counts most heavily in the placement of the group and in the determination of its assimilation.

The place of the English-speaking Protestant American Negro in our life yields the most eloquent testimony for this proposition. The Negro is culturally more like the white "old American" than the English and Scotch of Cultural Type 1, yet he occupies a very subordinate position where there is little likelihood of his ultimate assimilation unless our social order changes. Although the American Negro belongs to the same cultural type as the English and the Scotch, his racial ranking is near the bottom of the rank order.

These considerations of the relative rating of the cultural and social traits of American society bring us to consideration of the last column in Table 7. This has to do with the form of American ranking ultimately given each of these groups. All of the six cultural types in Racial Types I and II we predict will change from ethnic groups and become wholly a part of the American class order. The members of each group, our Yankee City evidence shows, are permitted to be upward mobile in the general class order. But all of the six cultural types in each of the Racial Types IV and V are likely to develop into castes or semi-castes like that of the American Negro. When the racial deviation reaches the Mongoloid and Negroid extremes the cultural factors are of little importance in the ranking of a particular group and race is all-important.

Racial Type III provides an interesting difference from the others. These ethno-racial groups are likely to divide into two parts: If and when the Spanish Americans and Mexicans lose their cultural identity, those of the more Caucasoid type will become a part of our class order and be capable of rising in our social hierarchy. The darker ones will probably become semi-caste. There is some evidence that it may be possible that this latter group will merge with the Mongoloid or Negroid groups. There is also fragmentary evidence which indicates that some of the Mongoloid groups may merge into the other dark-skinned castes.

The future of American ethnic groups seems to be limited; it is likely that they will be quickly absorbed. When this happens one of the great epochs of American history will have ended and another, that of race, will begin.

Paradoxically, the force of American equalitarianism, which attempts to make all men American and alike, and the force of our class order, which creates differences among ethnic peoples, have combined to dissolve our ethnic groups. Until now these same forces have not been successful in solving the problem of race. The Negro and other dark-skinned groups are still ranked as color castes.

How we will solve the problem of race in the future is problematical. The major areas of the earth, including the United States, are now closely interconnected into an interdependent totality. The effects of important racial and social movements in Europe, Asia, and South America are felt in the United States; our color-caste structure is an ever-present reality in the thoughts of the leaders of China, India, and Latin America. The dark-skinned races' struggle with the dominant whites for social equality is rapidly being organized on an international basis. To calculate the future we must interpret what happens in the United States in this larger setting. Whether we try forcibly to subordinate dark-skinned people, and thereby face certain failure, or use democratic methods, and thereby increase our chances of success, may depend more upon how this decision is made in the rest of the world than upon what happens in this country.

APPENDIX

DISTRIBUTION OF ETHNIC RESIDENCES

A MAP of Yankee City was made on which we spotted every ethnic residence, i.e., family household,[1] as of 1933. This represented a full coverage of ethnic families and provided a complete distribution of the ethnic groups throughout the city. Computation was then made of the proportions of each group in each of the areas defined in Chapter III. This made possible a comparative analysis of the residential status in 1933 of all the ethnic communities.

Almost ninety years of ethnic relations to the Yankee City society had preceded this analysis; and it was necessary to establish the successive antecedent stages in these relations. City directories, selected for decade intervals between 1850 and 1933, were the sources of residential data and of the occupational data to be analyzed. Lists were made for separate groups of the residence and occupation of each ethnic individual recorded; maps were then spotted for each decade, following the same procedure as for 1933. However, the directories did not include every family. It is our estimate, based upon a comparison of census figures and directory totals, that the directories generally covered 85–95 per cent of the adults of the city. Also, the directories did not include individuals below voting age, who have been covered in our 1933 data. Therefore, the area proportions for all the years before 1933 represent computations on large samples of each ethnic group.

For purposes of description we define two general types of residential pattern as follows:

1. The *nucleus,* 3 to 29 homes of the same ethnic group crowded together literally "within a stone's throw of each other." This is subdivided into:

    a. The small nucleus, 3 to 15 homes;

    b. The large nucleus, 16 to 29 homes.

2. The *cluster,* 30 to 150 homes, more loosely gathered in a larger area than that covered by a nucleus, but marked off spatially from other households of the same group. Subclasses are:

    a. The minor cluster, 30 to 50 homes;

    b. The major cluster, 51 to 150 homes.

1. Individuals who were in the city without family or kin have not been spotted on the map. These are all "boarders" in family households, either of their own or of other ethnic groups; hence they could not be accepted as equivalent with the family household which it is necessary to hold as the unit in the present context. Interviews, family diaries, and scrapbooks, genealogies as well as church records, were used to supplement data from the City Directory.

1. *The Irish*

ALTHOUGH there is evidence that there had been a few Irish in Yankee City from the beginning of the eighteenth century, they did not come in considerable numbers until the early 1840's. By 1848 the Irish group was sufficiently large to be organized by the Roman Catholic diocese into a parish serving the area for about ten miles around. A short history of the parish relates that the first permanent priest found "about one hundred Irish families in Yankee City." In the first Yankee City Directory, published in 1850, 104 Irish families were listed. The distribution of the Irish throughout the city from 1850 to 1933 is shown on the spot map in Chart VIII. This map indicates that while Irish entrance into the city was predominantly through the zone lowest in status—oldest, densest in population, and the most industrialized—a secondary mode of ingress was via the newest and least developed of the zones. In this connection, there is evidence that the Irish in Zone II at this early period were not new-comers but a portion of the earliest arrivals who had already progressed through Zone I. However, none of those found in Zone IV in 1864 had been in the city in 1850.

Between 1873 and 1903 there is almost no change in zone proportions except for a shift in the latter year between Zones IV and II, in spite of the fact that the Irish population had more than doubled in the interval. This is a period, then, of residential equilibrium for the Irish, during which each zone increases in Irish members at a rate no greater than that for the total Irish population. There is a family mobility, of course, but the residential status of the group as a whole remains unchanged.

The span between 1903 and 1933 covers the period in which all the other ethnic groups entered Yankee City. In 1913 the proportion of Irish families in Zone I begins to decline sharply by about 10 per cent a decade. This progressive reduction in the last three decades is accounted for by progressive infiltration into the three other zones.

In 1850, 85 per cent of Irish homes were in Zone I and the other 15 per cent in Zone II. More than eighty years later the distribution of Irish among the zones approximates that of the city's native population.

Up to this point our account has been exclusively in terms of gross proportions. We may now turn to an examination of the spot maps for the detail of the trends defined above, and for an analysis of the relations among the households of the Irish group.

Phase 1. In the period from 1850 to 1864 there were shifts of Irish among the three low-status areas of the city, but the fact of most significance in this decade is that the Irish appear in the first stage of developing a territorial base for their group, as seen in their various clusters and nuclei, and especially in their concentration along most of the waterfront within Zone I.

Phase 2. In the period from 1873 through 1893, during which the Irish population more than doubles in number, the six minor Zone I clusters

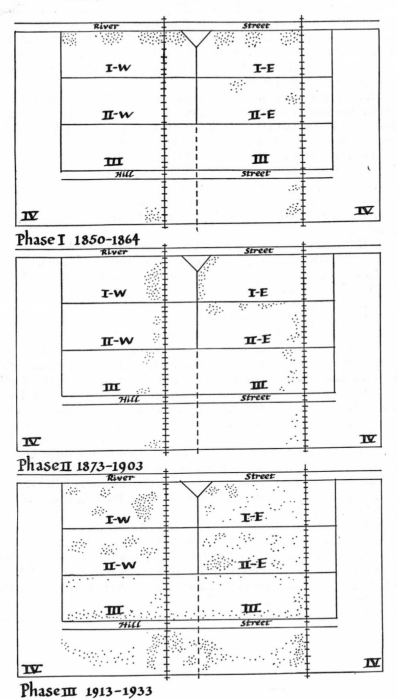

CHART VIII

SPOT MAPS OF IRISH RESIDENTIAL DISTRIBUTIONS

Phase I 1850–1864

Phase II 1873–1903

Phase III 1913–1933

coalesce into four major clusters. Three of these major clusters expand progressively in two directions—east-west along the main axis of the zone, and southward-upward on the incline of the city.

This second Irish phase is marked by the progressive formation of households into larger clusterings in Zone I and by intra-sectional movements started by the incursions of a second ethnic group, the French Canadian. Although the zone percentages have not changed markedly throughout the period, the Irish exhibit slow mobility toward Hill Street and higher residential status.

Phase 3. The years after 1903 end the previous thirty-year equilibrium among the various areas and constitute a period of regular infiltration into Zones II, IV, and III by Irish families from Zone I. The former Irish areas of residence were taken up by new ethnic groups.

The history of the Irish residential relations within Section I-W may be summarized as follows:

1. 1850, appearance of small nuclei;
2. 1864–1873, formation of two minor clusters;
3. 1883–1903, fusion into a single major cluster and progressive expansion;
4. 1913–1923, progressive shrinkage of cluster;
5. 1933, disintegration into one large and several small nuclei.

The development of the Irish residential relations in Section II-E can be summed up as follows:

1. 1850–1864, one small nucleus;
2. 1873–1893, complete scatter;
3. 1903–1913, one large and three small nuclei;
4. 1923–1933, complete scatter except for one small nucleus.

Section II-W tells another story. In 1913, much as in 1903, the Irish are dispersed, except for one large and two small nuclei, around the railroad tracks. Otherwise, they have made little advance over the lower threshold of the section since 1903. By 1923 the large nucleus of 1913 has been reduced by Greeks and Armenians from the section below. The two smaller nuclei of 1913 remain intact. However, a new large nucleus has formed farther west of the tracks. Also, there has been a slight upward movement to about the middle line of the section.

The history of the Irish in Section II-W, therefore is as follows:

1. 1850–1893, penetration just over the line from Section I-W—no nuclei whatever;
2. 1903–1923, one large nucleus and several small ones;
3. 1933, four large nuclei along the middle of the section.

Clearly the Irish penetration into this section has been laboriously slow over the entire period of eighty years. In contrast with Section II-E, in which the Irish have reached the middle half of the section by 1913, the Irish in II-W are still on the zone's lower border in 1913 and in 1933 are little beyond the section's middle line. Also, the Irish residential formations in II-E have been irregular, whereas in II-W, since 1903, residence nuclei of Irish have been progressively expanding.

Nuclear formation apparently results not only from increase in the number of ethnic households in an area but also from resistance on the part of native residents. This may be observed in comparing the development of the Irish in Sections I-E and I-W. With relatively large and approximately equal numbers in each, clusters and nuclei have far greater persistence in the latter than in the former. The same process is also evident in Zone II, where Section II-W, with only half the Irish numbers of its sister section, exhibits larger and more persistent nuclei.

Zone III, covering the area of Hill Street, has 2 per cent of the Irish in 1903. By 1923 this figure has doubled. Almost all these families are found either just over the zone line or in the two "depressed" areas where railroad tracks intersect the zone.

In 1933, 10 per cent of the Irish households are within Zone III, a striking advance in a decade. Many of these are still on the edge of the zone, some are in the track areas, but twenty are in the better portions of Hill Street, scattered singly along its entire length. These Hill Street families have reached the top of residential areas in the city. They are families which, as we shall see in another connection, have also climbed as far as an ethnic can climb in the Yankee City social-class system.

We may summarize the Irish residential history in Zone III by observing that it took from the early 1840's to 1893 for the Irish to penetrate the zone, and it took from 1893 to 1933 for them to "arrive" on Hill Street. These ninety years, therefore, are the equivalent in social time of the social space and social "distance" between River Street and Hill Street, Irish and native, lower class and upper class. The actual physical distance between the two streets is one-quarter mile.

2. *The French Canadians*

THE second ethnic group to enter Yankee City was the French Canadian, which appears on our very first map, 1850, with four household units, distributed in Section I-E, Wharf Square, Section I-W, and Section II-E.

In 1864, three are in Section I-W (widely apart, however) and one in II-E. Ten years later, two are in I-W and three in II-E—no two close to each other. And in 1883 three are in I-E, one in I-W, four in II-E, three in II-W, and two in IV—thirteen in all, but all still spatially remote from one another.

These data are presented here in spite of the fact that the enumerations are not statistically significant, because the French Canadians in this period of thirty years exhibit the first general phase of ethnic articulation to the Yankee City system, an amorphous phase marked by the following characteristics: (1) relatively few family units, (2) no residential congregation, and (3) relatively free movement through all zones except III.

Although there are only thirteen French-Canadian households in 1883, a decade later the number has increased to fifty-five. We shall therefore proceed with a description of French-Canadian relations, applying the same techniques used with the Irish.

This discussion will compare the second French-Canadian phase, that of 1893, with the corresponding phase of the Irish in 1850.[2] Certain parallelisms appear: (1) Zone III in both instances has 0 per cent; (2) Section II-W 2 per cent; and (3) Section II-E approximately 12 per cent. That is, in relation to the three highest of the city's areas, the French Canadians start their course in proportions almost identical with the Irish. The divergences, however, are more significant: (1) the ratio of Irish in Section I-E to those in Section I-W is about 1 to 1, whereas the French-Canadian ratio is about 3 to 1; and (2) 16 per cent of the French Canadians are in Zone IV, whereas there are no Irish here in 1850. But in 1864 the Irish reach a representation in Zone IV equivalent to that of the French Canadians in 1893.

In other words, the French Canadians exhibit a high concentration of house units in Section I-E, while Section I-W and Zone IV hold only 16 per cent each. Why should the French Canadians show such preference for I-E as against I-W, when the Irish, in a corresponding phase, have approximately equal distribution in these sections? Might it be due to the fact that the Irish in this decade year are concentrated in Section I-W, hence leaving open only I-E to the French Canadians? In 1893, 36 per cent of the 450 Irish residences are in Section I-W and 26 per cent in I-E. Certainly there is no great preponderance of Irish in I-W to close that section to the French Canadians, especially since the latter in 1893 are a small group, having only 12 per cent of the total number of Irish.

It is to be expected that Section I-E, being older and somewhat below Section I-W in status, would be more likely to draw a newly migrant ethnic group. This is only a partial explanation, especially since it does not hold for the Irish after 1850.

We have already observed that by 1883 the Irish in Section I-E have abandoned River Street and are moving up the side streets. In Section I-W, however, the Irish except at two cluster points are still concentrated along River Street. By 1893 the Irish in I-E have advanced still farther up the side streets, whereas those in I-W have made little progress. In 1893 the French Canadians in Section I-E are found ranged along River Street. Apparently the Irish, encountering difficulties in proceeding higher in Section I-W, are still "hemmed in" on River Street, thereby shutting off the French Canadians from a secure foothold on this lower threshold of the section. River Street along Section I-E, in contrast, recently deserted by the Irish for places higher in the section, is open. It is only here that a new ethnic group could establish itself in important num-

2. Although the evidence is lacking, it is assumed that in the first years after their arrival the Irish likewise passed through an amorphous residential phase.

bers. This is confirmed by an Irishman who, with reference to Section I-E, said: "The Irish did not move out because the French moved in, but the French moved in because the Irish moved out."

Except, then, for this difference between the Irish and the French Canadians in the ratio of their numbers in the two sections of Zone I, and in the fact that the Irish, by comparison with the French Canadians, are a decade late in finding their way into Zone IV, these two ethnic groups are distributed, on their first important appearance in Yankee City, in much the same manner.

The subsequent development of the French Canadians can be divided into two phases:

1. The period 1893–1913, Section I-E gains somewhat, as do most of the other areas except Zone IV, which falls sharply. On the whole, this is a period of relative stability.

2. 1913–1933, Section I-E drops in its proportion of French Canadians, with an approximately corresponding rise in Section II-E. Section I-W remains almost constant, as does Section II-W. Zone IV shifts from 4 (1913) to 14 per cent. No French Canadians appear in Zone III until 1933.

Thus, after a period of minor readjustment from 1893 to 1913, there is a movement of French Canadians from I-E into II-E, with secondary accessions in Zones IV and III.

Comparing these French-Canadian phases with the corresponding phases of the Irish, we note that the Irish pass through a phase between 1850 and 1873 in which Zone I remains numerically stable, although declining relatively, while Zone IV is being settled. The French Canadians, on the other hand, between 1893 and 1913 exhibit trends that are exactly the reverse. Zone I climbs somewhat in its representation of French Canadians, whereas Zone IV drops off considerably. Apparently Zone I—or more especially Section I-E in these years—is growing in French-Canadian units at the expense of Zone IV.

With the exception of readjustments in the proportions absorbed by Zone IV and Section I-E, the Irish show a sustained period of relative stability through 1903, a period of more than fifty years. The French Canadians, on the other hand, maintain this equilibrated phase (readjustments in areas IV and I-E excepted) for only twenty years (1893–1913). Further, whereas the Irish thereafter exhibit only moderate shifts between Zones I and II, the French-Canadian shifts are more marked. For example, the proportion of Irish in Zone I diminishes between 1903 and 1913 from 60 to 51 per cent, while in Zone II it increases from 25 to 30 per cent. In terms of sections, the percentages are:

Irish		*French Canadians*	
1903–1913		*1913–1923*	
I-E	25–20	I-E	58–39
II-E	16–20	II-E	11–25

This is evidence that the French Canadians have progressed in residential status, at least in these sections, at a faster pace than have the Irish. It will be remembered that the Irish numbers in Section II-E do not reach equivalence with those in Section I-E until 1913, i.e., until six decades have elapsed. French-Canadian numerical equivalence in Sections II-E and I-E is achieved in 1933—after four decades.

Phase 1. In 1893 the French Canadians are scattered along River Street, with the exception of a single nucleus just off this street in Section I-E. A decade later this small nucleus has expanded eastward and westward into a large nucleus, its movement upward being very slight. Single families here and there are edging their way up the side streets, although on the whole the group is still in the lower half of the section. Single French-Canadian residences are interspersed among the Irish nuclei, and a few Irish units are intermingled with the French-Canadian nucleus. In other words, there is no clear-cut separation of the French-Canadian vanguard from the rear-guard Irish, although the latter are in a period of residential dispersion in Section I-E, whereas the French Canadians are in a phase of consolidation.

The only other French-Canadian nuclei in 1903 are two small ones found in (1) Wharf Square and (2) Section I-W, on River Street, adjoining the tracks. The French Canadians, like the Irish before them, move into this section under the protective shadow of the railroad tracks. These French-Canadian groups resemble the Irish pattern in its small nucleus phase of 1850.

The French-Canadian households in the remaining zones are scattered, although many are located near Irish families. There are fully thirty of such tiny "mixed" nuclei, twenty of which are found in Zone II alone, suggesting that French-Canadian movement follows where an Irish wedge has already been driven.

With 1913, the large nucleus in I-E has expanded into a minor cluster, significantly in only one direction, upward on the city's incline, almost to the border of Zone II. Yet the cluster is somewhat diffuse and interspersed with Irish along three sides and recently arrived Poles on the River Street side. The small Wharf Square nucleus is almost gone, and the nucleus in I-W has moved west of the tracks. It is also apparent that the French Canadians in Section I-W have moved off River Street, to which they were confined in 1903, and are now almost halfway up the slope on the heels of the advancing Irish.

In Section II-E the French-Canadian units are still scattered and extend from the lower border to the upper. Here, as in II-W, there is not so marked a tendency as in 1903 for the French Canadians to settle hard by an Irish family. Generally, they now seem to be striking out by themselves. In Section II-W the few French Canadians have made no progress at all during the decade, still being restricted to the lower half of the section.

Phase 2. Between 1913 and 1923 Section I-E drops from 58 to 39 per cent of the French-Canadian households, and Section II-E jumps from 11 to 25 per cent. This is the decade of the first heavy Polish influx into Section I-E and of the final disintegration of the Irish formations here into small nuclei. The French Canadians, however, are also on the move, as indicated in their marked falling off in I-E. The Irish are moving upward into Zone II, cutting a swath behind which the French Canadians are following. And into the area left by the latter the Poles in turn are moving. Hence the arrangement of the ethnic groups in the city's residential system is roughly in the chronological order of their appearance.

In I-E the cluster of 1913 is now broken up into two nuclei, one large, on the upper edge of the section, and one small, still on River Street and blocked in by Poles. By 1933 both these nuclei are dispersed and the French-Canadian picture is one of complete residential scatter, the group being restricted largely to the upper half of the section.

These are the steps of French-Canadian residential groupings within Section I-E:

1. 1850–1883, amorphous;
2. 1893, small nucleus;
3. 1903, large nucleus;
4. 1913, cluster;
5. 1923, one large and one small nucleus;
6. 1933, dispersion.

Thus the French Canadians also have completed a cycle. The Irish in I-E went through identical phases of the cycle, the only difference being that the Irish cluster phase persisted through four decades, whereas the French-Canadian cluster lasted only one decade. The fact of the Irish pulling out on one side and the Poles pushing in on the other only partially serves to explain the premature disintegration of the French-Canadian cluster phase. For, as we shall see, mobility in the residential order beyond a certain point is a factor correlated with the break-up of residential juxtapositions among member families of an ethnic group.

Section I-W in 1933, as in 1923, is still negligible in its proportion of French Canadians. However, its single nucleus remains through 1933, with perceptible movement farther up the incline behind the Irish. Therefore, the French Canadians in I-W, amorphously settled in 1893, appear as a nucleus in 1903 and the nucleus moves progressively westward with each decade. Primary movement, however, is upward into the section and slow.

The French Canadians do not show a tendency to nuclear formation in II-E until 1933 when four small nuclei appear. From 1923 through 1933 the French Canadians are evenly distributed throughout the section. In Section II-W the French Canadians make no perceptible progress upward, either in 1923 or 1933, during which period they remain widely scattered. The French Canadians have here been "stopped in their tracks" for, as in the case of the Irish, they make little upward advance after crossing over the section's threshold. Thus Section II-W, like Zone III, has managed somewhat effectively to keep both the Irish and the French Canadians from getting much beyond the back door.

A handful of French Canadians appears on the edge of Zone III in 1903 but does not actually cross into this zone until 1933, at which time there are twenty-four families, or 4 per cent of the group total. However, twenty of these families are either on the border of the zone or in the track areas. Four have actually penetrated into Hill Street proper, and every one of these four is settled in a house immediately adjoining that of an Irish family. This was the mode by which the French Canadians first edged their way into Zone II. It represents the general method by which the more mobile families of each successive ethnic group tend to follow the course set by the preceding group.

Only in 1893 and 1933 have the French Canadians been as heavily represented in Zone IV as have the Irish. In 1893, 16 per cent of the French Canadians are settled here. In the next twenty years this figure falls to 4 per cent, rising in 1933 to 14 per cent. The French Canadians have been found on all three sides of the zone, always among Irish, with no nuclei formed until 1933 when three small, loose nuclei appear, one on each side of the city's periphery. This zone has been relatively unimportant and irregular in French-Canadian development.

It is apparent that the French Canadians in their own internal relations have gone through the same phases as the Irish, but at a somewhat accelerated pace, especially in the disintegrative stages. However, in 1933 the French Canadians do not have status equivalent to that of the Irish. In the first place, the Irish are rather evenly distributed throughout the whole residential system, whereas 57 per cent of the French Canadians are still in the eastern sections of Zones I and II, as against 24 per cent in the western sections. However similar their proportions in Section I-W may now be, the Irish exceed the French Canadians in Section II-W, although neither has penetrated very far; and in both Zones III and IV the Irish are more than double the proportions of French Canadians. In other words, the French Canadians are at a stage of specialization characteristic of the Irish in 1903.

3. *The Jews*

THE third group to make its way into Yankee City was the Jews. From 1893 through 1903 fifteen families of Polish Jews are recorded in the city. This is too small a number to be treated statistically. Here are their absolute distributions:

1893		1903	
I-E	2	I-E	6
I-W	6	I-W	2
II-E	3	II-E	4
II-W	4	II-W	3

CHART IX

SPOT MAPS OF JEWISH RESIDENTIAL DISTRIBUTIONS

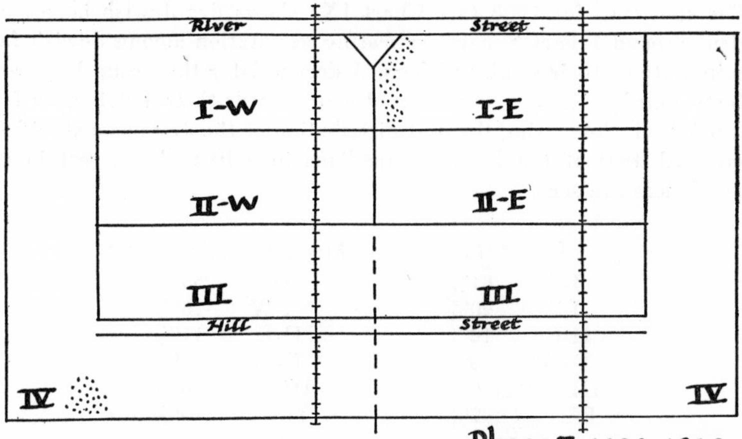

Phase I 1903-1913

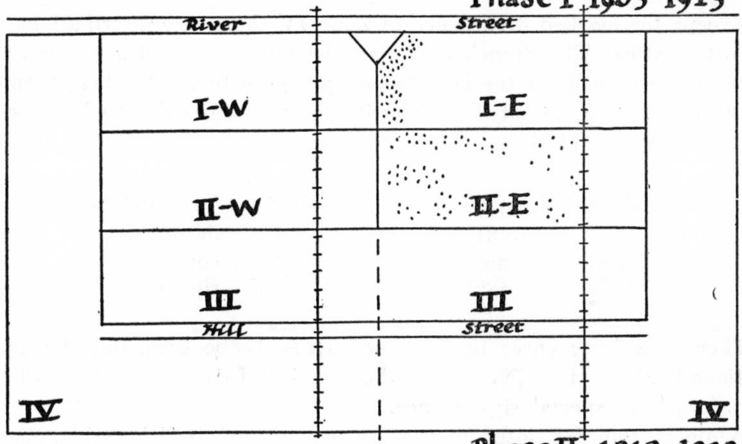

Phase II 1913-1923

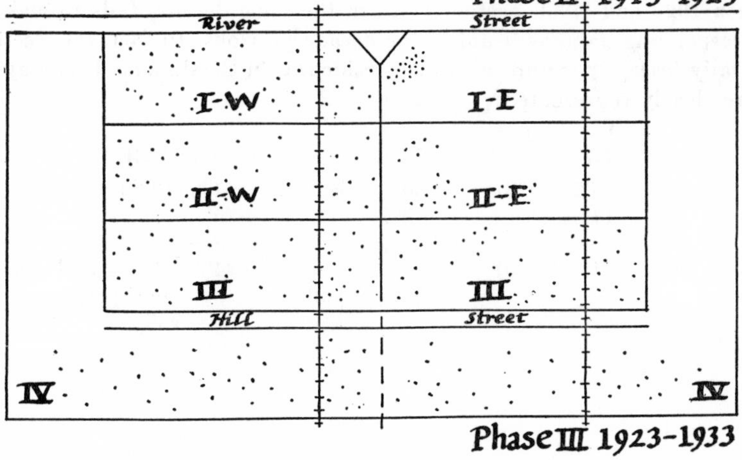

Phase III 1923-1933

Reference to the spot map of 1893 demonstrates the scatter characteristic of the amorphous phase. Typical of this phase also is the almost equal distribution between Zones I and II.

The spot map for 1903 (see Chart IX) shows five Jewish homes in a nucleus around Wharf Square, indicating gravitation among Jewish families in spite of their small numbers. A decade later the group has grown to forty-four households, and the spot map records their distribution from that point on. Comparing the first distribution of the Jews as a significant group with that of the French Canadians in a like phase, certain correspondences are seen:

	Jews, 1913		*French Canadians, 1893*
I-E	61%	I-E	55%
I-W	20%	I-W	16%
II-E	12%	II-E	11%
II-W	0%	II-W	2%
III	0%	III	0%
IV	7%	IV	16%

Except for marked divergence in Zone IV these two distributions are almost identical. The French-Canadian distribution, except in minor ways, remains unchanged for the next twenty years up to 1913. Then, between 1913 and 1933, accelerated movement follows, localized largely between Sections I-E and II-E.

	Jews, 1913–1933		*French Canadians, 1913–1933*
I-E	drops 31%	I-E	drops 31%
I-W	constant	I-W	constant
II-E	rises 13%	II-E	rises 19%

There are divergences in the other areas, to be sure, but the above sections hold about 90 per cent of the families of each group in 1913 and therefore have special significance.

While Section I-E loses another 15 per cent of Jewish residences between 1923 and 1933, Section II-E, in the same decade, fails to make a corresponding gain, as it did in the decade previous. In fact, this section actually loses 5 per cent of Jewish residences in the decade. This may be more clearly represented:

I-E	*II-E*	*III and II-W*
45% (1923)	30% (1923)	5% (1923)
−14%←	−19%	+19%
——→	→+14%	——
31% (1933)	——	24% (1933 actual combined proportion is 23%)
	25% (1933)	

But in terms of the relatively brief period the Jews have been resident in Yankee City, their upward mobility is the most rapid of any ethnic group.

We have already observed that the Irish exhibit a thirty-year period of distributional equilibrium before beginning a regular filtration out of Zone I into the other areas of the city, and that the French Canadians remain for twenty years in a phase of relative residential stability before there is concerted movement out of Zone I. The Jews show no such stable phase. No sooner are they settled in 1913 in a distribution among the areas almost identical with that of the French Canadians in 1893 than they proceed through shifts even more swift than those of the latter in the very same years.

As a special instance, it may be recalled that the Irish did not penetrate Zone III until they had been in the city more than fifty years, and the French Canadians not until after forty years. Within ten years after their first important appearance, 3 per cent of the Jews moved into this top area. In 1933 they actually exceed the Irish proportions in this area with 14 per cent of their households situated there.

A second divergence in the Jewish trends is in Zone IV. Among both the Irish and the French Canadians this area, secondary as a gateway for ingress into the city, is important. For example, the Irish have 26 per cent and the French Canadians 14 per cent of their households in this zone in 1933. The Jews, however, beginning here with 7 per cent in 1913, go to 4 per cent in 1923 and to 2 per cent in 1933. The trend of Jewish movements in this area is regularly downward, whereas that of the two antecedent groups, with some fluctuations, is upward.

In the case of the Irish, more than eighty years are required for the range in residential distribution to contract from 44 to 16 per cent. In the case of the French Canadians, forty years elapse in the tapering of the range from 53 to 26 per cent. But for the Jews, notwithstanding the descending trend of Zone IV at the lower extreme, only twenty years are necessary for the range to contract from 54 to 29 per cent. Excepting Zone IV, the range of the Jewish proportions among the areas in 1933 is 22 per cent, intermediate between the ranges of the Irish and the French Canadians in the same year. Thus it is apparent that the Jews, from overwhelming concentration (81 per cent) in Zone I in 1913, within twenty years have rapidly approached an even distribution through all areas of the city's residential system except Zone IV.

We may summarize the development of the Jews thus:

1. 1913, more or less typical first-decade distribution;

2. 1913–1933, concerted movement from areas I-E and IV into areas II-E, II-W, and III.

Hence the Jews telescope into thirty years the same phases which cover seventy years for the Irish and forty years for the French Canadians.

4. *All Subsequent Ethnic Groups*

ALTHOUGH there were nine Italian families in Yankee City in 1893, the group was not large enough to be significant until 1923. Similarly, Armenians and Greeks in 1903, and Poles and Russians in 1913, appeared in small numbers, but in no instance were their households significantly numerous until the decade year 1923. In addition, an interval of one decade, of course, is insufficient for the determination of trends.

One of the striking facts shown in Table 8 is that the Italians, the Armenians, and the Greeks—the ethnic groups to follow immediately after the Jews—are the first to make Section I-W rather than I-E the principal area of first settlement. The Poles and the Russians, on the other hand—the last of the ethnic groups to enter the city—are not only concentrated in Section I-E, but in greater proportions than any previous group.

Italians, Armenians, and Greeks have high representation in Zone II by 1923. Two factors seem to be involved. The first is that those who have pushed their way into this middle zone by 1923 are, with a few exceptions, the pioneers of their respective groups, many of whom have been in the city since 1903 and even earlier. The second factor is that by 1923

TABLE 8

Area Distributions of Five Most Recent Ethnic Groups

Group	Year	Percentages					
		I-E	*I-W*	*II-E*	*II-W*	*III*	*IV*
Italian.........	1923	17	58	6	9	3	6
	1933	10	52	7	10	3	18
Armenian.......	1923	0	77	11	10	2	0
	1933	0	62	15	18	1	4
Greek..........	1923	22	45	12	18	0	3
	1933	19	37	14	19	5	6
Polish..........	1923	83	4	5	0	0	8
	1933	75	7	9	1	0	8
Russian........	1933	88	0	3	0	0	9

the Irish, French Canadians, and Jews have progressed into Zone II so effectively that the older families among the newer groups have comparatively little difficulty in moving into the zone. Significantly, most of the Italians, Armenians, and Greeks in Zone II (and Zone III) are established close to the homes of either the Irish, French Canadians, or Jews.

A third element shown in the table is that the Italians and the Armenians appear in Zone III as early as 1923. But almost without exception they are found in the low evaluation spots in the zone and near the residences of one of the earlier groups. This is still the case for these two groups in 1933 and for the Greeks as well.

The Italians remain in an amorphous residential phase from 1893 through 1913. By 1913 the Italians in Section I-W are gathered in two tiny nuclei and are all members of the South Italian faction. In 1923, however, these nuclei have expanded into one large and one small nucleus, both still centered on River Street. In all other areas the Italian residences are spread about. This remains the situation in 1933 except that the South Italians in Section I-W have now formed a diffuse minor cluster. At no time has the smaller North Italian subgroup exhibited any residential confluence. In their own internal relations, therefore, the Italians, at least those of South Italian origin, are still in a consolidating stage.

The first decade year in which the Armenians are recorded in the city directories is 1903. In that year their thirteen families are all closely grouped beside a shoe factory in Section I-W. The Armenians appear not to have passed through the amorphous first phase observed among the other ethnic groups. Two explanations for this early nuclear formation are offered by Armenian informants. The first is that "most of the Armenian families at that time were kin." In that first period the small Armenian group was more closely bound by ties of kinship than we know to have been the case for any other ethnic group, with the result that residential juxtaposition took place almost immediately upon their arrival. A secondary explanation is that the Armenians at that time were almost exclusively employed in the shoe factory which their homes adjoined.

Two thirds of the Armenians in 1913 are found collected in the Section I-W nucleus. In 1923 this is supplemented by three small nuclei in the same section, a condition which prevails also in 1933.

Five Greeks are listed in the 1893 directory, but since all were unmarried and living in boarding houses, they cannot be considered as household units. In both 1903 and 1913 there is only a handful of Greek families in the city, the members of which are scattered between Wharf Square, Section I-W, and Section II-E, in what appears to be an amorphous phase. In 1923 they form a small nucleus on the western side of Wharf Square in Section I-W; a decade later this nucleus has grown to a minor cluster. In 1933 the Greeks are found in Section I-E in one large nucleus and in two small nuclei in each of Sections II-E and II-W. Although the Section I-E nucleus is already on the upper border of the section, the cluster in Section I-W is still fixed on River Street.

The few Polish families in Yankee City in 1903 are evenly divided between Sections I-E and II-E, with no two near each other. A decade later they have doubled in numbers and are principally on the lower edge of Section I-E, forming a small, loose nucleus which is mixed with a few

Irish and French-Canadian families. In 1923 the Poles, heavily concentrated in Section I-E, are arranged in a minor cluster and several large nuclei along River Street and the bottom half of the section. In the decade-year 1933 they number 154 families, 75 per cent of which are still in Section I-E. These latter are now in a major cluster of 85 households, ranging from River Street upward, and in two large nuclei. The balance of the Poles are scattered evenly among areas I-W, II-E, and IV. The Russians in both 1923 and 1933 are interspersed through the Polish cluster. With respect, then, to internal relations, the five newest ethnic groups in 1933 are in a final stage of residential consolidation.